OT Blues

Comical Stories from a Life on the Road

MARK,
What a RiDe! CongRATS! on
RetiRemenT.
ENJOY,
Barry Metzler

By:
Barry Metzler

Strategic Book Group

Strategic Book Group
P.O. Box 333
Durham CT 06422
www.StrategicBookClub.com

ISBN: 978-1-60911-678-1

Printed in the United States of America

To my wife, Cindy, who kept an uber-cool outlook running the household while I was travelling for so many years, missing babies first steps, birthdays and so many school plays. And thanks for keeping track of the missed anniversaries but only reminding me once in a while. Also, to our amazing kids, Kristy, Matthew, and Shannon, who missed their dad but listened to and learned from their mom.

Contents

Preface

PHILADELPHIA INTERNATIONAL AIRPORT
February, 2008

It's just before eight o'clock on a miserably cold Monday morning, and I'm already on my second leg of a long journey, coming in from Pittsburgh and trying to make a connecting flight from Philadelphia to Dallas. While making my way from gate B-Last to gate D-Last, I feel the familiar rumbling of my lower abdomen telling me *it's time.* Apparently, my internal body clock thinks it's noon.

Now if you've ever traveled though the Philly airport, you know it's not the cleanest of places to make a pit stop. In fact, it's probably one of the foulest smelling places on earth. But I really had no choice, so I begrudgingly head toward the nearest depository.

I enter the busy men's room, and, ah yes, I immediately recognize the familiar aroma. I'm tempted to call it the smell of death, but I really don't have anything against the smell of death and I don't want to give it a bad name. This is a stench all its own. Holding my breath, I start systematically bumping my way through the morning crowd, checking for feet under the doors until I spot an empty stall near the back. Way back. After squeezing through the human maze, I finally get there and open the door, and son of a bitch, it's a handicap stall. I think about the morality issue for about a half second, but again, I have no choice. Anyway, I'll be quick.

Airport etiquette requires this to be quick and to the point, so why not? (Airport restrooms are kind of like being in an Applebee's...

heavy walk-up traffic and high turnover.) I get in and go through the male ritual: Take off the suit coat and hang it on the hook. Swing the necktie over my shoulder, apply the paper cover to the seat, and assume the position.

If you want a miserable way to start a week, this was it. Wake up at three-thirty A.M., stumble into the bathroom, shower, shave, and head out for a five-thirty A.M. flight in the bitter cold and darkness. Step into the ankle deep snow and chip the ice off the car windows and door just so you can get in it—all in the same wet shoes and socks you'll be wearing for the next sixteen hours.

My reward for getting through this is that when I get to the airport, I strip halfway naked to get through security and follow the other lemmings to the gate. All before the sun rises.

So here I am, sitting on this porcelain throne, collecting my thoughts and hoping Larry Craig isn't in the stall next to me. Keeping my eyes trained on the floor, I see something odd and a bit upsetting—and my worst fear is realized. I see the distinct look of the rubber-coated steel wheels roll up to the door and stop right outside my ill-gotten space. Yes! Of course, it is indeed a wheelchair. *You gotta be shittin me...*

Being in this men's room in the first place is bad enough, but now I feel like a major asshole because there's a handicapped guy waiting and I'm in his space. What am I going to say to this poor guy? W*hy does everything have to happen to me?* I just stare at the floor for a while, but those shiny steel wheels don't move. I glance up at the wall and actually entertain the thought of hoisting my fat ass over it. *Yeah, right.*

After contemplating my dilemma for a little while, I decide there's only one way for a real man to handle this. I finish my task and put on the suit coat and fix my tie. I sling my computer bag over my right shoulder and grab the handle of my carry-on. I slowly open the door and gaze down at the handicapped guy. I look him right in the eyes and give him a quick, brotherly nod. I then turn away and exit the stall, dragging my right leg behind me like it was a dead fish.

I decided if you can't beat them, join them, so I pretend I'm handicapped and make my slow-speed getaway. I continue the trek with my left leg making the awkward buck-step required to pull my now-useless right leg through the never-ending men's room. I keep looking straight ahead, gimping my way out of there like I owned the place, proud as a one-legged peacock. I even dipped my shoulder with each lurch for added effect. Kind of like Bella Lugosi sprinkled with Jerry Lewis.

I never looked back, or left or right for that matter, and continued to limp my way out of the restroom, with a completely straight face and looking as serious as a heart attack. I feel the eyes on me, but I stay determined and gimp onward. Onward, that is, until I'm one drag-step out of the men's room and I bust out laughing as I realize what I just did. I must have looked like a complete idiot.

I get to the gate, still laughing at myself. Out loud. People are looking at me like I'm nuts. Thank god no one knows me here because I can't stop laughing. What the hell just happened? I mean, really? I know people get shit on all the time, but was I the shit-er or shit-ee?

As I sit down and wipe away the tears, it all comes back to me. Twenty-some years of traveling and the boat-load of absurd situations and events that I happened to be a part of. They all flash before my eyes, and right then and there, I decide that some of this stuff is pretty comical and I should write a book.

So that's what you will be reading about. Events and situations that various colleagues and I have found ourselves in throughout the years of traveling for business, and our life on the road. Keep in mind, most of these things weren't funny to us at the time; they just happened and we mostly didn't give them another thought. But now that I'm older, I can see that some of these things just weren't normal.

Introduction

A LITTLE BACKGROUND

For the last couple of decades, I've been in a field of work that has required a lot of travel. Back in the mid-eighties, I started out as an electrical engineering tech in the industrial field. That means I was responsible for start-ups and commissioning of industrial equipment projects throughout North America. The companies I worked for were located in Pittsburgh, PA, where most of the fabrication took place. The equipment was tested and then shipped to the final location, usually in the USA, and sometimes Canada and Mexico. My background covered the electrical and industrial software end of the equipment installations; I worked with many colleagues who worked in the mechanical and piping field. This made for teams of technicians that supposedly would cover the technical areas required to start up these systems.

We all took our work very seriously—well, kind of seriously—and most of us were good at what we did. It didn't hurt that we were all about the same age and had the same penchant for the after-work scene: bars, restaurants, clubs, bars, and more bars. We all worked hard, and it made for long hours. But, we also took the *off time* pretty serious, and we played hard, too. Did I mention the bars?

We actually thought of the night life and travel related activities as 'working overtime.' This 'OT,' for short, led to many mirthful situations and the inevitable rough mornings, which we simply called the 'Blues.' Thus the term 'OT Blues.' It could mean anything from waking up with bloodshot eyes and no cash left to missing your flight home.

When we went out after work, in whatever city or town we happened to be in, we had an unwritten code that we would have each other's backs. Of course, that kind of trust made the naïve and young ones among us easy targets for general ball busting bordering on sometimes cruel and unusual abuse.

The gist of this collection of stories is to entertain, and it's all based on actual events. What you'll read is the chronological telling of little stories and ditties that we either fell into or fell on us. I did change some names to protect the guilty. Check that—I changed ALL the names. The timeframes are basically correct, but keep in mind I didn't keep notes, and this is not a memoir. It's entertainment only, and I sure as hell don't want to find myself on Oprah's couch being shamed on national television. So read on and have a laugh or two, keeping in mind it's our American right to laugh at other people's embarrassment. Of course, it works both ways. We all get a turn being laughed at sometimes, too.

That's my story and I'm sticking to it.

Enjoy.

Chapter 1

THE EARLY YEARS

When this gig started, I was an unmarried, twenty-two-year-old punk who took a job at an electrical design company, often referred to as a systems house. (I didn't call myself single because I was engaged to my future wife, Cindy.) It was a small, family-run business and I took a position with this little outfit called Drive Systems, Inc. It was a great decision, with a great owner and a VP who both took me under their wings. I learned a lot from Phil Williams, the owner, and Bud Allen, the co-owner and VP, as they taught me the real-world points of the electrical engineering field, and industrial software and controls. I didn't get paid a lot, but it was better than paying for formal schooling.

I also learned from and worked with Phil's son, Greg. He was a few years older than I was, and the best way to describe him would be *deep*. Not a bad deep, but deep.

Phil and Bud taught me a lot of industrial engineering, and I tried to soak it all in. They also taught me how to live and work on the road, except we just didn't have anywhere to go. Anywhere cool, I mean. A lot of our work in the beginning was in the coal mining and coal prep plant industry, in West Virginia, Kentucky, and Virginia coal mines.

Our installs usually meant eight- to nine-hour drives into these god-forsaken Podunk towns where everyone worked at the local mine. Our systems included industrial computers that would auto-

1

mate the operations; they are called Programmable Logic Controllers, or PLCs.

I quickly found that this little glimpse of the 20th century was not welcome in most Podunk towns. It was assumed that the computers would take the job of ten guys. Not true, of course, but it's hard to argue with a rebel flag and a shotgun. I was taught to never use the word *computer.* It was always *controller,* or simply, *module.* It was basically the equivalent of spelling words in front of your kids so they couldn't get what you were saying.

One of the first trips I made was to a little town called Amherstdale, West Virginia. We were installing controls for a coal conveyor system in a coal plant near this little town hidden in bowels of West Virginia and a long drive from Pittsburgh, near the Kentucky border. It was a town with one traffic light and a motel.

It was late on a Sunday afternoon when I left the 'burgh to be onsite first thing Monday morning for the start-up. So I drove and drove, using the company station wagon to take a load of tools and parts down there. It was an uneventful trip, except for the huge box turtle I ran over. It made a unique crunching sound, actually a two-tone crunch followed by a slight *squish* sound. It left a blotch on the road and turtle guts all over the wheel, too.

After driving all day, I finally felt the relief of pulling in to my destination. It was the only motel in the town, and I was led to believe it was a nice place. I was feeling pretty good about myself when I finally spotted the sign. I pull into the lot. As I take a good look around, I get the, "I'm in a shit hole" feeling.

What I see is about ten rooms facing the parking lot and a small office with a black and white TV glowing through the window. A true No-tell Mo-tel. This is definitely the place, so I head to the office.

The little old lady at the desk was friendly as could be, calling me young Yankee and making small talk.

I sign the paper and she hands me the key attached to the plastic tag with the number 8 on it. She tells me where to find room 8 and off I go. There were only ten rooms, five on the bottom, five on the top. I'm confident I would have found it on my own, but I humored her. I stop at the car to grab my beer and suitcase—in that order, of course—and go to room number 8. I insert the key while juggling the bags, and I give a little shimmy to the door and push it wide open.

To my surprise, the room is not empty, and in fact it appears to be occupied by a local couple, rolling on the bed and going at it like drunk monkeys. The Pabst Blue Ribbon cans strewn about were obviously the fuel for this romantic interlude.

The girl turns her head a little and gives me a blank stare and I get a good look at her. Oh, sweet Jesus. The missing teeth are what I remember most about her, but the bulging eyeballs were a close second. This poor girl was like ugliness dipped in misery, and at first I wanted to congratulate her on getting laid, but the cross-eyed stare with the mouth hanging open kind of froze me in my tracks.

No words are spoken as I just stand there, not knowing if I should cry or wind my watch. I've never really seen a train wreck, but I'm thinking this is pretty goddam close.

Finally, the guy gives me a quick little look, with his ass bouncing up and down, the bed squeaking and the occasional grunting of Broom Hilda. He calmly says to me, "We was here first. Go away."

So I did. Quickly.

I walk back down to the office, bags in hand, and I smile at the little lady and explain to her that I just interrupted a form of local procreation and would need another room.

She suddenly recalled that, "Oh, yeah, number 8 is taken," and said she was very sorry. She then says, "Take room number 10," and gives me a polite wave and nothing more.

"Okay. But I'll need another key."

"Oh, honey, that there key will work in every door in this building."

You gotta be shittin me. "Is that the same with all the keys?"

"Summa them, yeah. Can't keep track of 'em all anymores. G'night, sonny…"

Ten freakin' keys and you can't keep track of 'em all? It was obvious that this discussion was over, so I shut up, smiled and left. Sometimes less is more, as they say.

So I go to number 10, slowly open the door, and to my relief, it's empty, so that's a good thing. I finally put my stuff down and I chuckle to myself as I pull the little chain across the latch and realize it's my only form of security. Welcome to the glamorous world of travel.

I wonder to myself if this was payback for the turtle.

§ § § § §

One of my functions on this job was to verify that all the devices and control components were installed and wired correctly. This meant "walking the system," checking each and every device on this job. For the most part, it was the same on all of our start-ups.

This was not a problem until I got to what was referred to as the *stretch conveyor.* This was a four-foot wide conveyor that *stretched* at least a quarter to half a mile between two mountain tops. High in the air. Really high. And since this conveyor had a number of tension and web switches, it meant I had to climb up and check them all. Fortunately, there was a catwalk that ran the length of this thing, with a railing that I could clutch.

As I prepared to do this, I suspect the local electrical contractors had an inkling that I was not fully prepared for this task. They giggled a lot as they kept telling me, "Don't look dahn, Yankee."

Of course, I was hell-bent on proving I was cool with the whole thing, which I wasn't, but I had to put up a front.

I climbed up the never-ending stairs until I was what seemed like a thousand feet above the valley below. It was probably more like five hundred, but after four ninety-nine, who's counting? I could see the road far below and the occasional passing of the coal truck. I took my tools and began going through the system, checking the devices. After a couple of minutes (which seemed like hours), I started to feel the wind, my legs started shaking, and I swear that catwalk started to sway and I did it—I looked down.

BIG mistake. Immediate pre-upchucking began, first with small spasms, but I was able to retain it. I continued on a little bit, but as I looked down again, I saw the roadway below—far, far below—and I let loose. I barfed everything in my system right onto the shiny new conveyor belt. Holding on to the railing with both hands, I heaved like a champ for what seemed like an hour, but was probably closer to two or three minutes.

I regained my composure, and kind of stood still for a minute to get my shit together. But at least now I had an empty tank, so I didn't fear another come-uppance. I continued on with only the occasional dry heave, finishing my high altitude duties.

I climbed back down to the starting point, and was quite pleased, as apparently nobody had binoculars to witness my christening of the conveyor. This little yak-fest was my own little secret. In actuality, I was pretty damn proud of myself that I had only puked and nothing more.

Since I had finished checking the devices, it was now time to do a test run of this conveyor belt. This meant the pile-o-puke would make its way to the plant where it would be conveniently and efficiently deposited into the holding cell, which had a giant scale built in to weigh the puke—I mean coal. Probably a six-foot drop or so from the conveyor to the scale, which was actually set on the floor. The sixth floor, that is.

I liked to believe I was a pretty quick thinker, so I tried to delay the start-up of this particular belt, knowing the treasure that was up there. I pulled a main fuse and made like I couldn't understand why this thing wouldn't start. This backfired on me, as the electrician in charge put another fuse in and he started the belt.

As the conveyor belt ran toward the plant and the small group of us watching this thing run, I estimated my drop zone and kind of eye-balled it as it made its way toward us. Seconds before it arrived, in a rush of panic, I sprung to action. In one sweeping motion, I spread my arms wide and pushed the guys back and made sure they were all safely out of the danger zone.

The conveyor belt didn't disappoint me, and the second coming of my breakfast splattered right before our feet. By my estimate, the closest pair of shoes to this little surprise was about four and a half inches.

No one said a word as we stood there. The locals just stared at me for what seemed like an eternity. Finally, one of them spoke up. "Thanks."

"You betcha," I said.

That was that and we all went about our business.

A little while later, the foreman came up to me and repeated his earlier advice: "I told y'all not to look dahn."

§ § § § §

The plan was usually for me to show up first, to make sure everything was installed correctly and ready to start up, thus the term, *start-up*. This would typically take about a week or so.

We were at that stage of things when Greg showed up. Now, Greg was a very intelligent guy, but without the hands-on, industrial experience. He knew how everything worked, or was supposed to work, but the actual hardware and component design and installation was not his forte´.

Greg showed up and I took him around to meet the people on site and give him the basic nickel tour. After that, we split up so Greg could get his computer and things and bring them to the control room.

To give you a little mental picture of the building, we were on the second level of a six story, corrugated steel platform building structure. The building was installed next to a set of railroad tracks that we had to cross to get to the building and the stairs. We had to duck around and through the crossbeams and knee braces, which were steel angle irons installed to hold up the rest of the structure. The coal would drop from the conveyor belt (the one I had already tagged) to the drop area; it would be cleaned and weighed, then fed into a waiting rail car below.

Everything made of steel was painted drab green, and there was a lot of it.

As I waited with the others, making small talk, I saw through the window that Greg was making his way toward the control room from the parking lot about a hundred feet away. As we stood around the room bullshitting, we heard (and felt) a deep, echoing thud. Actually, more like a *bong*.

At first I didn't think much of it, as loud noises were common on this job. That is, until the foreman tapped me on the shoulder and pointed out the window. "Isn't that your buddy down there?"

I looked out the window and saw Greg staggering around, hunched over with his hands clutching his forehead. His computer and other things were scattered next to the tracks. I suddenly put two and two together and knew what had happened. Before I could say anything, one of the workers looked out the window and asked, "What the hell happened to him?"

To which the foreman quickly answered, "The smartest guy here just walked into the building column."

I ran down the stairs to help him, quickly glancing at his dropped gear as I made my way over to him.

"Greg, are you okay?"

"Fuck no! Ah SHIT! I hit my fuckin' head! I think I'm gonna fucking pass out! Ah…fuck! Fuck!"

I'm toning it down quite a bit, but he was hurling expletives that would have made a longshoreman blush, all while firmly clutching his injured melon. He dropped to his knees, rubbing his forehead and screaming the word *fuck* at varying decibels for a few minutes.

He was obviously in a lot of pain and apparently very pissed off. I looked over again at his dropped belongings scattered in the gravel and took a mental inventory:

- One computer in a square black nylon case
- One brown leather briefcase
- One standard issue, yellow hard hat

"Greg, were you wearing your hard hat?" I asked.

"I was carrying the goddam thing!"

"Carrying it?"

"Yeah, it's too fucking tight on my head," he yelled back to me.

I just looked at him for second but I had to say something. "Well, congratulations! Thank god you weren't wearing it, otherwise you might have scratched it and we wouldn't want that now, would we?"

So, instead of wearing the too-tight hardhat or even adjusting the goddam strap, he carried it. He had a nice lump going on there, and he was a bit nauseous for a while, but eventually he was okay and the golf ball sized egg on his gourd went down in a couple of days.

BIG STONE GAP

One of these jobs took me to a town called Big Stone Gap, Virginia, a quiet little town nestled next to Black Mountain, where there was coal to be had. This job was a huge prep plant, one that received the raw coal straight from the mine and prepped it for sale and usage. The prep part of it was basically cleaning the dirt and other impurities from it so it would burn.

Our job was the electrical panels and control of the systems conveyor belts, pumps, and other automated moving parts. Not unlike any other coal project, but this was deeper in the south and a really big project, overall. I planned on being stationed there for at least three weeks or so, to get the system ready for starting, and then my boss, Phil, would show up to load the software and start the commissioning.

This was the plan, at least.

When I showed up on day one, the electrical foreman, whose name was Daryl Baner, was waiting for me with open arms. Problem was, as I found out a little later, Daryl was a few days behind schedule and forgot to mention that to us, or to the general contractor.

I arrived at the home base around one o'clock in the afternoon on a Tuesday. Home base, by the way, was actually a rented construction trailer with power hook-ups, a desk, a phone, and a few chairs.

I arrived in one piece and quickly was introduced to Daryl. We sat down at the makeshift desk and started looking over the blueprints so I could get familiar with the lay of the land, so to speak.

It wasn't long before Daryl pulls out a couple of cans of Mountain Dew and some ice cubes from his cooler and pours a couple drinks in the standard, red plastic cups. I thought this was nice of the guy, but a little bit odd that he's set up with ice cubes and cups like we were at a backyard barbeque.

It all came together, though, when Daryl reaches down and pulls out a clear glass Mason jar filled with the local hooch. I was told by Phil and Bud to beware of this local hooch, more commonly known as moonshine, and Yankees like me needed to take it easy with this stuff.

Daryl asks if I'd care to join him a small sample of the local's finest. I accepted, of course, and we talked on about the job.

One turned into two, two into three, three into…well, you get the picture. It was about four-thirty when I realized this was a stall tactic; but I mostly didn't care at this point, which I later realized was his plan.

Wednesday morning was when I realized I could have stayed home a couple more days, but it was too late now. Of course, the management didn't know he was this far behind schedule, and having this little morsel on Daryl didn't escape me, either, so I blackmailed him into giving me two bottles of shine to keep me quiet. He thought that was a fair price, so he was more than willing to pay the piper. I figured I could take the shine home for Christmas with the in-laws. If that didn't work out, I could always find some paint to strip, or possibly even fuel my lawn mower with it.

§ § § § § §

The guys used to spend their lunch breaks hunting for snapping turtles in the creek beside the plant. They really liked their turtle soup, but it was the first experience I'd had with this. One day, they finally got me to go with them, and it was quite an experience. To catch the snapping turtles, which can actually take a finger off with relative ease, you go knee deep into the water, armed only with a broomstick, and start blindly reaching into the side of the creek bed, in the natural little caverns and indentations below the water line. Apparently, snapping turtles burrow themselves head first into the dirt walls. You just have to assume that they all got the memo and do, in fact, go in head first. You reach in as far as you can, and if/when you feel what may be a turtle's tail, you grab it quickly and pull hard. This was their daily routine.

When a turtle was caught, you take the broomstick, but no, you don't hit the turtle with it. You just wave it in front of his nose and *snap,* he reaches out and bites it. Hard. So hard you can twirl the stick around and ol' Mr. Turtle doesn't let go.

While he has a grip on the wooden stick, you pull on it a little, and with your free hand, take your buck knife and slice his head right off.

I've always wondered, "Just how do you get turtle meat out of a snapping turtle?" It's simple. With the help of an everyday garden hose.

Yes, a hose. Hold the now-dead turtle by the tail, and shove the end of the hose hard and deep into the turtle's ass. The true professional can do this in one swift motion.

The next step is to turn on the water. Mr. Turtle expands like a balloon, and then you again take your buck knife and slice around the middle, just where skin meets shell. It'll pop right open at that point, exposing the guts and what the locals called "the meat." They actually did this every day, and every day they were eating turtle soup, turtle stew, or just plain ol' turtle chunks. I tried it once or twice, but the thought of eating a decapitated, sodomized turtle didn't really appeal to me. It's probably an acquired taste. I preferred traveling the twenty miles round trip to the local Hardee's

§ § § § §

Phil showed up after a couple of weeks, and my man Daryl and I welcomed him with a moonshine afternoon. Another wasted day that I'll never get back, but it was now a tradition.

Phil and I spent most of the time in the control room, with Angelo, the operator. Angelo had a ritual of feeding the stray dogs at the plant with his lunch scraps every day. It was a good thing, I guess; otherwise, they might have left. Anyway, Phil, in his twisted sense of humor, programmed the color-graphic computer screen to display a colorful message every day, precisely at noon: "ANGELO—FEED THE DOGS!"

This was cute, and after a while, we kind of didn't pay any attention to it.

Then one day, long after we were gone from the job site, one of the corporate Vice President of-Something-or-Other was in the control room at precisely noon, saw the screen, and just blew a gasket over it. He raised all kinds of hell with just about everyone within earshot. When the dust settled, I was sent back to Big Stone Gap to re-program this little ditty. Another three days I'll never get back, and Daryl wasn't even there anymore, so we couldn't drink in the trailer.

I did what I was sent to do. Angelo apologized to me and was actually very sad that his name was not up in lights anymore.

I left the job site, but it took 365 days for Angelo to see his name again, as I programmed the color screen to display his name for sixty seconds, once a year, at exactly noon on the anniversary of my recall visit. Kind of my way of sticking it to the man.

§ § § § § §

As I mentioned, this was a really big project, and I had been there over five weeks without a break and I was simply burned out. Plus, I was young and in love and hadn't seen my girl in a month. We were making progress, but with so many devices, and the fact that the general consulting firm didn't have a real clue on how the process really had to work, we pieced it together day by day. We would start around six A.M. each day and work until dark. Phil knew I had hit the wall, so to speak, so he had called Bud to come down and assist him. (Actually, Phil didn't need assistance at this point—just someone to keep him company and drink with at night.) Plus, we had other jobs that I was scheduled to be on, so I got cut loose.

I got my marching orders and they had one of the plant engineers ride me to the Tri-Cities airport in Johnson City, Tennessee, where I caught a flight home to Pittsburgh.

The little bit of irony with this is that at the ripe old age of twenty-five, this was my first flight on an airplane. The first of thousands to come.

I had heard that the drink cart had beer, so I struck up a conversation with the waitress, I mean stewardess (as they were called in 1985), and she showed a lot of compassion and sympathy, and slipped me free beers all the way to Pittsburgh. I was also in the smoking section, so I lit up a Marlboro, sipped a beer, and made myself comfy on the way home. The stewardess actually sat down and joined me when she was done serving the other passengers. She bummed a 'Boro from me, and we chatted our way across the friendly skies.

This was the way to fly. I felt like I was back home hanging out at Bobby's Lounge. Twenty-four hours earlier, I had never been on an airplane, and now I have a favorite airline and I was having a cold one at thirty thousand feet. Gotta love it.

Chapter 2

THE BIG GUYS

In 1985, I was assigned to work on a project that would eventually change my entire career path. We were contracted to do the engineering for an Italian-based company that was headquartered near our office in the northern suburbs of Pittsburgh. The company was called Kanton USA, and they specialized in designing and making equipment for the production of polyurethane foam products. This was an up and coming industry, and there were only a few players in this market.

My first taste of this industry was a job we did for them that required us to design and supply the panels and software for the assembly of the equipment in Pittsburgh. We would test it there, and they would then dismantle it, ship it to the factory location, and reassemble it. Once it was fully reassembled, I would show up to start the debugging of the system so the software could be started and commissioned by the lead engineer, in this case, my colleague, Greg Williams.

This particular project was a production line of industrial mold carriers and chemical pumping systems to manufacture windshields for automobiles. The plant was in the Baltimore, Maryland, area.

On this job, I met the Kanton Technical Service manager, a guy about my age with a lot of knowledge of the process and systems. Jake Otum was the guy in charge on this job site, and this was clear. He made damn sure of it. Jake and I had similar interests, namely the hotel bar after work, and we got along just fine for the short time I was there.

He also rented a big car and drove me around, as he did with Greg when he showed up. Jake stressed the need to drive a Town Car whenever possible, and I made a mental note and duly filed this little morsel of advice.

Greg and I were scheduled to overlap by two days, so when he got there, I was a happy boy, knowing I was almost home.

The first day there, Greg kind of walked around getting his equipment set up and looking over the job. He really didn't seem interested in being told what to do, especially by a younger-than-him guy like Jake.

Jake is an intense kind of guy with a hot temper and short fuse. Being of Italian-American ancestry, he didn't take a whole lotta shit from anyone. On Greg's first day, I could see he was getting a little hot under the collar with the lackadaisical pace Greg was setting. Sure enough, at the hotel bar that night, he told me he'd let it slide on Day One, but it had better get a little more urgent the next day.

I assured him it would, but since Greg didn't really like to drink, he wasn't there to hear this little speech/warning. Since I was going home, I could basically make any promise that needed to be made, especially when Jake was buying. I wasn't going to be the one to have to follow through.

The next morning comes and the three of us meet in the lobby, and Jake rides us to the plant, which was about a half hour drive down the highway, followed by a quarter-mile gravel road to the plant.

Things are going much like the day before, and I can really see Jake's face turning subtle shades of red. He was like a human mood ring. Jake also had a penchant for the word *fuck* and just about every variation of the word. He could use it as a verb, adjective, noun, or predicate.

Just after lunch on Day Two, we still hadn't applied full power to the control system. Jake was getting pissed and I knew it was only a matter of time until he blew.

I wasn't wrong.

At about two-thirty in the afternoon, Jake storms into the control room and starts letting Greg have it. It went something like this: "Alright, Greg, What the fuck is going on here? We're waiting two fucking days to get this powered up! When the fuck are you gonna start this fuckin' system?"

Greg had a wee bit o' temper himself, if you recall.

"Who the fuck do you think you're talking to? I'll get going when it's time to get going. You're not going to tell me when to do my job. If you don't like it, do it your fucking self!"

Jake responded with his own obscenity-laced retort, which was expected. Like a good tennis match, this went back and forth for a while until it came to match point.

We now had hit an impasse and I tried to make some peace. It didn't work, and I only hoped now that it didn't come to blows. Greg, although a few years older, would lose.

Just at that point, Greg slammed his tablet to the floor and grabbed his coat. I guess he decided that when the going gets tough, leave. He shouted out two parting words, one of them obscene, and off he went. We watched from the control room as he stormed across the plant floor toward the door.

Jake was absolutely livid about this. His face was so red I thought his head was going to blow right off his neck.

I calmed him down, offering words like, "Relax, Jake. We need to get him back to finish this job and get out of here." I was only hours from leaving, myself, and there was no way Greg was leaving before me.

Jake calmed down after about ten minutes and realized he needed to be a bit diplomatic. I was certain Greg was doing the same. Or not. But Jake was our customer, for Christ's sake. Yeah, right. I knew even then I was lying to myself. Greg was leaving. Not just the plant, but the whole goddam town, city, whatever. He didn't give a shit.

Jake and I sat there for a few minutes, alone, as the room had cleared out in a hurry when the *fucks* had started flying.

Jake asked me if I knew where he went, and if he would come back. He was worried that Greg had gone to the airport and headed home. I let Jake stew over this for a little while, and then I hit him with the most logical of scenarios.

"Jake, you have the car, the keys to the car, and we're in the middle of nowhere. My guess is that he didn't get very far."

Jake realized he'd had the last laugh. I'll never forget his shit-eating grin. He slowly made his way out of the plant, alone, as I sat and waited.

Twenty minutes later, Jake and Greg walked in together. Apparently, Greg had started walking toward the hotel, down the gravel road, and damn if he didn't make it to the highway. He must've been really hustling to make it that far.

Jake caught up to him while he was walking down the four-lane highway; a lone figure, pissed off and determined to keep on walking. Apparently, Jake oozed some words of comfort and got him into the car.

Both of these guys had calmed down, and we got back to work. This ended up being a real turning point, as those two were chummy enough now that I could go home and know they were cool. That day, Jake and I became good friends, and that continues to this day. Greg was also baptized into the customer relations side of these business trips.

The next day, I got the hell out of Dodge.

MISSOURI BIN BURGERS

One of the jobs DSI did for Kanton was located in a small town called Perryville, Missouri. This was a small town about two and a half hours south of St. Louis. I spent some time on a job there working with Greg, who had been there before and was well liked by the client. This particular outfit was a Japanese owned company that supplied steering wheels to Honda and Mazda. It was completely Japanese owned but staffed by mostly Americans.

I mention this now because I ended up doing a lot of jobs for this customer, whose steady growth had me returning for many years to come.

My first trip, however, was with Greg to assist in the start-up of the system. Not a big system or particularly complex, so it was an easy one. No pressure.

Greg and I went through the start-up process without any issues, but one day, I witnessed an unprovoked flip-out of monumental proportions.

We went to lunch one day, and Greg was really fond of fast food burgers. Fresh ones, though. Going through the drive-through of the local McDonald's, Greg pulled up to the window and I told him, "I'll take a number three with a Coke."

Greg leaned into the speaker and ordered. "We need one number three with a Coke, and two quarter pounders with cheese and a Coke. But I want them made fresh."

To which the speaker replied, "Sir, all of our sandwiches are made fresh and are served within ten minutes of being wrapped."

That was it. I'm still not sure what set it off, but he was about to explode. I was not prepared for what was to follow.

He leaned closer to the speaker. "I DON'T WANT ANY FUCKIN' BIN BURGERS! MAKE THE GODDAM THINGS FRESH OR I DON'T WANT THEM!

I was speechless. Stunned. I just looked him in wide-eyed silence. I told you about the temper, but Greg had other issues, I guess, and apparently the high volume burger-making process was one of them. But back to the drive-through.

"Sir, there is no need for cussing. This is a family restaurant. We will gladly make you fresh sandwiches, but please pull forward. Our associate will bring them out to you."

Greg wanted the last word. "DON'T MAKE US WAIT FOR A FUCKIN' HALF HOUR, EITHER!"

As we waited for the food, not a word was spoken. Out of the clear blue, this guy just did a Jekyll and Hyde on me, and Hyde had just verbally assaulted the faceless McDonald's speaker.

I quietly tried to come to terms with this. *Bin burger? What the fuck is a bin burger? Who demands fresh at McDonald's? Why does everything have to happen to me?* I'm guessing the McDonald's window jockey was thinking the same thing.

After a few minutes of staring out the window wondering what just happened and why, I spoke up. "Don't care for the pre-made burgers, huh"?

"Nah, you don't know how long they've been sitting there."

He was calm as a cucumber, but I was a mess and had finally found words to share. "You know why we're waiting here now, don't you? They're probably rounding up every last crew member to hocker on our food. Seriously, man, do you think you might have over reacted a bit?" I was fishing for any kind of answer, but got nothing but a shrug.

We sat there for a few minutes in silence, when finally out comes McFrightened with our food. The awkward transaction happens, and the poor kid goes back into the building. Quickly.

We pull into a parking spot, and I watched as Greg wolfed down his freshly made booger burgers while I sat there staring into the sky and wondering what the fuck I was doing there. Needless to say, I didn't even touch my McLunch that day. I was still pretty much in awe as to what actually happened. Bin burger? I never heard of that before, but I guaran-goddam-tee you, I never forgot it.

Note to self: Avoid the drive-through with Greg.

WELCOME TO OHIO, DUDE

Somewhere around the middle of 1986, I was sent to a steel mill near Canton, Ohio. We had a job to automate a part of the steel making process, and I was designing the control panels and the installation.

Phil sent me to the mill to lay out and prepare for the installation of the panels and other hardware. One of my jobs included planning for the field installation, with the location and routing of the electrical conduits that connected the panels to all the devices. This way we could figure out how much material to buy.

When I arrived, I met the plant engineer and we talked for a little while. He gave me a plant layout drawing and a visitor's badge, and pointed me toward the area where we would be working. He told me to have a nice day and wished me luck.

As I walked around the plant, climbing over rails, walking down dark corridors, and taking measurements, I noticed I wasn't seeing a lot of other people. This was a busy plant, and not a single person stopped me to ask who I was and what I was doing.

I continued on, and about two hours into my mission, I found out why I was alone. I was walking a conduit route, and it took me into a remote area of the plant where I came upon a little room that was not on the drawing. No problem, probably just a storage room or closet. I opened the door and walked in, and what I saw can best be described as an opium den. There were ten to twelve guys in there smoking dope, playing cards, and generally just hanging out. One of them got a little startled when he saw me, and jumped up like I was someone who actually gave a shit. Of course, I didn't.

We chatted for a little bit and he was comfortable that I was just a contractor minding my own business. He shook my hand and said, "Welcome, dude."

The guys were actually pretty cool. I sat down and had a cup of coffee and bullshitted with a couple of them for a few minutes. This was kind of like sitting in the corner bar and killing time with some buddies. Problem is, this was a busy steel mill, mid-morning on a normal weekday.

One guy was telling me that he had made sixty grand the year before, and he was a second-year millwright. This was 1986, and that was a hell of a lot of money—for smoking dope, anyway. I sincerely congratulated him and asked if he whistled "God Bless America" when he cashed his paycheck. He laughed a little, missing the irony.

I finished up and left, heading back home thinking I'd had a fairly easy day but actually worked my ass off compared to the new friends I made that day.

I never did make it back to that plant, which was later closed in the evaporation of the American steel industry.

Chapter 3

MOVING ON

In the time I was doing these coal jobs that nobody else wanted, Greg did a lot of work for Kanton, until they finally offered him a job and a bunch more money, so off he went.

I still worked with him some, but now I was really working for him. Not a problem, and we actually had some good times in towns like Nashville, Dallas, and a few others.

Phil needed to fill the slot left open, and he eventually hired a clean-cut kid from a local Christian college. His name was Andrew Peterson. He was young and naïve, but he was a computer geek with short hair, he didn't smoke, and didn't drink. A complete opposite of every single person at DSI.

He was willing to learn, so we tried to get him to fit in. Phil gave him some small stuff to get his feet wet, and a year or so later he got his first big job. This was a huge project for Kanton, in the appliance industry. The end customer was a big-name refrigerator manufacturer, located in a little town in Illinois called Galesburg, not far from Peoria.

This project was designed to inject foam insulation into a refrigerator cabinet with complete automation. This included a maze of conveyors to move these things around on their backs and keep them moving at a pace of about 900 units per shift.

My job, as usual, was the overall system checkout before the new guy showed up to download and start debugging the software. This is one job that was a true beast, and it would separate the men from the boys in more ways than one.

When we would get deployed on these jobs, the first thing we would think of when we got on the job site was, "When can I get home?" That was typical for all of us, but in between was usually an enormous amount of pressure, since everything seemed to be late and the deadlines were absolutely critical. Usually, the customer's financing and release of funding was tied to a start-up date or some kind of production milestone.

Since the start-up guys were the last ones on the job site, any delays by the mechanical or installation team was shoved on us as the start date was pushed back, but the end date wasn't.

This usually just meant we had less time to do our jobs. This would mean that twelve, fourteen, or even sixteen hour days were not uncommon. We tried to pace ourselves, knowing that the bars needed our business as well.

This particular economic support package started in the summer of 1988 and continued well into 1989. We supported the local dining and beverage industry with a lot of cash and business in that time.

It was late August in 1989 when I got my orders and flew off to Galesburg. I arrived one day in the late afternoon and found my way to the plant. Our usual style at the time was to find a back door where we didn't have to sign in or get a badge. I had a map sent to me from the guys at Kanton, and they were expecting me.

I found the entrance to the plant and made my way to the back lot. The route I had to travel was a temporary dirt road since the main road was under heavy construction at the time. The plant security was one up on me, though, as they had a little guard shack in the back of the plant with a single guard on duty. I quickly found out his name was Charlie, and he pretty much didn't give a shit about too much. He was a retiree, just working a few hours a day for something to do. He showed up every morning with a thermos full of coffee and a couple of raw eggs he would fry on the little skillet and hot plate combo he kept in the guard shack.

I got there in mid-afternoon, and was met by the lead electrician for Kanton, a guy named Kenny Toll. Kenny was a small guy, with sandy blonde hair and a round face. He was trying to grow a beard, but it only grew down the side of his face and under his chin, kind of like an Amish guy. He spoke quietly and had a very reserved type of personality. As we talked, he let me know the status of where everything stood, what was still being installed, and a general lay of the land. We went over the project drawings on the trunk of my rental car out in the back forty.

It wasn't long before I figured out that Kenny was a good electrician and was probably a good foreman, but he was a lousy bullshitter. After he went through his spiel, I interrupted him by asking, "How far behind are you?"

"Two weeks."

Of course; two weeks. The industry-standard answer.

This pissed me off a little bit, but I was smart enough now to at least expect it. Kenny helped me bring my things into the plant, and we did a walk-through to see exactly where things stood.

This was a big project, and it covered a lot of floor space in the plant. The client gave us use of these little motorized carts—the orange Cushman vehicles common in industrial plants and factories. These little babies would bring us much joy over the next few months.

When we started in the back end of the plant, making our way to the install area, I noticed another big piece of machinery being installed. I asked Kenny about this, but he didn't know what the deal was over there. I put it in my cranium file to look into this.

He then took me to the equipment area and the control room, on the second level of the mezzanine, which was a part of the new equipment package. It was a nice big area, with a chair and a giant console-type main control panel that would house the computer and all the status lights for the ten individual lines below us. This would be my home for the next few months.

Kenny introduced me to the installation superintendent, who was actually his boss. I was a contractor, so nobody worked for me directly, but rather they were my customers. Technically, I worked for them, but I was the lead guy who was responsible for getting the equipment ready to run, or at least checked out to the point to download the software and let Andrew take over.

The superintendent's name was Douglas Michaels. "Not Doug. It's Douglas." Kenny warned me he was a little weird about his moniker and insisted on Douglas.

Doug was a chain-smoker who was thrust into this position. I remember meeting him because he was a tall, thin guy, with a neatly trimmed beard with a slight touch of gray. He was wearing a white, long sleeve, button-down shirt, faded straight leg blue jeans, and worn-in cowboy-like boots.

He did a good job, though, and apparently the customers loved him. And he was good to work for because he knew how to keep things moving and basically knew how to deal with people. Usually.

After I got the walk-through and the basic feel of the land from Kenny, I headed to the hotel and got checked in.

I signed in, setting up a long term account and arranging to keep the room for a couple months. This would allow me to keep my things in the room when I went home every other weekend.

I checked in, got my key, and immediately began the next order of business, which was finding and checking out the hotel bar. I found it quickly, making note of the location and layout. It was only four P.M., but the bar was already half full. That's usually a good sign to the road whore, as we called ourselves. Fellow travelers could form an immediate bond in the hotel bar, and a good bartender could see this and capitalize on it. That's because there's one thing we all have in common: We're all on expense accounts.

I eventually strolled down there and found a stool with my name on it and sat down. Turns out, I was next to Doug, I mean Douglas, in his white, long sleeve, button-down shirt, faded straight leg blue jeans, and worn-in cowboy-like boots.

He welcomed me with open arms and a loud, boisterous, "HELLO, BARRY!"

He then proceeded to introduce me to the entire staff. The bartenders, hostesses, busboys, and even the hotel manager. It was obvious he was a regular, and the staff loved him. I made it a point to make them love me, too. Find common ground and form a bond with the customer, your basic Business 101.

We formed a bond that evening until one A.M.

Forming that bond made for a slow start the next day, but I got to the plant around seven A.M., and met up with Kenny. He asked me how I spent my evening, and I told him about the seven-hour chat in the bar with Michael. He looked at me in a little disbelief and said he didn't like to go there, especially since Doug was always there. He was a bit intimidated by him, but I would work on that.

Shortly thereafter, Doug came strolling in, wearing a white, long sleeve, button-down shirt, faded straight leg blue jeans, and worn-in cowboy-like boots.

The plan was for me and Kenny to start the debug, and two more electricians would be deployed the following week. We were each given an FM transmitting radio so we could maintain contact with each other over this massive equipment site. With the control room upstairs and a lot of the machinery downstairs, this was an absolute necessity.

These radios provided a huge benefit to the job; they also provided the same degree, if not more, of amusement for our little group of morons.

Kenny and I did fine, though, and throughout the week, he was kind enough to show me around town to some of the establishments.

The first week there, we hit three or four of the better bars in town, and it became apparent Kenny was a little shy with the ladies. He was single, and everywhere we went, I would pressure him into going over and talking to a possible companion. He mostly declined, but that was okay, since I didn't want to drink alone, anyway.

I quickly realized during week one that Kenny was a bit gullible. He was a good electrician, but his karma was such that he could get shit on at any time by any one.

One afternoon, we were in radio contact checking some devices, and we quickly found a couple things that needed replaced. This was his job, so I left him alone to do his thing. As for myself, I realized that I was in the control room and hadn't attended to one of my rituals, and that was munchables in the control room. I decided that, with Kenny knee deep in his repairs, I could sneak out of the plant and head down the road to the local grocery store to take care of my immediate problem. So I left without a word.

Fifteen minutes later, I'm in the snack aisle at the local Food Lion looking for pretzel stix and pistachio nuts. I'm standing there in aisle nine with a stupid look on my face when my radio starts squawking, with Kenny trying to contact me with some sort of emergency. My fellow shoppers all looked at me with quizzical puppy dog faces as my radio blared obscenities when Kenny discovered that he hadn't shut off the power source, and he was currently getting 120 volts of electricity running through his fingers.

Our radios were the clip-on type with the flexible phone cord wire with a microphone/speaker on the end. The little end would clip on your collar, with the cord running down your back. This way, when Kenny started yelling, "Son of a bitch! Turn off the fucking power! Now!" it was a very loud and very clear broadcast to all my fellow shoppers. You've got to love this FM radio technology. It's a very clear, crisp transmission.

Embarrassed as all hell, I turned the volume down and slid toward the produce aisle before these kind-hearted Midwestern ladies let me have it. Finding a quiet corner, I keyed the mike and asked him if he was okay.

"I'm fine. But please turn off the power. I'm not sure where the main switch is."

I did know, but I wasn't much help here at the Food Lion. "Kenny, come up to the control room and we can go over it. I'm going to the restroom, so I'll meet you there in a minute."

"10–4."

The line at the checkout was a little longer than I would have liked. Sure as shit, Kenny squawked over the radio again and again. "Where are you?"

I finally shot back at him, "I'm making my way over there now. Give me a minute. Go get a Coke and I'll see you there."

Fifteen minutes later, I was getting out of my car in the back of the plant and heading in to the control room. Walking up the stairs to the second level with my bag of groceries, Kenny spotted me, and finally realized he had been hosed.

"Where were you really at?" Kenny asked me.

"Care for some pretzel stix?"

He was not amused, and apparently he wasn't in the mood for a snack, either.

We sat down and he told me all about his brush with live current, and then we shut off the power and got back to business.

§ § § § §

There were two main customer contacts we worked with. The leader was Dave Lacher, and his right hand man was Stu Kapinski. Dave was the patriarch of the engineering department, and he was very adept at getting his way with suppliers. He was a master at beating the vendors down until he either got his way or at least a bit of something for nothing.

Dave was in his early sixties, the grandfatherly leader of the company's foam group. So much so that the guys under him called him Dad, but not to his face. He could be a nice guy, but he could also be a real son of a bitch when he wanted to.

Stu, on the other hand, was in his late thirties and was technically sound, but didn't much care for the political side of the project installation process. He wanted to make good product and learn as much as he could.

Whenever Dad would come into the control room screaming and bitching about the schedule, Stu usually stood two steps behind him and admired the ceiling. This was actually quite impressive because there were many times when Dad flipped out like a lunatic but Stu stood stoic and silent, usually admiring the light fixtures or some other far away object. Some of us were convinced he just went to his happy place. Then again, maybe this was his happy place.

Most of the high octane complaining was aimed at Douglas, since he was the leader, and Doug would offer the usual retorts of, "Yes, Dave. Okay, Dave. Will do, Dave."

This was also a source of amusement for us, but occasionally it was pretty heated. Ol' Dave had a low tolerance for delays and any general bad news in the schedule update meetings. Of course, this, too, would be a source of our entertainment in the months to come.

When Kenny and I had gotten to a point where we could use a chase team to start testing, Kanton sent a few more electricians and a couple of tech service guys. The tech guys were responsible to actually start the equipment and make sure it was working correctly and the sequencing was correct. That was Jake Otum and his guys, and they would soon be joining us in our little Midwestern fling.

They also had another electrician take over the completion of the install work and the overseeing of the contractors. Jim Stanton was the guy. He was a little older than us, a family man who previously worked at a nuclear power plant. He was also a part-time preacher in his church. Jim was an average sized Africa-American guy with short hair and a low tolerance for "shenanigans," as he liked to call it. We, on the other hand, had not only condoned shenanigans, but encouraged it. He did his own thing, arriving at six o'clock versus our six-thirty, and preferring not to join us for our nightly drinking festivals, or even dinner, for that matter. Of course, we wouldn't be good road whores if we didn't exploit this once in a while.

One of the things that used to piss Jim off was our frequent use of cocktail napkins. I would use these to design circuits, write software codes, or make general notes. A lot of things came to me as we would be drinking a beer after work. (This is basically why we called it OT.) I guess once we left the plant and stopped pressing to solve a problem, the relaxed atmosphere and the prudent use of Miller Time would make the creativity flow.

The first time this happened, Jim was going though his routine in the plant, when Kenny and I strolled over to talk to him about an electrical design problem with all the lines, for which we had the fix. We went to the blueprint table, and carefully opened the roll of blueprints to the page in question.

Pointing with my pencil, I started. "See this wire here, number 45?"

"Yes."

"Well, it doesn't go there anymore. Scratch that off. It now has to go over here…kind of like this." I spoke as I was drawing a red line on the blueprint.

I then proceeded to pull six cocktail napkins out of my pocket. I unfolded them and arranged them in the proper order to cover the blueprint. Without saying a word, I pulled some tape out and put these little napkins together, all taped up nice and neat, and attached them to the print. "There you go, Jim," I said. "Piece of cake."

Kenny chimed in with, "It's official."

Jim was incensed. He stared down at the print, too pissed off to speak. Of course, that wasn't the point. The main point was to fix the circuit problem; it was just a nice little bonus that it pissed him off to such an extent.

"You ARE NOT going to put cocktail napkins on this blueprint and expect me to re-work these circuits like this. I refuse. This is not the proper way to engineer something. If we were in a nuclear power plant, this would take three days to get approved," Jim said.

"Well, Jim, take a look around. We're in a goddam refrigerator factory in the middle of nowhere. If you want to get home to see Mrs. Stanton, I'm thinking you should just go with it."

Kenny added, "Yeah." He always had my back.

Jim then stormed off to complain to Doug, and one of our guys was there to hear it. Jim started complaining to Douglas, who was wearing a white, long sleeve, button-down shirt, faded straight leg blue jeans, and worn-in cowboy-like boots.

Doug let him get half of his complaint out before he teed off on him, telling him "not to question the guy who's responsible for getting us out of here."

This was basically for our amusement, and the next day, I called our offices, told them of this change, and had revised prints Fed Ex'd to us from HQ.

§ § § § §

One night, after hitting the local pub for a few, Kenny and I pulled into the hotel parking lot somewhere around midnight. When I pulled in, I saw Jim's car sitting all by itself in the front row. Without speaking a word, I pulled next to Jim's car, getting my car about an inch from his driver side door. Again, without a spoken word, I got out of my door, and Kenny instinctively climbed over the front seat and exited my car from the back door.

He pulled out his car keys and walked over to his rental car in silence. He got in, started it up, and pulled it over to the other side of Jim's car, leaving about an inch between the doors. Actually, looked pretty funny, now that I think about it. Kenny and I were driving Lincoln Town Cars. Jim had a Taurus. Kenny exited his car from the passenger side, and we walked inside and went to our rooms without so much as a word about the cars.

§ § § § §

One of the claims to fame in the town of Galesburg was that it was the birthplace of Carl Sandburg. None of us actually knew who he was, but we felt proud to be in his hometown. Actually, I knew he was a poet, but can honestly say I didn't know—or care—where he was born. Until now. I put this in the old memory bank for a future game of Trivial Pursuit.

The big sign on Main Street reminded us every day that the museum and birth house of Carl Sandburg was only 1.1 miles south. Kenny would occasionally declare his desire to visit this morsel of Americana, but I told him I wouldn't go until he knew who Carl Sandburg was.

§ § § § §

One of Kenny's favorite pastimes was smoking a little pot. He didn't drink as much as most of us, so he preferred the occasional getaway with Mr. Green Jeans. A few of the boys would partake, just not as often as the masteris cannabis.

We used to kid him about this. A lot. Knowing the paranoia effect of weed, I would occasionally walk down the hall and pound on his door and scream, "Security!" He admitted the first couple of times I did it, he about shit his pants. But not any longer. Once he came to expect it, though, I gave it up. It was enough for me just knowing he was tip-toeing around his room and peeking out the peep hole trying to bust me. Mental masturbation was just another form of entertainment to us.

§ § § § §

The plant had given Kanton an unused office on the second floor to use while we were there. Nothing fancy, just a desk, phone, and fax, with a little file cabinet. Doug spent a lot of time there, doing whatever it was he had to do at the time. Probably sleep.

One morning, I was walking toward the office to use the phone, when I heard Jim in the office talking to Douglas. Being part neb-shit,

I stopped to listen. I heard Jim telling Doug he believed he smelled marijuana in the hotel hallway last night, in the area of Kenny's room, or the maybe the "guy from DSI." That would be me. And it wasn't.

I was getting ready to read the ol' Rev the riot act when I heard Doug start talking in his raised tone usually reserved for foreigners. "What are you doing, snooping around the halls like a hound dog? This is none of your business, and it's none of my goddam business either."

"Well, Doug, I..."

"Forget it, Jim. I have a lot more to worry about than you *MAYBE* smelling pot in a hotel that holds hundreds of people. And for Christ's sake, if you don't have anything more to worry about than coming in here and trying to rat out your co-workers, then maybe we should get you a little more to do"

I was almost pissing myself laughing. I could hear the chairs starting to move, so I turned tail and shuffled my fat ass down the steps as quickly as I could. I got to the bottom, regained my composure, and walked slowly back up, like I had just gotten there. Halfway up, here comes Jim, halfway down, right on cue.

"Hey, Jim. What's up, buddy?"

Not a word as he walked right past me.

I got up to the office, and there was Douglas, smoking a Marlboro. I lit one up and sat down. I couldn't help but notice that he was wearing his white, long sleeve, button-down shirt, faded straight leg blue jeans, and worn-in cowboy-like boots.

"What's going on, Doug?" I asked.

"Your buddy Jim thinks he smelled dope in the hotel and thought he needed to tell me, for some reason," Doug said.

"Jesus Christ, you gotta be shittin' me. Doesn't he have anything better to worry about?"

"I guess not. I'll make sure he does from now on," Doug said.

"There ya go," I said.

Doug had one more question. "What the hell did you and Kenny do to him the other night?"

"Not a thing," I answered.

Doug kept talking. "He was bitching to high heaven the other morning. Something about his car in the hotel parking lot. Said he was going to bring the fear of Jesus into your lives."

I about choked on my cigarette when he said that. I had completely forgotten about the nocturnal parking lot shenanigans. I was smart enough to wait a little bit before leaving the hotel the next morning, guessing that Kenny wouldn't be. I was right, and he didn't, and he caught Jim's wrath right there and then. I hadn't heard a word about it until now.

All I could do was chuckle at that point.

Recalling the "less is more" thing, I exited stage left.

When I got back to the control room, I made it a point to tell Kenny to open his freakin' window next time he wanted to burn one in his room. Maybe a towel under the door wouldn't hurt, either.

§ § § § §

One morning I was heading toward the restroom, making my way to the entrance to the plant where the other equipment was being installed. A group of Italians were installing machinery similar to what we were doing. Our equipment was built to blow the foam insulation in the refrigerator cabinets, and their equipment was to foam the doors. Kanton was an Italian company as well, but these guys were right off the boat. There was a group of four of them, and two of them didn't speak a word of English.

The one I remember most was Giorgio, a big, dumb looking guy with a giant smile. He was the spitting image of Jethro Bodine, the educated nephew of Jed Clampett of *The Beverly Hillbillies* fame. These two could've passed for twins. Apparently he was the laborer of the bunch. Nice as could be, I think. He smiled a lot and said *ciao* whenever we crossed paths, and we became good wave buddies. I'd wave to him, and he'd wave back. My impression was he was a hard worker, but dumber than a box of rocks, and he obviously didn't care to bathe daily. Of course, this wasn't just Giorgio; this was a Euro thing. He was kind of the poster boy for this phenomenon, though. If you ran into him mid to late week, he was usually pretty ripe. But he seemed harmless.

§ § § § §

Things moved along pretty well, and it was time to call in the rest of the crew. My man Jake Otum was the first to arrive, with a couple of start-up technicians to get the equipment operational. We also called in a couple more electricians to work with us, since we were still way late on the schedule.

Jake showed up with little fanfare, but that soon changed. He immediately took control of the start-up, allowing me and Kenny to concentrate on the machinery, instead of who was taking a break at the wrong time or who showed up late.

I basically gave the guys a little leeway when we did these jobs, trying to treat them like men. I made it clear that they were allowed two pees and a poop, which translates into two fifteen minute breaks and a half-hour lunch. Now they were answering to Jake, and I knew they would be missing me and Kenny REAL soon.

The electricians who were sent down fit right in. The first guy was Tony Allemino, whom we called Alley. The other guy was a con-tracted guy named Paul Vucich. Alley was a year or two older than I, and he was a full blown Italian-American. He was a long-hair, worn in the mullet that was prevalent in the '80s. Paul was about the same age, but he was tall with short hair. An ex-Navy guy. These guys were quite a pair, as they obviously had grown up together and had known each other for quite a while.

Jake showed up with another one of his guys, Jack Cambo. At first glance, Jack was an imposing sight: long dark hair parted in the mid-dle, wire rim glasses, a thick mustache and a full facial beard. And I mean FULL. He was usually wearing his trademark black jeans with either a Harley Davidson T-shirt or a long sleeve Kanton uniform shirt with the Harley shirt underneath. Jack was a good technician, very analytical and extremely mild-tempered. He looked like a bad-ass but was really a quiet guy, a family man with a wife and a kid on the way. He also was from the same town as Paul and Alley, so it was like a ready-made party showed up on our doorstep.

Toward the end of the first full twelve-hour day, the new guys started asking the inevitable question: "What are you guys doing tonight?" The proper answer, of course, was, "Working overtime." This was the generic term for "going out drinking for most of the night." They learned fast. Kenny and I took them to the hotel bar for starters, where we met up with Douglas, who, not surprisingly, was wearing a white, long sleeve, button-down shirt, faded straight leg blue jeans, and worn-in cowboy-like boots.

After a couple hours at this gin mill, the bartender gave us a tip that there was a neighborhood bar down the road from the hotel—away from town—which explains why me and Kenny hadn't found it yet. We never made a right turn when we left the hotel, always a left. This would change.

We got to the bar, called Phil's Lookout, and we walked in like we owned the place, all six of us. We got the customary glares and stares from the locals, but after a few beers and ten bucks in the jukebox, they loved us. Phil, the owner of this fine establishment, quickly became our buddy. And why not? We were pounding cans of beer like we were going to the electric chair in the morning.

And we had to pound cans since that was the only way he sold beer. Strange. No taps, no bottles. Just cans. And each empty was systematically shaken empty in the sink, taken over to the wall-mounted can crusher, crushed and thrown into a thirty-gallon garbage can for recycling. Don't get the wrong idea here; Phil was NOT into the earth and a big fan of recycling. He was cheap. A good cheap, even a funny cheap, but these cans were taken back for the cash. Actually, coin, to be more precise.

We met a few of the locals that night, including the bar maid whose name was Katy. Katy was also about our age, but very naïve. She was amazed at our crew and the ability to spend expense money without counting the change, stacking coins, or hiding the bills.

At the end of the night, we got up to leave, and we all instinctively left all the change and a few dollars each on the bar; nothing extraordinary, and nothing even discussed—just the customary gratuity from our part of the world.

§ § § § §

The next day, it was obvious who's been on-site for a couple months and who had just showed up. The new guys looked like hell and I'm sure they felt even worse. It was actually funny for Kenny and me to watch. Alley and Jack were miserable. Jake wasn't too bad, or maybe he was just a great actor. Paul was in bad shape and wasn't even trying to hide it. His eyes were so glassy we thought he was wearing goggles. It wasn't just him, though. To a man they all looked like they were rode hard and put away wet.

I tried to make light of their misery, explaining to them that what they were feeling had a name. "The problem you have is the aftereffects of working overtime."

They just looked at me through their bloodshot eyes.

"You got the OT Blues." And a phrase was born.

§ § § § §

Day Two finally ended, and about seven P.M., everybody was feeling great and ready to put in another OT shift. It started with dinner at a local rib joint, followed by a visit back to our new favorite place, Phil's.

Only a few of us made it that second night, though. Jake, Alley, and I all continued to the bar while the others called it a night. When we entered, there was Phil, half shit-faced and smiling.

Katy saw us and jumped to her feet. "I'm so glad you guys are here!"

We sat down, and Katy came over to us with a handful of white envelopes, and she leaned across the bar and started whispering to us. "You guys left last night and you forgot your money. I kept it all in the stacks that were on the bar. I think I got everyone's name right. Here, take these." She pushed this stack of envelopes at us.

We looked at each other in stunned silence. I looked at Katy with mixed emotions. What she lacked in the sense of the real world was clearly trumped by her overwhelming honesty.

I spoke up first. "Katy, that money is yours. It's a tip, hun."

"Really? There's over twenty dollars here."

"Katy, believe me, it's yours. There was six of us here and you served us for three hours or so." I pushed the stack back at her.

Jake started chuckling, and finally chimed in. "It's your tip, Katy. Keep it. Please. But if you ever want to see another one, quit arguing and get us a beer."

She smiled like a little girl at Christmas and put the money behind the bar. She got us our beers, and it was clear we were big shit now. These guys from Pennsylvania were cool. Way cool.

I guess it's like the old saying: "In the land of the blind, the one-eyed man is king."

But these were good people, and we had a great time hanging out with Phil and his regulars.

§ § § § §

After a week or so with our newly formed group, it was time to call in the actual software engineer from DSI, the guy who was going to replace me and set me free.

Andrew Petersen showed up one fine afternoon. I had tried to pre-warn the guys about Andrew, that he was not a party guy. He was a clean-cut young college grad who wasn't well versed in the ways of the world. He was a nice enough kid, but he was not going to fit in, and I tried to buffer this, since he was my ticket home.

I was deathly afraid these guys were going to walk all over him take his lunch money, but hey, it really wasn't my problem. Either way, the worst case, in my mind, was that I would overlap him by two weeks and then get the hell out of there.

Andrew showed up and I promptly showed him around, introducing him to the group. He arrived clean-cut and full of hopes and dreams. His first full blown start-up. I had already given the guys a heads-up on ol' Andrew's background and Boy Scout upbringing. When I introduced him to Doug, who was wearing a white, long sleeve, button-down shirt, faded straight leg blue jeans, and worn-in cowboy-like boots, you could feel the skepticism in the room from the get go. Douglas thought he was too young, too green to write the software for a job this big.

Time would tell, but he was my ticket out of there so I talked him up like he was Bill Fuckin' Gates.

§ § § § §

My buddy Andrew got a little taste of our lack of respect for the rental car industry on his second day. We all left the plant together and headed back to the hotel. Kenny was first in line, (in his maroon Town Car), I was behind him (in a brown Town Car) and Jake and the rest of the boys behind me in his white Caddy.

Pulling up to a red light in the heart of Main Street, I got within three feet of Kenny's bumper and *forgot* to hit the brakes. Bang! Andrew shrieked like a little girl. Actually shrieked. I don't think I ever actually used that word, but I'm telling you, he shrieked. Kenny looked at me in his rear view mirror and, with a gleam in his eyes, he jammed his car into reverse. Bang!

Yet another pitiful shriek from my frightened passenger. I couldn't let Kenny get away with this, so I went back at him…bang! Then he went again…bang!

Andrew didn't know if he should cry or hide. Thank god at least the shrieking stopped.

That's when I looked past the passenger side window and saw the other folks in traffic watching, with gaping mouths, what they must have thought was a gang war in progress. They were more frightened than Andrew. Once I saw these people staring at us, I figured it was time to end the Town Car pinball, and Kenny picked up on it about the same time. The light changed and off we went like nothing happened.

Andrew looked over and asked, "What was THAT all about?"

"He looked at me funny. I don't take that shit from anybody." I said this to add fuel to the fire, but there wasn't really a fire. Just messing with him. Andrew, that is.

§ § § § §

As the time went by, and we got further behind schedule, it became pretty clear that Andrew was pissing off just about everybody there, especially Jake. This worried me big time. It could seriously affect my go home plan.

On top of his stubbornness and shitty attitude, Andrew had a habit of wearing ridiculous wool sweaters with little deer on the front. Not a mean or valiant looking buck, but cute little dancing reindeer. This earned him the nickname, Deerski, usually said three times, in rhythm. "Deerski, Deerski, Deerski."

He never figured out why they called him that. Alley invented it, and occasionally he would even put his fingers up over his ears. He even started taking bets on, "Deerski Day."

§ § § § §

We had no choice but to take Andrew with us when we worked OT. It wasn't really a problem, but he was a lightweight with the beers, and we found out that even a peach schnapps was out of the question.

One particular evening, whilst working our typical OT shift, we struck gold. We were all out at one of the nightclubs, with a DJ and dance floor in the back. In the front was a nice big bar where the older guys could have a few cocktails and actually carry on a conversation. This particular evening, Jack, Kenny, Paul, and I were sitting at a corner of the bar, just BS'n as usual. Andrew, on the other hand, had a few drinks in him and was feeling fine. He was gonna try to find himself a local gal and have at it.

Problem was, and this was obvious, Mrs. Peterson's baby boy couldn't get laid in a whorehouse with a fist full of fifties.

As the night wore on, Andrew would come back from the dance floor for the occasional refill, telling us how he was "on a trail," his actual words.

We kind of blew him off, but finally the barmaid asked me if he was with us. I told her the story of his boy-scouting background and his lack of experience in the lovin' area. His sweater told the rest of the story.

This led to the idea of the night, possibly the year. I asked each of the guys for a couple of bucks, and they handed them over and we kind of pooled a beer fund. I called the barmaid over, and told her our plan. "Next time Andrew comes over for a beer, give him one and tell him it's from an admirer." I handed her the cash.

She looked at me like I was from Mars. "I can't do that. That's mean."

Paul threw her a ten-spot.

"Okay, I'm in," she said.

We introduced ourselves and she told us her name was Cassie.

The first time he came over, we kept our conversation going, pretending we were engrossed in some deep subject and not paying any attention. Mr. Peterson got his beer and was told it was from his *admirer.* He perked up like a puppy and tried to pry out of her who it was, but she was pretty cool with it, telling him, "She's on the dance floor. Go find her."

He ran to the dance floor. I mean he actually *ran* to the dance floor. We all looked at her and we knew this was going to be a good one. We tossed her another ten dollar bill.

This went on all night, and he never had a clue. Each time, Cassie handed him a free beer and came up with a new clue as to where his love connection was, telling him things like him she was shy, or embarrassed, or she needed some courage. All the while, we were acting oblivious to the whole thing. He finally came over to us to fill us in. We all pumped him up, trying to feed this flame. He was FINALLY going to get a girl.

This went on for a couple of hours, and he kept scouring the dance floor, making it a point to walk up to every available girl there and flash his stupid-looking grin.

The crescendo of this farce was nothing like any of us could have dreamed up. With the DJ calling it a night, Andrew came over to the bar, pleading with Cassie to tell him who this girl was. He needed to meet her.

She finally gave in and said okay. She walked over to him, putting her arm around his shoulder, and within earshot of us, she pointed to the back of the bar and said to him, "There she is, in the corner over there. Go get her."

We all looked over. There, sitting in the corner, was an honest to god four-hundred-pound woman with frizzy hair wearing a man's flannel shirt.

Before we could even start laughing at him, he let out a drunken, "AH!" and he was gone. Ran right out the front door. Pretty quick, too. Ran just like a, well, a deer.

We stayed there laughing our asses off. This was too sweet. We sat there for a while laughing, especially Cassie. She became our newest buddy, and we made it a point to tip her well. She made a nice buck from us that night, and we got a bargain.

To this day, Andrew doesn't know he was set up.

On top of that, he got pretty drunk, too. Driving into the plant the next day, he kept repeating, "The bed was spinning. I couldn't get it to stop."

§ § § § §

During these extended stays in the factories, we would typically befriend the workers in the plant, especially the ones in the maintenance and production groups for the areas we were working. This time was no exception.

We became friends with most of the maintenance department; it was not unusual that we would need their help occasionally, like when we would need a special tool or a component we didn't have with us. We, in turn, would buy lunch or give them hats, T-shirts, and other promo items. We also made it a point to have them drop by the control room and have some of our coffee. "Good relations," we called it.

One day a group of the guys were standing around talking, and I couldn't help but overhear their topic. Someone was pooping on the toilets. Not *in* the toilets, but *on* the toilets. Apparently it had been going on for a few weeks, but it was now escalating and really pissing off the housekeeping staff. When I first overheard them, I thought it was a joke or that surely I had misunderstood what they were saying, so I asked about it.

It was true, they told me. Someone was actually dropping turds on the outer rim of the toilet bowl and even on the seat. *Unbelievable.* There was no real pattern or particular time of day this was happening. The only thing they knew was that he was targeting the south and central men's rooms on the plant floor.

They called this felon the Mad Shitter.

They asked us to be on the lookout for this bastard, and to let them know if we saw anything suspicious. I was going to ask them to define *suspicious,* but I let it go.

§ § § § §

As the days passed, it became apparent that Andrew had worn out his welcome and wasn't keeping the schedule moving fast enough. Even Douglas, knowing he was supposed to be the main guy, pulled me aside and told me that he had contacted my boss, Phil, telling him he needed to get Andrew out of the picture, and I would need to stay. Wonderful.

Sure enough, Andrew got his marching orders, obviously a little shocked that he was thrown off his first job site. I tried to comfort him, but this pompous asshole had just added months to my already-been-here-too-long stay.

In true road whore fashion, we told Andrew we would take him out for a going away party. We went down to Phil's Lookout, and our old friend Katy was working that night and we explained that Andrew was going home. It was a fairly full house that night, with a lot of locals gathered around the bar. Andrew was getting buzzed and feeling quite sorry for himself.

As we sat around pretending to commiserate with him, all of us had pretty much had enough of his whining, but we endured it. The first time he got up, I called Katy over to ask her for a favor. On the other side of the bar was a young, local girl, a little on the homely side. Not ugly per se, just homely, and obviously single.

I realized this would be my last time to screw with Andrew, so I put the wheels in motion. I gave Katy a twenty-dollar bill, and asked her to get the young lady a drink and tell her it was from Andrew. Likewise, she needed to get Andrew his next drink and tell him it was from the young lady.

She kind of hedged, obviously on the fence as to whether she wanted to be a part of this. Turns out she was a decent person, unlike us assholes. Paul and Alley started laughing, prodding and encouraging her. They helped the cause, each throwing her some cash, which pushed her over the edge.

When Andrew came back and sat down, Katy took a drink over to the girl, and we saw her talking and pointing toward Andrew. She walked back toward us, giving Andrew a drink and telling him it was from "the young lady over there."

He looked over at her, and go figure, she was looking at him and smiling. He held up his Coors Light and gave a little salute to her, and, amazingly, she did the same. He was smiling from ear to ear. He looked over at Paul and me, and asked us if we had anything to do with this. The balls of this guy.

We denied it, of course, and he hem-hawed around for a while, not sure what to do next. Alley did. He slid down the bar a few spots and had Katy buy the young lass another drink from Andrew. Again she looked over at him and gave a smile and a nod.

Andrew tensed up, again asking, "What did you guys do"?

Paul delivered a straight faced lie, telling him in a stern voice, "This is for real and you better not blow it. Go TALK to her."

Paul all but grabbed him by the neck and dragged his ass over to her. If nothing else, we wouldn't have to put up with his whining anymore. He mustered up the courage and went over on his own, and actually started talking to this young local.

Sonofabitch. Could this be a love connection in the making?

We ended up leaving him there, and he found his own way back, apparently. We saw him the next morning in the lobby, and we were all pretty curious about his night. When Paul asked him if he got any, he replied, "Oh yeah, I got it."

"Oh, yeah, what did you get, big boy?"

"Her phone number."

Poor geek. He'll never be back in this town again, but he got himself a phone number.

§ § § § §

The Mad Shitter had struck again, and these guys were really getting pissed.

If—I mean when—they catch this guy, it ain't going to be pretty. I'm guessing the shit's really going to hit the fan.

It was becoming an obsession with a couple of the maintenance guys. They were talking about look-outs, spying, you name it. I think they may have even started a pool for the one who catches him. I didn't want to use the word *bounty,* but…

§ § § § §

Even after a few months on this job, Kenny was still talking about seeing the Carl Sandburg house. He even read about him, which made him the resident expert on this guy. He was spewing facts and little tidbits of information he picked up.

His constant nagging finally took its toll on me, and I gave him what he wanted to hear. "Jesus Christ, Kenny. I'll go with you. Next time we're here on a weekend, I'll go. I promise."

Hearing this, he was now officially a happy boy. I figured I owed it to him.

§ § § § §

Douglas came in one fine morning, and gathered us all together. Not surprisingly, he was wearing a, well, you get it. He was going to the airport to pick up a guy from Italy, and we should be cool to him.

His name was Giuseppe, and he was a tooling technician. His job would be to make sure all the molds were within tolerance of the models they were supposed to manufacture. This was a huge task, as we came to find out. The molds that were supplied, and there was a shitload of them, would all need to be shaped and adjusted to meet the specifications. Or better yet, for customer Dave to approve them. Another step in getting our asses home.

Douglas came back with our brand new Italian, one Mr. Giuseppe DeRossi. He seemed like a nice enough guy, but spoke very little English. About as much as my wave buddy, Giorgio, but about a hundred and fifty times smarter. Giuseppe was in his mid-thirties, probably ten years or so older than me.

Our man Giuseppe worked like a dog. He was like a machine, grinding, measuring, filing, measuring, more grinding, measure again, on and on and on. He worked up a pretty respectable sweat each day, and we were constantly reminded of the Euro-habit of bathing weekly whether you needed it or not. Holy shit, this poor guy stunk to high heaven.

We gathered Doug one morning and told him it was his job to talk to him, in whatever language worked best. "Take him to the Food Lion and get him some soap and shampoo, for Christ's sake," Paul said.

"I know. I know. I'll talk to him. Believe me, I know. I'm the one who drives him everywhere," Doug replied.

It sucks to be the boss, but you have to take the good with the bad. We were going to ask Doug to show him how the laundry service works, but we weren't sure he knew about it himself.

I made it a point to introduce him to the other Italians working near the back of the plant. I showed him around and let him meet them. First, I took him to Massimo, who was the boss, and finally, my smile buddy, Giorgio. After they talked for a while, I kind of asked Giuseppe what he thought of those guys. Turns out, they all worked in the same small town outside of Milan, Italy. Giuseppe filled me in a little bit, telling me how they were coming along and what-not. He also mentioned the pecking order. "Massimo is boss of men. Giorgio, he not so bright but good at working."

Not that it mattered, but I felt a little impressed with myself at my take on those guys.

§ § § § §

One of the fun things to do with Giuseppe was to teach him English words that he thought were appropriate, but of course, they weren't.

For example, one afternoon we were getting ready to wrap for the day, just at six. I went to where Giuseppe was working like a dog, and I called his name. "Giuseppe! Giuseppe!"

He looked at me. I lifted my left arm and started tapping my watch. "Fuck it!"

He looked a little confused, so I said it again, still tapping my watch. "Fuck it!"

I then added the slashing motion across my neck, hoping it was an internationally recognizable signal for "quitting for the day."

He got it! He looked at his watch, tapped, and said, "Okay, Barry…fook it."

Still tapping my watch, I confirmed back. "Yeah, fook it."

He smiled and started packing up his tools to leave.

My only intention was to show him it was quitting time. He took it one step further and, in his mind, assumed that when the hands on his watch were straight up and down, the English word for this time was, "Fuck it."

Kind of like fuck it A.M. and fuck it P.M.

Of course, we didn't realize this right away. Apparently over the next couple of weeks, he showed off his new English word to the hotel staff, and as we found out, he had no problem communicating this to Dave and Stu, particularly when our two customer friends were watching him and the clock struck six.

Right in the middle of a conversation he and Doug were having with the customers Dave and Stu, he saw it was six o'clock, and suddenly ended the conversation with polite tap of his watch, a smile and a, "Fuck it."

We had to promise Douglas we wouldn't teach Giuseppe any more English.

§ § § § §

It turns out our new Italian friend was a drinker. He had little choice. It was either drink with the rest of us or sit in his room and watch a TV that he couldn't understand. Doug and I took him to the hotel bar for a few, and from there we went out to eat and have a few more cocktails.

We went to a neighborhood joint near the main part of town, a little more classy than I usually did with the boys. But the three of us sat at the bar, and we ordered some steak sandwiches and fries, typical American dinner. Our boy loved it. He also loved Budweiser. In his limited English, we were able to decipher that he usually drank wine, as most Italians do. He was married and had two children, and never got a chance to go out and drink beer with friends.

So the beers were flowing freely, and he was getting a little wound up. It was cute.

We did, of course, explain to the barmaids that our friend was from Italy, and new to the States. Most of the locals had never met a European, so they usually took to our guy pretty quickly.

With Giuseppe enjoying the expense account beers, he started getting a little more loosened up, and was actually becoming kind of talkative, but we only understood a quarter of what he said. And Douglas's thoughts on speaking to a foreigner were to use small English words but SAY THEM VERY LOUDLY!

"GUISEPPE! WOULD YOU LIKE ANOTHER BEER?"

"GUISEPPE! THESE ARE CALLED FRENCH FRIES!"

At one point I couldn't take it anymore. "Doug, He's Italian, not deaf. Quit screaming at the poor bastard. Just talk slow. And only use verbs and nouns until he catches on, but stop yelling at him."

Giuseppe sat there smiling. And drinking.

When he needed a refill, he leaned toward me. "Barry. How you say more beer?" he asked in his broken English.

He needed to know how to order a beer. Of course. The basic survival words.

I held my empty bottle off the bar a little, showing him to do the same. I then said, quietly, to him, "Beer wench."

"Beer wench?" he said.

"Yes. Beer wench." I repeated this while waving my empty toward the bar maid, who was at the other end. I motioned to Giuseppe to wave the bottle and say, "Beer wench." He gave it a dry run and I nodded my head in approval.

When the young lady looked our way, Giuseppe stood halfway up on his bar stool, waved his bottle like a flag, and started yelling, "BEER WENCH! BEER WENCH!"

Douglas almost shit his pants. The girl behind the bar gave him a death look, while Douglas held Giuseppe's arm down saying, "No! No!"

All the conversations around us stopped, and everyone on our end of the bar looked at Giuseppe.

I started laughing to myself, and the guys sitting around me started laughing, too, which saved Giuseppe from getting his first bitch slap. The barmaid looked at me and knew what was going on. Thankfully, she was pretty cool about it, pointing at me and shaking her head. I think Giuseppe figured out he was just set up, and he did the only thing he could do. He put this dumb-fuck look on his face, which all but proclaimed his innocence.

The barmaid was a good sport, though. She leaned forward and showed him her name tag. "Sandy."

"Zan-dee?"

"Sandy. Not beer wench."

He looked at me and said something in Italian. I'm thinking it was some sort of invitation for me to have sex with myself.

That was fun. It's those unplanned little things that mean the most.

§ § § § §

The days were getting longer for us, as we kept falling more and more behind schedule. There were days that nothing would go right for us and it seemed we would take one step forward and two steps back.

Thank god I had my Jimmy Buffet tapes to listen to after work. Jimmy had an amazing way of helping me clear my head after a brutalizing day at the office. Debugging software and electronic components all day got to be mind-numbing. I would see these lines of code in my sleep, so I needed a neutralizer, and being a long-time Parrothead, Jimmy usually made the trips with me. Most of the guys enjoyed my JB routine after work. Except Kenny.

At the beginning he did, but one night he took issue to one of the lines in one of the tunes. It was "Son of a Son of a Sailor," and one particular evening, we left the plant and were headed back to the hotel, when I shoved the tape in and the song flooded the Town Car's airspace. I wasn't really paying attention, but when the line played, "the seas in my veins, my tradition remains, I'm just glad I don't live in a trailer," he got noticeably pissed and started bad-mouthing the song, then the tape, then the car, then me, then the two guys in the back.

Paul and Alley started laughing, since they knew why he had suddenly turned into Colonel Bummerinski. Turns out Kenny lived in a trailer—a little one, too. Not even a double wide.

Ouch. Who knew?

§ § § § §

When these long days really hit us, we just couldn't go out and party like we wanted to. One of those nights, it caught up to me.

We got cleaned up after work and went out for a bite. We ate and had a few drinks, but we were all dragging some serious ass so we called it an early night. Must have only been around ten P.M.

I got back to the hotel, turned on the TV, and crawled into bed. This was a good time to call home and check in on things with the missus, so I wedged the phone against the side of my head and got into the phone conversation. I remember the call started with me whining about being tired, miserable, and sick of the job in general.

The next thing I know, I'm being shaken in my bed. Scared the living shit out of me. I open my eyes, as I think I see and feel this figure in the dark trying to wake me up. It takes me a few seconds get my bearings, but I do. I then reach up and grab the bastard by the vest and start a stream of obscenities that flowed from my mouth like I was speaking in foreign tongue. I was getting ready to free up an arm to start swinging, when I finally hear the guy and understand the words coming from his mouth:

"Mr. Metzler! Mr. Metzler! Barry! It's me, Jerry. The manager, Jerry."

I gaze at him with my own version of the dumb-fuck look and ask him what the hell he was doing.

He looks at me sheepishly. "Your wife called us. She was afraid something happened to you. You were on the phone and then stopped talking."

I look down and saw the phone handset lying next to me in bed.

He continued. "You must have fallen asleep when you were talking to her. She called us really worried about you."

I didn't know what to say, so I kind of just half-sat there (in my underwear, no less) for a minute. I quickly got my shit together, and decided it was time to speak. "Thanks, I guess. Jerry, I'm okay. You can go. Thanks. I'll call her."

I had known Jerry for a few months, so I guess he felt he did the right thing. He was a brave man, that one there.

I still laugh when I think back at this middle-aged, slightly balding guy who looked like Mr. French coming into my room to wake me up as I lay there in my underwear, to make sure I wasn't dead.

I called home to talk to the wife, and I was kind of kind of pissed, but I couldn't really act like it. She was just worried.

Totally fucking embarrassing, but hey, what comes around goes around. I guess it was just my turn. I made it a point to call home early in the evenings from that point on.

§ § § § §

Kanton sent down a couple more guys for us to put to work. One was a service tech named Shawn Miller. He was a little older than me, but he seemed pretty sharp. He was hired to work for Jake, so his gig was to get things in production-ready mode. It was obvious he knew what he was doing and would hit the ground with his feet moving, as they say. The other guy was a different story. This kid came in with wide eyes and little else. His name was Chris something-or-other. He was hired as an electrician, on a contract basis, and he was sent down for Kenny to lead around and train. This always scared us a little, as this was a dangerous place if you didn't know what you were doing.

When Kenny brought him into the control room, he introduced him around a little and we started to chat. It was obvious he was young and green, so I wanted to check out his tools. (This was usually a good indicator of a guy's experience level.)

Looking through his tool box, I saw the basics of a couple screwdrivers, wire cutters, etc. I didn't see voltage testers or, preferably, a voltmeter, which was the one that was really needed. As we gathered around the table, I asked him if he had any type of voltage testers.

His answer was one we weren't expecting. "I have these right here." He reached into his little tool box and pulled out this little toy which he proudly held up for all to see.

"You gotta be shitting me," I said to him.

He looked at me with a confused little look. "What's wrong with these?"

What he was holding up was this little Handy-Andy tester, about four inches long, with this tiny little pair of leads coming out of the center piece, with a tiny little light in the center. I really think they sell these in the grocery stores.

"You ain't using these on this job site. You'll get electrocuted and we'll all be here longer than we need to be. Let me see those."

He handed them to me, and I, too, held them up for all to see. I then dropped his pride and joy onto the floor and stomped them a few times with my right boot.

The boys started laughing. Hard. And loud.

"Sorry, dude. There ain't no way in hell we can have you running around here with even the potential to use those things."

The problem was that we had a system that was 480 volts of electricity with no conscience.

"You need to get a real set"

"Well, I do. At home. I'll call my mother to send them overnight mail to me."

Great. He's going to call his mother to send his tools to him.

Kenny, who was actually the kid's boss, finally spoke up. "You don't need to call your mother. You can borrow mine. I have an extra set."

As they walked away, I called back to Kenny, and he came over to us. "Kenny, watch this guy. He could get killed or worse."

"I know. I know. See what I have to deal with?"

So Kenny set him up, and we all understood that this kid was not to be left alone for any reason in this plant. Not that we were worried about his health; it was the schedule problem and we were all ready to blow out of this place. But we figured the life we saved might be one of our own. Besides, a dead body might slow us down.

§§§§§

Like all young kids who were away from home for the first time, our boy Chris couldn't wait to get done with work and go out on the town. Well, he got his wish.

We left the plant in the evening, got cleaned up, and went out for dinner. We ended up at one of the bars in town, where it was kind of relaxing, with a couple pool tables and tunes playing. There were four of us, with me and Kenny, Shawn, and the youngster.

We stayed and relaxed for a little while, calling it a night a little after eleven. We told Chris we were leaving, and he gave Kenny a bit of an attitude. He apparently wanted to stay.

"C'mon, why are we leaving? It's only eleven."

"Five o'clock comes pretty quick. Come on, chief, you'll thank me in the morning."

He kept giving Kenny some shit about leaving, and I joined in. "Chris, we have a lot of things to get done tomorrow. We can come back tomorrow night."

He looked at us like a kid who was just told "no more candy."

He looked Kenny right in the eyes. "You party pussies."

"What?" Kenny asked, insulted.

"You guys are party pussies. "You're too fuckin' old to hang. Party pussies."

Kenny looked at me and Shawn. We kind of looked at each other, and we knew the gauntlet had been thrown down. We took off our jackets and sat back down.

"Okay, kid, you win. Let's see who's a party pussy."

So we all sat back down and ordered a few more beers. Difference was, we knew how to take it easy on a school night. The rookie was drinking like a rock star. It was obvious that he was away from his home and his mommy, and he was ready to party. He lost track of why he was here. We stayed until closing time, with three of us in good shape and one of us plastered. Guess who that was? He was babbling all the way back to the hotel.

We knew he was not going to have fun the next day.

The morning came as predicted, and we got to the cars, all a little curious as to how the youngster was feeling.

It was worse than we ever could have imagined. This kid was still three sheets to the wind. He actually looked like he might bleed to death through his eyes. He was moaning and groaning as he got in Kenny's car. Shawn and Paul jumped in my car, and off we went.

We left the lot at the same time, but Kenny and his party boy showed up about twenty minutes later.

"We had to stop so this party pussy could puke his guts out on the side of the road."

"Well, well, well, Chris. You want to call mom and ask her for a cure?"

He just groaned. And groaned.

There were some union plumbers and painters working around the site, and they immediately saw the kid in his bad shape, and took it upon themselves to let him have it. I, for one, did not try to stop them.

About mid-morning, Kenny found me and we went looking for the party boy. There he was, lying on the floor under a conveyor with a paper bucket next to him, like his own personal puke pail.

Kenny was relentless. "Hey, Chris. Sorry you don't feel well. But you weren't hired to come down here and puke all day. You need to get to work and get those wires pulled to these boxes. You also need to clean up any puke you get on the floor"

Ouch.

I couldn't resist. "Hey, party pussy...who's the party pussy now? You know we're taking you out again tonight and you're going to drink some more."

This brought an instant heave into the bucket.

"Party pussy, huh?" We were moving in for the kill.

The sight of this kid slithering on the filthy plant floor in his coat, with a puke bucket next to him was an open invitation from just about anyone working on this job or even in this plant. We tried to hide him deep in the bowels of the equipment, but we couldn't hide the constant moaning. My god, the moaning.

As bad as we were, the plumbers really gave it to him.

We stood there watching on the floor as one of the guys yelled at him. "Hey, kid! If you feel something furry in your throat, you better swallow hard. It's your asshole!"

Ouch.

One of them got really creative, and showed up with a little Styrofoam bowl from the lunch room. We actually had Chris up on his feet, and although he still looked like shit, he was at least walking erect. That didn't last long.

The guy walked over to the kid with the bowl behind his back. "Hey, kid. Seriously, I know how you feel. We've all been there. I have this sure-fire recipe to cure a hangover." He talked to him in a gentle, fatherly voice that sounded like he'd been there before.

"Okay, I'll try anything," replied our puke-osaurus.

"Okay, eat this as fast as you can." He then proceeded to put this bowl filled with creamy, white mayonnaise in front of the party boy's face. "Go ahead, eat this. Quick."

The scent and sight of the bowl of mayo and the thought of swallowing it made this kid go into an instant puke fit that lasted for fifteen minutes or so. He ended up on his knees looking like he was going into convulsions.

It was pure joy, a well-deserved opportunity to laugh at someone else's misfortune. The whole group of us just couldn't stop laughing or come up with a shred of sympathy. Kenny was relentless. "Party pussy, huh? Who's the party pussy now?"

All good things must come to an end, though, and Doug finally stepped in and asked Kenny to take him back to the hotel.

He was still sick two days after that. On Friday, he flew home, got fired, and we never saw him again.

§ § § § §

The crew had shriveled down to about five of us, but we were still way late on the overall schedule, so we started working earlier to try to gain some ground. If nothing else, it gave the appearance that we were trying.

One evening, we decided we would start at five A.M. instead of the usual six or six-thirty. Not a problem, we all agreed.

Of course, someone had to screw it up, and it was me. I didn't get up on the first ring, so when I did get up, I realized I was already late. I looked into the parking lot and saw the cars gone. No problem, I'll drive myself.

I threw on some clothes and ran to the car. I jumped in and hauled ass all the way to the plant. I got to the property and pulled onto the temporary road they had plowed for us as they rebuilt the real road around the back of the plant. It was dark, and I was still moving at a pretty good clip when I hit the dirt. I weaved the Town Car around and through the track like I was in a tank. I should have slowed down, but obviously didn't, and sure enough, there was a nice big dip in the road. I hit it with some serious force, and the car went nose first into the ground. Next thing I heard was a this-can't-be-good *ca-LANG! ShKech!* I knew it was a steel-ripping sort of noise and it was pretty obvious that something wasn't there anymore.

Fortunately, or unfortunately, the car pulled out of the dip and never stopped, so I kept on going. I got to the back entrance and parked as usual. I looked at the front end of the car and what do you know, the bumper was gone. The chrome front bumper had been the only casualty. *No big deal,* I thought, *it's a rental.* I got into the plant and made my way to the control room. Just another day, and by nine-thirty, I had forgotten all about it.

We finished up for the day around eight P.M., and we made the decision that it would be a rib night. We made our way out of the plant, and I honestly had forgotten about the missing bumper. I get in the car, start my trek back to the hotel, but as it turns out, the road workers were a kind bunch, and apparently one of them had found the bumper and set it, nice and neat, next to the dirt road where it was easy to spot. Actually, it was pretty hard to miss. A shiny new chrome bumper that really didn't have any damage to it.

When I saw it sitting there by the side of the road, the morning's events all came back to me so I stopped the car. I got out, walked back to it, and grabbed it, as the guys in the car behind me just watched in silence and waited. I opened the back door of the car and chucked Mr. Bumper into the back seat like it was a part of the family. We got back to the hotel, did our thing, and headed out for our OT shift at the Rib Shack, as we usually did. Nobody ever mentioned it.

I drove around with this thing in my back seat all week. When Friday came, it was a go-home weekend, so I headed for the airport. I took the car keys back to the counter and handed over the paperwork. The folks there knew me by now, so we made small talk about the weather, flights, the usual.

"How was the car, Mr. Metzler? Any problems?"

"Perfect," I said, flashing a big smile and giving the "Okay" sign. "ar," I continued. "See you Monday."

"Okay! Thank you, Mr. Metzler!"

Ha ha; now that's customer service. They actually thanked me.

I never heard another word about that car or the bumper.

§ § § § §

They sent down another new guy, this time a service tech, working for Jake. The guy was about ten years older than us, and he was apparently somebody's brother-in-law. He had a haircut like Elvis with a well-maintained beer belly and a big red nose. When he smiled, he showed off his *summer teeth*…some are here and some are there.

When I first met him, Shawn and I were in the control room and Jake brought him in and introduced him as Bob Waller. We said hello and talked for about fifteen minutes. Long enough for Bob to smoke two cigarettes in a row. Jake made Shawn take him around and show him what was what.

A little while later, I ran into them downstairs just as Shawn was introducing him to Stu. Problem was Shawn didn't remember his name and kind of just mumbled to him. Just as I walked by, I heard Bob introduce himself as John.

He was shaking Stu's hand as I stopped and turned toward them. "I thought your name was Bob."

Shawn suddenly had a flashback to thirty minutes ago and chimed in. "Yeah, it's Bob. You told us your name is Bob."

"John or Bob, I don't care."

This pissed Shawn off for some reason. "Well, what the fuck is it, Bob or John?"

"It doesn't matter."

"What do you mean it doesn't matter? What's your name?"

"John or Bob, I really don't care."

"Jesus Christ, it's a simple question. Which name do you prefer?"

"It doesn't matter."

"Okay, then, How about John-Bob? We'll just call you John-Bob. See ya later, John-Bob."

This exchange really pissed him off. Shawn would not care for our John-Bob. Not now, not never. Another annoyance to Shawn was John-Bob's chain smoking. He always had an extra-long cigarette hanging out of his mouth and he apparently didn't get the memo about flicking the ash, thus his extra-long smoke was usually sporting a nice long ash that would eventually fall onto his shirt. It was all a part of the look.

It got worse when we took John-Bob out with us for OT a couple of nights later. As we sat around bullshitting, John-Bob told us about his dream vacation. He wanted to rent a "big ass van" and drive with his whole family to the Bahamas. This declaration pissed off Shawn even more. The last straw was later that night when we were talking about work-related things, like new technology, when John-Bob informed us of his idea to invent the first solar powered flashlight. This almost had Shawn hyperventilating. Really, a solar powered flashlight. The man was dead serious about this.

"For Christ's sake, John-Bob, think about that. How the fuck is a solar powered flashlight going to work in the dark? You moron. I'm done here." And he got up and left in a huff.

Between the van ride across the Atlantic Ocean and the idiotic flashlight idea, John-Bob had dug himself quite a hole. We all kind of knew we'd have to keep our eye on him and not let him get hurt. Simple jobs only, and not around Shawn.

§ § § § §

The Mad Shitter made another hit and run in the same men's room. This time, though, they had a clue. It definitely happened midway through the second shift, between six and seven-fifteen P.M. This was a fact that the housekeeping crew uncovered, since they were on the hunt, and they were making repeated visits to the crime scenes, even though they weren't told to do so. A check at six uncovered nothing unusual; however, at seven-fifteen, it was discovered that the rogue defecator left a turd on the porcelain in stall number 3. This got the cleaning and maintenance crews as excited as I had ever seen them. It was actually kind of ironic that the Mad Shitter, as hated as he was, had lit a fire under these folks that actually had them working harder. If their management had asked them to do this, there probably would have been a wild-cat strike.

§ § § § §

The time had come that I had been putting off for as long as I could. Kenny and I made a plan to visit the Carl Sandburg house. He and I volunteered to work through another weekend, while everyone else went home. We couldn't get into the plant on that Sunday until after twelve noon because they were installing some kind of overhead sprinkler system. This gave Kenny the grand idea that we could go visit this piece of Americana and god-dammit it would be fun.

Kenny was unusually pumped up for this, and it was actually kind of cute. He wanted to go out and get a disposal camera to record this momentous event in his young life. So we went camera shopping on a Saturday evening.

To give an example of Kenny's gullibility and/or dumb luck, even a trip to Wal-Mart is an opportunity to get shit on.

We were walking into the store minding our own business. We weren't doing anything in particular, just talking between us and heading for the doors. Kenny was a step ahead of me and he reached for the door, kind of looking back toward me as we kept talking about something or other. A split second after he grabs the door handle, a woman in her mid-thirties, with a couple of little red-headed kids about eight or ten years old, also went for the same door handle at the exact same time. He never saw her.

She must have really needed to get in there because she let him have it, launching a verbal assault on him without breaking stride. She gave him a death look and a, "That's garbage, guy! Who the hell do you think you are?"

Kenny was stunned. He just looked at her. He made his best decision of the week at that precise moment and said nothing. She and her miniature posse walked through the door he was now holding open.

The little boy, walking behind the pack, turned back toward Kenny and stuck his little tongue out at him with his scrunched up freckled face. No "thank you" or "excuse me;" nothing from the mother. As she passed him and walked into the vestibule, she told her kids, "That son of a bitch is dumber than a stick."

I stood there with my mouth open and just looked at Kenny. I mouthed the words to him; *"dumber—than—a—stick."*

He got over it and we laughed it off, but we used both of those phrases ever since. "That's garbage, guy," and "dumber than a stick."

Sunday morning came pretty quickly, but it certainly wasn't quick or pretty. A shitty day that was cold and gray, with light rain every now and then. Add to this the fact that Kenny and I were sporting pretty significant hangovers with splitting headaches. He still wanted to go and I still didn't. But I made him a promise and he got the camera and all, so off we went. Being as we were both suffering from the head-pounding after-effects of Saturday night, we basically bitched at each other all the way there.

We get to the famous house on Third Street and entered through the visitors' doors. As we entered, it was pretty obvious we were the only ones there. Go figure.

I mentioned this to Kenny, actually quite a few times.

We got in and were greeted by a member of the Carl Sandburg Historic Society, a woman in her mid-seventies dressed in old-time period garb. She welcomed us in her very quiet voice, and told us there was a two-dollar donation to take the tour.

Tour? It's a four room house, for Pete's sake.

We paid the two bucks and she started talking about Carl Sandburg, how he was born in this house in 1867, became a poet, songwriter, yadda, yadda, yadda. She really knew her stuff. Problem was we mostly didn't care. She could have said anything to us and we would have nodded in agreement. She led us around the little place slowly, of course, starting in the kitchen. A modest little eight-foot-square room where Mrs. Sandburg did her thing.

We get to the actual bedroom, and we both stood in the doorway as our host started the speech. It was an eight-foot by ten-foot room with a bed, a dresser, a sewing machine, and a cradle on the floor. The nice old lady gave a rundown on the four things we were looking at, in case we were brain dead and didn't know a bed from a dresser.

We stood there looking around like we were really impressed. At least I did, anyway. That's when Kenny pulled out his new camera and started taking pictures.

I stood there, leaning against the door jamb, watching in stone cold silence. I'm not sure what it was, but something in me snapped. I finally couldn't take it anymore.

"Jesus Christ, Kenny." I said in a slightly hushed but angry voice. "What are you doing?" He kept snapping his pictures as I gave him more attitude. "Oh yeah, get the bed. You can show your friends Carl Sandburg's bed! Don't forget the dresser. What a bed, though, huh? Snap another one. Try another angle. Make sure the lighting is just right. Make sure you get the pillow, too."

"Shut up, asshole. What else do we have to do?" He snipped at me, but I kept going at him.

"What could be better than this, a picture of Carl Sandburg's bed? That picture could be worth a lot of money some day. You can tell all your friends you made the big time at last!"

"You're an asshole. Just shut the fuck up, Okay? Shut the fuck up." He kind of growled that one at me and he wasn't whispering anymore.

From out of nowhere, the old woman (the one we forgot was there) spoke up in her quiet little voice. "I think you boys better leave. Right now. This way, please," and she pointed to the door.

Kenny looked at me like I just kicked his dog. With his round Amish face starting to get red, he just glared at me.

Hells bells, we're getting thrown out of Carl Sandburg's house! We were getting the bum's rush to the door by a seventy-five-year-old woman! In an eighteenth century costume no less.

As we got to the exit, Kenny, with his cardboard camera in hand, took the high road and tried to make nice with the old lady. "Thank you, ma'am. It was very informative." He was a terrible liar.

I, on the other hand, wasn't as stoic. Going through the door, I stopped for a second and winked at her. "We've been thrown out of better places than this, you know."

Kenny bitched at me all the way back to the hotel. Kept telling me how much I embarrassed him, he's so sick of being here, he wants to go home, wah, wah, wah.

I told him his pictures would comfort him for years to come, so get over it.

Later that day, as we were in the plant and I was sitting at the desk, staring into space, I had a premonition. The kindly old lady got home from her volunteer job, and it probably went something like this: "Hi, Marge, how was your day?" her hubby would ask.

She would answer him in her crackly voice. "Hi, honey. It was very slow, as usual. Except for this morning. Two young men came in. They weren't from around here, though. I told them a little about the house, and they seemed polite enough. Then they went into the bedroom and they just started cursing at each other. I still don't know what started it, but they just began cussing at each other, using the foulest language you could imagine. I finally had to ask them to leave."

"You're kidding me."

"No. One of them thanked me and the other told me he's been thrown out of better places than that. They just left—still cursing each other all the way to their car. It was a bit frightening."

I ran this in my mind and started chuckling to myself. Thankfully I was alone at the time.

§ § § § § §

We decided to do something worthwhile for a change, so Paul, Alley, Kenny, and I decided to go to a hockey game in the big city of Peoria. Alley and I were big hockey fans, especially of the Pittsburgh Penguins. Turns out, the Pens farm team at the time, the Muskegon (Michigan) Lumberjacks were playing the Peoria Rivermen in a minor league game in Peoria. We left the plant a little early and headed to the arena about an hour away.

We had never been to a minor league game, so we were looking forward to it. And as it was the Penguins affiliate, it was like having a little piece of home for a change.

We got our tickets and made our way to our seats, with a stop at the beer stand, of course. We sat down, and the game started. *All right,* I thought, *something constructive.*

About a minute into the game, Alley stands up and screams, "PEORIA SUCKS!"

You gotta be shittin' me. I think to myself that this can't be good.

"Alley, no!" It was too late. As they say, you can't un-ring a bell.

We got our first taste of the minor league hockey fan mentality, because as soon as he sat down with his shit-eating grin, it all started. We got barraged with food, garbage, you name it. Shit rained down on us and we were cursed like I've never been before. These people were ruthless. And mean.

Popcorn pelted us; French fries were hitting us like little missiles. Alley took a full Coke on the shoulder; Kenny caught a half-eaten hot dog loaded with ketchup right on his neck. I felt bad for the poor kid; he didn't like hockey or ketchup.

I was able to knock away an almost-empty beer cup, but the follow-up pizza crust got me in the temple.

Paul finally gave the order. "Let's get the hell outta here!"

We jumped out of the seats and made our way to the concourse, all the while being cursed and pelted with more missiles.

We wiped and dried ourselves off, now able to laugh at it all. Alley admitted it wasn't the smartest thing he did all day.

We decided to go to the visitors' side of the arena and see if we could watch the game in peace. We did, but the ushers wouldn't let us sit anywhere since our tickets were for the other side. And we would be assholes to even think about going back. So we decided we would stand and watch for a while. That seemed to work out a lot better for us, and we agreed no more yelling of obscenities. Problem was, standing around and getting shoo'd around by the ushers got old, and we ended up leaving halfway through the game. So much for constructive OT. Back to the bar it was.

§ § § § §

Every now and then we got a visit from the Kanton salesman who sold the project. His name was Don Dooley. A very nice guy, liked his gin and Marlboros, but had a habit of getting in the way. He liked to make like he was technically oriented, but in actuality he wasn't. But I knew he had to make like he did in front of the customers. The thing was, though, that he had this whiny, effeminate voice. The voice that elongated words at the end of the sentence, and had the soft "S's" mixed in with a slight dose of the "th" sound. We've all heard it. For example, when he said my name, it wasn't just "Barry," it was "Beer-rrrrry." Very womanly.

During one of his unannounced trips, we were knee deep in things and he suddenly shows up. The electricians and techs couldn't stand him, basically because of the feminine voice thing. Then he started. He's standing on the ground floor, with the customers Dave and Stu, and he starts calling for me up on the second level. "Beer-rrrrry! Beer-rrrrry!"

I let it go for a while, but he kept yodeling for me in that irritating girlish voice. Shawn, who was standing near me gave me a stern, "Jesus Christ, will you answer him?"

"All right," I said, and got up and slowly started walking over to the railing as he lets out another "Beerrrrrrry!"

Just as I reach the railing and lean forward so I can see him, Shawn, who is behind me and out of sight, yells out a very loud, "Talk like a man!"

The timing was impeccable. Shawn yelled just as I lean over and make eye contact with Don and everybody else standing down there with him. No doubt to all the folks below, it was, of course, me who just hurled the insult at Don. I could tell by the frightened looks on all their faces. I completely froze for a moment, as did they. We stared at each other for what felt like an hour, but he finally spoke. "Can we cal-li-brate?"

"No!" was all I said. I turned around and there was Shawn, and now Kenny, too, standing behind me, still out of sight of the group below us, and damn near pissing themselves from laughter.

I looked at Shawn and let him know what I thought of his actions. "You're an asshole."

He laughed even harder but was able to get in the last word. "I guess you won't be getting a Christmas card from ol' Donny boy this year."

§ § § § §

One unassuming day, about mid-morning, it happened. I was in the main restroom, alone, standing at the round hand-wash station in the middle of the room. There I was washing my hands when I heard some footsteps drawing closer. I casually look up, and it's my wave buddy, Giorgio.

"Hi, Giorgio! How are you?" I asked him without stopping my hand washing.

"Hi, Barr-ry." He smiled and waved, as was his style, and headed into a stall. I really didn't give it another thought.

I finished washing my hands, and I went to the paper towel dispenser, near the entrance. I looked around, kind of casually. Not really looking, just kind of there.

I heard a little rustling from Giorgio's stall, as one normally would. I looked down and scanned to my right for really no reason at all, giving the room a little, quick scan.

I was starting to walk out when it hit me. There were no feet under the stall Giorgio was in. I stopped, turned, and went back in. I looked at the stalls along the back wall. No feet.

What the hell?

It became quite evident. Giorgio was standing on the toilet to take his dump. Then it suddenly hit me like a ton of bricks: *It's the Mad Shitter! It's him! It's fucking Giorgio! Giorgio's the Mad Shitter!*

I started to panic, my heart started racing, and I actually had to stop and catch my breath. I looked at the entrance, and, thankfully, no one was coming.

My mind started racing. *I gotta get outta here...they'll think it's me. They'll fry me. Giorgio...holy shit, they'll kill this poor slob. Oh well, that's his problem, I guess. Run away! Run away!*

It seems the 'equipment' in this restroom was of the old fashioned industrial variety seldom seen anywhere. Being as the plant was probably built in the forties, the shit houses had these extremely old style commodes. They sat kind of high up, shaped like a giant pear. Nothing like the modern day Ferguson's we relate to nowadays.

But Giorgio? What the hell is going on here? Is he spiteful or just plain stupid? I was hoping for the latter, but I had to do something, anything, quickly. So I left the restroom as quick and calm as I could. I made my way back to our work area, trying not to be noticed and went directly to the control room. Didn't pass Go. Didn't collect $200.

I thought for a minute, and decided I should mention to Douglas and Giuseppe what I had just witnessed. Doug was friends with the Italian guys, and I could bring in our Giuseppe to help coordinate things.

I called Doug on our two-way radios, and he and Giuseppe showed up in a few minutes. I started to explain to Doug that we had a situation, and I thought I found the Mad Shitter.

"Who is it? Who is it?" he asked me.

I started to tell him how I was minding my own business in the bathroom when the guy walked in and headed for the stalls. I told them about the "'no feet showing" thing, and finally Doug exploded and interrupted me right there and then.

"Who the fuck is it? Is it one of our guys? Please tell me it's not one of our guys."

I looked him in the eye and calmly stated, "It's Giorgio."

"No!"

"Yep. I busted him, Doug. I don't think he knows that I know. I don't think he even knows he's him. The Mad Shitter, I mean."

About this point, Shawn walked in and he's sharp enough to know something was going on. He pressed us, and I finally had to fill him in. He reacted about the same as Doug, with shock and dismay, and then finally relief that it wasn't one of us.

He also knew Giorgio, and like us, he was stunned. It was the why that bothered us.

We talked for a little bit, and we decided it would stay our little secret. Giuseppe would talk to Giorgio's boss and see what the deal was. I wanted no part of this, but I was already involved. Pretty deep, too.

Giuseppe and I made a plan that he would talk to them at lunch time, which was actually in about fifteen minutes.

We headed toward their work area, and Giuseppe called his fellow Italians over. He started speaking to them in Italian, and I kind of just stood there looking stupid. A few sentences into the discussion, I heard a few gasps and knew he was getting to the point.

Giorgio's boss started asking him direct questions and they commenced to yakking back and forth, voices raising, and their hands were flying around like they were swatting flies at a redneck wedding.

After their discussions in their native tongue, Giuseppe looked at me with sad eyes. "Barr-ry, here is the problem. Giorgio, he don't know any better. He don't shit on the seat on purpose. He think he supposed to stand over the hole, just like in Italy. Like the same in the factory where he work. He ask me why there no hose with water to spray after he finish. Is normal for Italy. For factory, only the hole on the floor and some paper and hose with water."

So there you have it. Giuseppe explained to me the whole sad, pathetic situation.

It seems that Giorgio, the guy who never left his village, was trained to shit into a hole in the floor, and upon completion of the task, grab the water hose hanging on the wall and squirt the remnants into the hole in the porcelain floor. I was told that this is the typical factory shithouse etiquette in Italy. I suspected it was a nothing more than a crude ploy to keep them from writing on the walls, but who knows?

That might have been the case, but there were a whole lot of people looking for this guy, and they were NOT a happy bunch.

We decided that the best thing to do was to instruct Giorgio on the proper method of interacting with modern day plumbing fixtures, and we would all just let it go. No problem with me, but we needed to be sure the five us knew it was REALLY important to keep this covered up, so to speak. So there we were, five grown men having a sit down to discuss the action plan for getting a simple Italian man up to speed on shithouse etiquette. We decided that the most inconspicuous plan of attack was for Giuseppe and Giorgio's boss to take him down to the restroom and give him a quick lesson, and maybe we could all get back to work. Somewhere in Italy there was a village in search of its idiot, and we were determined that one day they would be reunited. So that's what they did.

And that was that with that.

Over time, as the Mad Shitter incidents stopped, the furor died down, and the plant folks blamed it on one of their co-workers who was recently fired. It seemed the episodes came to an end about the same time this guy was canned. Another lucky break for the visiting team.

I couldn't help but think, though, that this was a small town, and eventually one of the pissed-off cleaner-uppers would run into this poor innocent schmuck walking down the street and probably beat the snot out of him.

§ § § § §

It got to the point that the customer was in production, but we still had issues to fix. The crew was a little lighter now, and the customer's man, Dave, was getting hot headed with us; we all knew the urgency of the situation. We started in August, and it was now December. The routine was a drag, and I, for one, was sick of not being home. The weekends were our best time to get things done, but we still wanted to go home every other weekend. One Wednesday evening, I made it a point to go to the hotel bar and run into Doug. I got there, and low and behold, there he was. In them same fuckin' ratty blue jeans, the same fucking boots, and that same fucking shirt. Not that I held it against him. He was still a good superintendent. I was just in a beaten mood, pretty much sick of it all. I sat next to him at the bar and the barmaid got me a Miller Lite without asking.

"Douglas," I started.

"What's up, Barr?"

"Douglas, I have a deal for you."

"Go on," he muttered while looking straight ahead.

"I'm due to go home this weekend, but I'll stay and work since were making the final push. All I ask in return is you fly my wife here. She'll stay for a few days and it'll save Kanton time and money."

Douglas didn't say a word, but started squeezing his chin with his right hand, like he was in deep contemplation. The other hand spun the ashtray. "Okay." he said. "On one condition."

"What condition?" I asked him.

"We will do this if you agree to come to work directly for Kanton. You work for us directly and we'll fly your wife in any time you want."

I hadn't really considered this, and I was happy at my job as it was. I liked the guys I was working for, and I really wasn't looking to make a switch. But I was tired, lonely, and basically sick of the current situation. So I agreed.

"All right, Douglas. I'll do it."

His reaction startled me and everyone around us. "YES! I'm calling Bryce right now."

Bryce Hunter was the president and CEO of Kanton. It was nine o'clock in the evening, and Douglas ran out to the lobby for a pay phone. (This was 1988, when the word *cell phone* referred to something a guy in jail used to call his lawyer.)

While Douglas was on the phone, the barmaid, Dottie I believe it was, came over to me with a puzzled look in her eye. "Did I just see happen what I think I saw happen?" She knew the situation, that I was a contractor working for Kanton—she also knew Phil, since he, too, was a barfly like the rest of us.

I didn't speak for a minute, but I looked at her. "I guess you did. Looks like I just got a new job."

Dottie, a young lady about my age, took this as a cue to work the crowd. She announced to the bar what had just happened and informed the crowd that it would now be an official party.

While the shots and beers started flowing, Douglas came in and whispered to me. "Bryce wants to talk to you on the phone."

I went to the lobby payphones, and picked up the one that was obviously in use. I spoke to Bryce for a few minutes, and we basically decided that we would work out details in the next couple of days.

When I looked up, who was walking through the lobby but Kenny, Shawn, and Alley. They came over to me, saw and heard the commotion in the bar, and asked me what the occasion was. I explained to them that I took a job with Kanton in return for an air strike—that being my wife coming in for the weekend.

It turns out they were on their way to the horse track, about forty-five minutes north in Moline. I decided to join them, since it seemed like fun. Never mind I was blowing off my own party, but I'm sure they would get over it.

We went to the track, and had a good but uneventful time. When we got back to the hotel, the party was still going on in the bar. We went in, and Douglas started yelling, "He's here! He's here!"

Of course, that meant another round of drinks. And another, and so on.

The guys who actually had work to do the next day (us) ended up leaving, but I hear they partied long into the night. Apparently, the manager and employees locked the doors and joined the fun. That was kind of cool, though, having the staff and unknown guests have a party for a guy who wasn't there.

§ § § § §

Cindy got a flight from Pittsburgh and made it in for the weekend. I gave her the tour of the hotel, the pool, spa, and so on. She spent the day there while we all went to work.

That night, she and I were in the hotel bar, relaxing a bit and getting her introduced to the locals. At about ten o'clock in the evening, Shawn came in, looking a little pale. He was worried big time about something. He then proceeded to tell me that he was in the plant, alone, trying to fix some of the issues we were still fighting with. God bless him for trying, but I could sense the next part that was coming. Maybe it was the beads of sweat forming on his mostly exposed forehead.

"I think I fucked up, Barr," was all he said.

"What happened?" I asked.

He proceeded to tell me he was changing a pump and ended up faulting the system out, and now it wouldn't re-start. The plant people were starting their shifts at six A.M., and having that system running was pretty important. So the three of us went into the plant, straight from the bar, at ten-thirty at night. The security guards didn't even ask us why, who, nothing. Just a nice wave and a smile, and in we went.

Turns out there was a component that failed. I was able to patch the software to allow for the morning start-up, but we agreed that Shawn would have to be there and watch the process all day since there was now no safety back-up system. We also agreed it would be our little secret.

That was not the unusual part, though. The strange part was that the three of us were able to walk into this huge factory unescorted, damn near midnight, and have our way with the machinery. We laughed at the security force and their lack of giving a shit. Mission accomplished, we went back to the bar.

§ § § § §

Another Friday night came along, and after work, when we were walking through the hotel lobby, the girl behind the desk called out to us. "Barry! Kenny!"

We walked over to the counter.

"I have a message here for you guys. Katy called from Phil's bar. She said to tell you guys it's all-you-can-eat-fish night at Phil's, starting at four. We all looked at each other and kind of nodded. There you go; we now had plans for Friday night in Galesburg.

We cleaned up and went to the fish fry. We sat at the bar and were immediately handed cold beers, without ordering, I might add, and we all ordered the fish, thanking the folks for thinking of us and calling the hotel.

I got a plate of fish and started digging in. I had a hard time chewing, though, as the fish was pretty tough. Kenny, too. We chewed it for a while, and I recall I had to load it up with tartar and hot sauce as it was perhaps, no, make that without a doubt, the worst fish I'd ever had. But they called us, for Christ sake, so we really couldn't complain.

Phil came out from the kitchen and started making small talk. "How's the fish, boys?"

We both kind of politely nodded our heads as we chewed. Finally, I got the mouthful down and looked over at Phil. "Hey, Phil, what kind of fish is this?"

"Scored carp."

"Whattya mean, scored carp?"

"It's carp that's scored with rows of blades to kind of soften it. We love it around here."

I thought I was going to puke. *Carp? Did he say carp?* I looked over at Kenny and Shawn.

Kenny was actually green. Shawn was spitting food onto his plate.

Phil looked at us with great bewilderment. "What's the problem, fellas?"

Shawn jumped in first. "Phil, no one eats carp. Are you kidding me? Carp? It's a shit eating garbage fish." He ran to the bathroom to finish regurgitating. Kenny and I pushed our plates away and guzzled our beers.

"Phil," I said, being polite and trying to build a bridge between *thanks a lot* and *we ain't eating this shit.* "Thanks for the call, but we're from the east. We don't eat carp. We won't even use carp for bait. For us, carp is basically a rat with gills."

Phil looked he was going to cry. "Sorry, guys. I didn't know. We eat it all the time around here."

He was such a nice guy that not only was he not insulted by our reaction, he was truly apologetic. He even made us all cheeseburgers, but we did verify that it was beef we were eating.

Twenty years later and I can still taste that carp. Nasty.

§ § § § §

The project was starting to wrap up, and we were down to just a few of us on site. One particular Monday morning, Kenny, Alley, and me all flew into Peoria on the same flight. We were walking to our rental cars when, out of nowhere, a local reporter and her cameraman appeared in the parking lot. They stopped us, but luckily, the gal went to Kenny and Alley first. I stood there and watched as she asked them if they would mind answering a few questions.

"Sure," said Alley. He was a ham anyway, and wanted to be on TV. She positioned the cameraman, got them standing in just the right position, and started telling them not to be nervous, that she was going to ask them about the new rental car tax that just went into effect. It wasn't like any of us knew this, or actually gave a rat's ass.

The cameraman says "go" and she starts her schtick. "This is so-and-so at the Peoria airport, and we're here to talk to car renters about the new tax that went into effect at midnight." She leaned the microphone toward Kenny, and proceeds with her Emmy-caliber -interview. "Tell me, sir, what do you think of the new rental car tax that you're now paying on top of your rental fee?"

Kenny looked directly into the camera. "Well, to be honest with you, we were never informed of any new tax, so this is news to me. But what the fuck. I mostly don't give a shit. It's all a bunch of fucking bullshit anyway. Fucking taxes are fucking taxes. What the fuck do I care about a fucking new tax that's a bunch of fucking bullshit?"

I almost peed my pants. Alley was bent over laughing.

The cameraman slowly lowered his camera as the reporter calmly said, "Cut."

She was glaring at Kenny, who'd just done us proud.

"How was that?" he asked her, very politely.

Apparently she was so impressed she couldn't speak.

We got into our respective Town Cars, and the cameraman must not have learned his lesson. He was still filming us, looking to get an action shot of us as we pulled the cars out of the lot. Not us. Not today.

I backed the car out and turned the wheel. I then revved up the engine as I dropped it into drive, laying a loud and thick patch of rubber as I sped out of the lot. Kenny did the same in his car. As with just about every other situation we had gotten into, we never mentioned that debacle again.

§ § § § § §

One early morning, and I mean really early, my phone rang. Kenny was calling with distressing news. I answered in the dark and his voice was somber and his tone was serious. "Barr, Kenny. Our cars were broken into in the parking lot."

"What happened?" I asked with my eyes still closed.

"Both of our cars were broken into. Did you have anything valuable in there?"

"No, Kenny. Not a thing, nothing, and it's a rental car. Is it drivable?"

"Well, yeah. The cops are on their way. You should come down and talk to them."

"Kenny. It's a rental car, for Christ's sake. There's nothing to talk about. What about your car? Did they take anything?"

"Yeah; a pack of gum and my disposable camera."

"THE camera? Your little disposable camera?"

"Yeah."

"Oh, god! No!" I feigned. "Not the pictures of Carl Sandburg's bed? You mean THAT camera?"

"Yep. It's gone. All my pictures."

I started laughing my ass off. "No more pictures of Carl Sandburg's bed. Now your friends will never believe you were really there! They're going to call you a liar! And the gum! How will you replace it?"

After all I endured, with him whining about wanting to go there, and the actual visit itself, and now some slob stole the camera. I almost wanted to get out of bed to see the cops reaction to the list of stolen goods: One pack of Juicy Fruit gum and a disposable camera with pictures of Carl Sandburg's bed.

The irony of the whole situation made me laugh all day. Only Kenny.

§ § § § § §

The job was winding down, finally, and now it was only Alley, Kenny, and me left to button things up. Dave was still ornery as hell, but that was his nature. Of course, it's not like we didn't give him any ammunition. One morning I was at the control desk, looking into the screen for something, when I hear the familiar foot stomps coming up the stairs. It was Dave and he was pissed. His face was red as a beet as he huffed and puffed his way over to me.

"That's it! That is it! I'm fed up with you people. This is the last straw, do you hear me? The last straw!" This was as pissed off as I'd ever seen the ol' boy.

"Dave," I asked, "what the matter? Holy smokes, what could be so bad?"

"You have to do something with these guys. They're out of control!"

"Dave, what guys?"

"Those guys. Them!" He was waving his arms around trying to point at somebody, somewhere.

"What happened, Dave?" I was trying to calm him down.

"One of your men drove into the guard shack out back. Drove right into it. Almost hit poor Charlie out there. Drove the car right into his shack. What are you going to do about it!?" He was giving me his attitude like I was Doug.

"Hold on, Dave. First, is Charlie okay?"

He didn't answer but he appeared to nod slightly.

"Second, and this is kind of important Dave, they are not my guys. Talk to Douglas. I don't even work for Kanton. I'm a contractor, remember? Go find Douglas."

He stormed away and I think he was even more pissed now, but this was not my problem. Potty training a grown man, maybe, but not policing the parking lot.

I was dying to find out what the hell happened, so I walked out to the back parking area where Charlie held his post. The shack was pushed off its foundation a few feet, but still standing. No one was there, so I walked over and peeked into the window. There was poor Charlie's radio and little hot plate on the ground. Next to the hot plate was his little skillet with a half-cooked egg hanging halfway out of it. Holy shit…the guy was probably minding his own business frying his morning egg when one of the guys rammed the shack. Poor guy must have shit himself. The thought of it happening was kind of funny, though.

I got on my radio and called for Kenny and Alley and we met up in the control room.

When they got there, I was short and to the point. "Who hit Charlie's love shack?"

Alley stepped up. "I did. It wasn't that bad, though. I was a little late and I accidentally slid into the hut. I just bumped it, though."

"Did you see Charlie?"

"No. I didn't think he was in there."

"Well, Jesus Christ, Alley. He WAS in there and I think he shit himself, too. His little hot plate and egg are still on the ground out there. And I gotta tell you, Dave is really pissed. You need to hide for a while."

And that he did, and did well, because we didn't see him for three days. To this day, I think he went to Chicago and partied, but he denied it.

When the dust settled, it ended up Kanton had to apologize to Charlie, pay for a new guard shack, and install protective concrete pillars around it. They also had to get Charlie a new hotplate.

That was our swan song, as we wrapped it up and left the job site. I returned to Pittsburgh and started working directly for Kanton, but it was hard leaving Phil and DSI. But we would cross paths again, many times, and I was going to partner up with Greg again.

Chapter 4

THE NEXT PHASE

Starting a new job is usually a little uneasy and nerve racking, but not this time. It was the spring of 1989, and I was basically continuing what I had been doing for the last seven months, except now I was getting paid more. Same bunch of guys, same job description, same drinking habits, and I was even reunited with my old buddy, Greg. This would start ten years of installs and start-ups, from coast to coast and even across continents and borders.

My first assignment was a familiar one. We were supplying another system to our customer in Missouri. I inherited this job mainly because Greg was not very fond of this town and their "fuckin' bin burgers." Since he was the leader of this department of two, it was his call on how the projects were staffed. No problem, though, since I was comfortable with these guys and their town.

The guys in this plant were a good group of young locals, learning as they go and working for the Japanese. Every day, they started off with the mandatory morning exercise. This was apparently a Japanese ritual where the entire plant work force would line up in rows near the front of the plant, and a few Japanese leaders would lead them through various calisthenics. To see these people, basically mild mannered rednecks, following Japanese exercises was quite entertaining. It was even more entertaining to see the likes of Paul and Alley mooning them from afar as they did their thing. We were working in the middle of the plant, and our control equipment was located on the second level of a mezzanine. So being up this high, the plant exercisers could see us, but not the Japanese leaders since they had their backs to us. It became a ritual. We actually made sure we were in the plant by seven A.M. to make it for the morning mooning. The plant workers actually told us they looked forward to it and helped them through the indignity of being led through jumping jacks by a four-foot tall Japanese guy.

§ § § § §

Melvin Moore was a young maintenance guy who was kind of simple but did a decent job. As a young local, this was the first real job he'd had. He was moving into his own place, a rental duplex just outside of town. All he could talk about was his new apartment. More importantly, after two weeks on his own, he was getting cable TV installed. He couldn't wait, and he made it a point to invite all of us to his place after work to drink a few beers and watch the Cardinals baseball game on cable TV.

He was so excited, we couldn't say no. So after our day shift, we planned on OT at Melvin's. We even offered to buy the beer and snacks. This kid was damn near giddy all day. The workday ended, and we all headed to Melvin's for the party.

Since the cable guy was there that day, Melvin was anxious to see their work and turn on the nineteen-inch Magna-Vision.

We walked onto the little porch, following Melvin, and he unlocked his door and swung it wide open. We entered the living room, only to hear our host shout out a couple of choice obscenities. We looked in the room and we all just stared for a couple of minutes. At first it was complete silence quickly followed with uncontrollable laughter from everyone except Melvin. The cable was installed alright, but it wasn't what one would call a professional installation.

The black cable was run through a screen in a window on the far left side of the room, where the window was then simply closed on the cable. From there, it was run on the wall, down to the floor. It made a left turn at the baseboard and then came up the wall on the left, with staples holding it in place right on the wall. It didn't stop there, though, as it was stapled across the middle of the ceiling and down the opposite wall to the spot where the TV was. It must have taken all of fifteen minutes to install. It looked like a hillbilly shack with the clean white walls divided by a black cable with a bunch of staples stuck in the drywall.

Melvin was furious, and embarrassed, I guess. We calmed him down, though, and he eventually dealt with it. Until, that is, we were a few beers into the night when Paul decided he would stir the pot. He got Melvin stoked again and again with his trademark laugh and the, "Melvin, you can't let them get away with this. They hosed you, man. You can't take this. You have to kick some ass. C'mon, Melvin, you have to be pissed. This is a disgrace."

And on and on he went. He got Melvin hotter than hot, which was his intention. After a while, we convinced Paul to let it go, for the sake of Melvin's blood pressure.

Poor kid, though. The look on his face when he walked in that house was unforgettable. He was on pins and needles all day waiting for the cable guy—and having a party with his Pittsburgh buddies. Meanwhile, the cable guy showed up with a spool of wire and a staple gun. It was like he just found out the truth about Santa Claus. We liked the kid, so the next day we left the plant a little early and went back to the Moore residence and fixed the wiring so it looked a little more professional.

§ § § § § §

There was one hotel in this little town, and it sat next to the only bar, which was attached to the only restaurant. The bar was our domain, of course, a cozy little place called the Back Door Lounge. Cute name, since it was attached to the back of the eatery. Clark was the bartender's name, and he quickly became our good buddy. Clark was actually the bartender, manager, and head waiter. There were a few waitresses who came back once in a while getting cocktails for the real customers who were out front.

One particular evening, while we were imbibing and keeping to ourselves, Clark came over and mentioned to me that he had fifteen or so Japanese guys in the private room, having a group dinner. He knew they were from TeeJay, and he mentioned they were just finishing with dinner I took this as an opportunity to make friends with the right people, so I told him to head back in and offer drinks to the entire room, mentioning they were from Kanton. Clark disappeared for a few minutes and then returned with a shit-eating grin on his face.

"You asked for it, Barry," he says to me. I looked at him with raised eyebrows. He continued. "They accept your offer. They really accept your offer. They all want Scotch. The good stuff, too," and with that, he grabbed a bottle of single malt and headed to the party room.

When he returned empty handed, I knew it was going to be an expensive gesture.

"How much are we talking about, C-man?" I asked him, almost knowing the answer.

"That bottle is $50. That's because it wasn't full. The next one will be about $80."

I almost shit myself. "The NEXT one?"

"Yeah, man. These little guys came to party. They told me to send you back there to join them."

That was a given, of course. If I'm buying bottles of Scotch, I'm sure as hell drinking some of it. So I head back to the party room where the waitresses were just clearing the dinner plates. The little guys were wound up and ready to let loose. I went back and found the top guy, and planted myself right next to him. I gave him my card and introduced myself and he introduced me in broken English, and then to the rest of his buddies, in Japanese, of course. I remember hearing a lot of "Hiyas!" and assorted grunting sounds, but since they were all smiling, I figured it was all good. I tried to stick to the Miller Lites, but my new friends didn't, and they were completely shit-faced by the time the eleven o'clock news came on.

Halfway through the second bottle, I had them singing "Got Bress America" and they tried to teach me a Japanese ditty, but I just couldn't get it. They must have had fun, though, seeing as how they staggered out the door well past midnight after socking me with a $300 bar bill.

It ended up being a good move, though, since the top guy was the US president of operations and now a good ally of mine. This was the first time I witnessed a Japanese posse getting all boogered up and trying to hit on American waitresses. It was kind of comical, being in the no-nonsense Midwest. Clark later told me it was the new age, and they had better learn to like it since they brought hundreds of jobs to the community.

GROUNDED, PART 1

I figured out a great way to get a pass on travel for a while. It was pretty simple, and all I had to do was stand around looking stupid while my wife had a baby. With my wife, Cindy, pregnant and due in late October, I was pulled off the road from mid-October until December. I thanked my daughter Kristy for this when she was born on October 30, 1989. Being a new father seemed pretty cool, and my bosses were great about letting me stay home for a while, as this was the longest I had been grounded. This worked out pretty well, so we figured we should do it again sometime.

OH, CANADA

In the late summer of 1990, Canada came a-calling. We had a fairly big project to install for a Canadian auto products supplier just outside of Hamilton, Ontario, in a little town called Guelph. The project itself was considered big, with a lot of interfacing equipment and automation. Nothing really new there, except it was my first real experience in the great north, and it was just that—an experience.

With a job this size, I really wasn't surprised when the installation crew ran a few weeks behind schedule putting it back together. Nothing really new there. When I did finally show up, the majority of the crew was sent back home, leaving my man Paul as the electrician and Jack Cambo as the technical guru.

Day One started when I arrived at the plant about three in the afternoon. I was introduced to the plant manager and the lead engineer, Ken Cramer and Gerry Moyne. Both good guys, and this was clear in the first ten minutes upon my arrival. I met Gerry on the plant floor, and we talked a little in the control room. Mostly small talk and scheduling.

He then took me to meet Ken; we caught up with him in his office. We made a little more small talk, and after about ten minutes, Ken gives it the old, "Well, it's too late in the day to start anything now," (it was three-thirty), "so whattya say we go get a cold one?" No one said a word, so it was obviously a unanimous yes.

Right on cue, we went to the closest bar, which happened to be a fairly decent pub and grub, as they say. It was a cool place, in what looked to be an old house and it was called the Northern Light. When we walked in, it was apparent that this was not the first time these guys had been here. The bar maid had a beer on the bar for Ken before he even sat down. I noticed my guys didn't have to order either.

The layout of this place was such that the DJ and dance area were in the back, and the bar area up front was a regular looking tavern. Not too loud, nice décor, but the kicker was that they had the best steak sandwiches around. Absolutely killer. Jack turned me on to this. Gerry and Paul disappeared to the back, so Ken, Jack, and I stayed at the bar and talked shop. But we couldn't help but notice that Ken was inhaling his beers at a two-to-one rate on us. When he finally went to the men's rooms, Jack quietly told me to make sure I go slow, that the Canadian beers were a lot more potent than the US versions we were used to. A valuable morsel of information, indeed.

We hung around for a little while, but it was eventually time for us to start saying our goodbyes. Gerry came up from the dance area, asking Ken if he was ready. Ken nodded and immediately stood up from his stool. The quick movements must have triggered something in his equilibrium, because when he stood, he did a very bad hula-dance impersonation, took two awkward steps backward, and fell flat on his back.

I was in a panic. *Holy shit! The customer just did a header in the bar!* Apparently this was not unusual, though, as nobody else had any kind of reaction. Gerry just calmly walked over and picked him up by his armpits and helped him out the door. The bar staff didn't react either, just saying, "Goodbye, Ken!" when they left.

I asked Jack, "What the hell was that?"

Jack kind of gave me a nonchalant look. "Now you've been properly introduced to Ken. That was his usual dance, man. I don't really like going out with him unless Gerry is with us. Notice he didn't pay his bill. You're the leader now, so you might as well take care of it."

Son of a bitch, he was right. I kind of chuckled to myself, but now I knew the gig. Gotta love these automotive guys. They can work a vendor for everything from a free machine upgrade to Class 5 hangover.

§ § § § §

A couple of weeks into our start-up, Kanton hired a new technical service guy, and they sent him to us for a little hands-on training. Danny Serba was a little older than us, not much, but a few years. A tall and thin guy, with short red hair and round eyeglasses. He was a laid-off steelworker (not uncommon in Pittsburgh) who went back to trade school for electronics. He was a quiet guy, seemed like a good worker, and he had a strange level of intelligence. He had a deep sense of humor, which was cool. He handled the working hours just fine. The extended OT gave him fits, though.

His first day was a long twelve-hour marathon in the plant, followed by a visit to the Northern Light. Paul was determined to break him in, and Jack and I mostly didn't care. I had discovered that the bar had a few video poker machines, and that was right up my alley.

We were only there for about an hour, when Paul came over to Jack and me, laughing that the new guy was ready to go and stumbling over the tables. Since he was a passenger, though, he wasn't going anywhere. So we all kind of just did our thing. This Canadian beer was taking another victim.

By the time we were ready to go, our man Danny was obliterated. No problem, though. We were there to help.

After he paid our bar tab, we escorted him to Paul's car and chumped him into the back seat for the fifteen-minute drive to the hotel. When we got there, Paul and Jack each grabbed an armpit and dragged him to the elevator. Paul propped him against the back wall for the trip up to the eighth floor, where he gave us his key and we all went to his room. Turned out it was right next to my room, but at this point, he didn't know it. Advantage, me.

With Danny safely in his room, they kind of just pushed him slightly so he fell back onto his bed. Nice placement for a big guy. Jack was nice enough to start taking his work boots off his big feet, but Paul and I each had different ideas.

Paul grabbed his TV remote, and immediately put it on the porno channel. "I'll bet he'd want to watch this if he was conscious. It'll loop all night, so in case he wakes up in a few hours, it'll still be on for him."

We laughed to each other, knowing it would probably cost him fifty or sixty bucks when he checked out. I picked up the phone next to the bed and dialed "0."

"Front desk, how may I help you?"

"Hello, this is Dan Serba in room 812, and I need a wake-up call."

"Yes, sir, Mr. Serba. What time would you like your wake-up call?"

"Well, this is a little odd, but I hit my head at work today and the doctor thinks I may have a concussion. Can I get a call once every hour, starting at one?"

"Absolutely, Mr. Serba. I'm so sorry to hear that. Is there anything we can do for you?"

"No, thanks, I'm okay, really. Just a precaution. You know how doctors are."

"Yes, sir. We'll have you called every hour. Please let us know if there is anything else we can do for you."

"Thanks a lot. I appreciate it." I hung up and looked at my partners in crime.

Paul and Jack looked at me like I was a ghost. Wide eyes and open mouths.

Paul spoke first. "Excellent! Barr, fuckin' excellent. Oh, my god, you are a bastard."

We all laughed as we left his room and went our separate ways.

I usually got up early to put the coffee on and get the paper that they delivered every morning. This was a nice hotel, and they delivered the newspaper every morning in a little bag and hung it on the door handle. I got up and got my paper, and pulled it out of the little plastic bag. As I walked back into my room, I saw the day-old, yesterday's newspaper on the dresser and yet another way to screw the new guy hit me. I took the previous day's paper, put it in the bag, and headed for hall. I quickly stepped next door, took Danny's paper from his door, and replaced it with the old one. *Old news is good news,* I thought to myself.

We met for breakfast around seven in the restaurant. The three of were sitting there wondering how the new guy would look, feel, sound, walk, etc. He showed up trying to look bright eyed and bushy-tailed, but we knew better. The Canadian beer was brutal in the morning, especially the first morning. Danny sat down and picked up the menu without saying a word.

Paul went first. "How'd you sleep, Dan?"

"Uh, I feel like shit, thank you. Why'd you guys keep me out so late? And I'm going to give the manager of this place an earful. I swear my phone rang every hour. And nobody was on the other end. I finally unplugged it around four o'clock this morning."

"You're kidding me?" he answered with a straight face.

"No, I'm not. Total bullshit."

And that was it. No mention of the bar tab, the porno channel, or newspaper.

"I'm not going out with you guys tonight, I can tell you that now. I'm not used to this kind of life."

It showed, believe me. He looked like he was in serious misery.

We all chuckled at the time, but he kept his word. He would only come out with us once in a while. Dinner and then snuggle up with a book. That was his night.

§ § § § §

The plant we were working had hundreds of workers, but the housekeeping crew really stood out. Literally. It was a pair, or rather a couple, of locals who were responsible for the housekeeping and cleaning throughout the plant, in the lunchroom, restrooms, and the area we were working in. These two were quite a pair, though. A him and her tag team that seemed to be attached at the hip. Well, not actually the hip, but maybe the top of the head and the hip. Gerry had told us they were "special." Hard workers, but "special."

She was tall, maybe six-feet four, very thin, with long, scraggly red hair and a bony nose that stuck out like a beak. He stood around four feet tall, with dirty blond hair that formed a classic mullet, an always-open asymmetric mouth and thick, Coke-bottle glasses. The look was topped off with his hunched over frame, tiny little alligator arms, and bow-legged gait. These two would always be together, and they could show up and vanish like the wind. It was creepy; you could be walking one direction and see them flash across the aisle, and when you were walking back, they would be on the other side of plant with brooms in hand. Never more the two feet from each other. Her at over six feet, and him at his four.

Poor bastard, though. He was too tall to be considered a little person and too short to be considered a regular person. He was shunned by both groups. The guys had nicknamed her the Missing Link, probably for lack of anything quite right, but never tagged him with a moniker. Until Danny came along.

We were having a little meeting in the control room one morning, as we occasionally did. As we finished up, the guys left their coffee cups lying around and Jack made a comment for them to pick them up. As he was walking out the door, Danny made the inconspicuous comment. "Let Quasimodo and Esmeralda take care of it. They'll clean it up without ever being seen."

I started laughing my ass off at the comparison. One by one, as soon as the realization of who he meant set in, Paul and Jack did the same. Pretty soon, the four of us were in tears in the control room. The Hunchback of Notre Dame and his mate. That was it. Perfect! They were tagged forever. Danny had never even mentioned these two before that day, but he had felt the same creepiness we all did. He just had a better tag.

§ § § § §

Since his first drunken night, I had made it a point every morning to replace Danny's newspaper with my day-old version. He never knew I was next door, and I never bothered to mention it to him. I did mention it to Paul and Jack, and we kept our ears open for some kind of comment.

We knew he was an avid reader and current events junkie, so we prepared ourselves to deny everything in case he brought it up, which he didn't, at least for the first week. Until one morning at breakfast, that is, as we were sitting there and Jack noticed Danny at the front desk, holding a neatly folded newspaper and waving his arms like he was really trying to make a point. When he finally came over and sat down, Jack threw the first line out. "What's up, Dan? Problem with your room?"

"No, the room's fine. These assholes deliver the paper every morning but it's always yesterday's paper. Every goddam day since I got here. Look." And he showed us his day-old newspaper.

We all looked at the newspaper like we were interested in his dilemma.

Paul asked him, "What'd they say?"

"They denied everything, of course. It's fucking magic. They deliver a fresh newspaper but it turns into an old one while it hangs on my door."

I almost choked on my coffee and I have to give us credit for all keeping a straight face.

He kept going. "I asked them what time they deliver these things and I'm going to be there waiting tomorrow. I don't care if it's four A.M. or not. Maybe my phone will ring all night again and I'll be up anyway."

That was way too early for me, so I assumed my prank had run its course. Of course, if he was going to start waking up at four in the morning to check his newspaper, I guess it's still a prank in progress. Paul and Jack agreed and congratulated me on a fine example of one-upsmanship.

§ § § § §

Over the couple of months we were there, Jack and I had become pretty good friends with the manger of the pub, Dale, and his fiancée, Sherry, who happened to be the nighttime bar maid. This paid off on one of the last nights we were in town.

We were about finished up, so Gerry and Ken wanted to go out, and that we did. Late in the evening, the four of us were at the bar getting ready to leave. We had a problem, though, was we didn't have much cash, and Sherry informed us that their credit card system was down. Ken and Gerry started to panic a little, realizing they were the locals in this group.

Sherry went over to Dale, and they chatted for a minute before coming over to us. Dale smiled at me and Jack, and said, "I hear we have a little problem, guys." We kind of smiled back, but our friends decided to stare at the floor.

"Tell you what, guys," he said. "This ones on me tonight. You guys have been really good customers so I'd like to say thanks. Tonight's on the house."

Jack and I shook his hand and thanked him. Ken and Gerry gave a wave and a thank you, as well.

As we left, Ken was just this side of giddy. "Holy shit! I've been coming here for five years and that's the first time I got a free drink from anyone. And it took you gypsies to do it."

Gerry put it a little simpler. "That's the first time I got a free drink from any bar owner in this town, period."

We heard it from them for quite a while after that, even years later when we ran in to each other at trade shows or what have you. It pays to be a good guy when you travel.

BAG SHOTS

I did a quick little service job in Johnson City, Tennessee, at a plant that made residential water heaters. It was just a small little machine, and the customer was having issues of some sort. I was scheduled to be in the area for some other reason, so I volunteered to go in and look at this problem. Being in the south, the plant was, of course, filled with locals. Locals who spoke with a southern twang.

I looked the machine over and found a software glitch, so I made a little program change but needed to test what I did. This machine was set up so the machine base sat in one area, and the chemical pipes ran up and over a work area, with the injection head hanging over the production line where water heaters would be run underneath. An operator would hold the dispense head over a hole in the top of the heater, push a button, and the insulating foam would be poured into the appliance. When one was finished, another would come along, and so on and so on.

To do my testing, I put a very large garbage bag over the injection nozzle and held it with one hand. With my free hand, I could push the button to make a *pour,* as we called it. This operation was called a bag shot, for the obvious reasons.

So, I'm doing my thing, looking up in the air at the valves while holding the bag and pushing the button over and over, with each push of the button pouring more liquid foam into the bag. After a couple of minutes of this, I felt a tap on my shoulder. I look over and one of the plant guys starts talking to me in southern twang.

"Yerbadda olint."

"Excuse me?" I asked as I kept pushing the button, looking up at the valves and filling the bag with foam.

"YERbadda olint."

I looked at him again, kind of irked.

"Huh?"

YerBADDA Olint."

Now I'm visibly irked bordering on pissed. I stopped pushing the button, leaned my head closely to him, and said, "I'm sorry, man. I can't understand what you're saying."

He was irked now, too, and it showed on his face and in his voice. "YOUR—BAG—HAS—A—HOLE—IN—IT."

I heard it that time.

The bag was leaking from the get go, and I was now standing in twelve inches of rising foam that was encasing me up to my shins. I pulled my feet, hard, and managed to get out of the hardening white muck with big chunks of this stuff molded around both ankles. I was officially foamed. My work boots were toast. After peeling chunks of foam off the tops of my feet, I borrowed a knife from Cousin Fiscus and cut through the laces of my boots so I could get my feet out of them.

Now standing there in my socks, I felt like a complete idiot. The bottoms of my pant legs were also encrusted in a white film that experience told me would never come off. I thanked the guy, told him the machine was fixed, and said goodbye. I grabbed my briefcase, leaving the gigantic mess, along with my foamed-in boots and my dignity, in a pile on the floor. I sock-walked through the plant, out to the parking lot and into my Town Car. I drove immediately to the closest Wal-Mart, where I walked in, in just my socks, scowled at the greeter, and headed right to the shoe department. I bought a cheap pair of work boots and wore them out of there. The boots were covered on the expense account, of course, but my dignity wasn't. I felt like I set Yankee-dom back a hundred years.

MEXICAN NIGHTMARE

I had to take on a job in Mexico that wasn't mine from the start, so I had a lot of catching up to do. When I was assigned, it was already installed and only a day or two from the start-up. I packed my bags and headed for the deep south. The plant itself was in Matamoras, Mexico, just across the border from Brownsville, Texas. I was given a brief run-down on the project and handed my plane tickets. The last thing they told me was our very own John-Bob Waller was the technician on the job. He was waiting for me in the bowels of Texas. Wonderful.

The hellish trip to Brownsville, Texas, was unlike anything I had ever experienced before. Flight number one was from Pittsburgh to Dallas. No problem there. Flight number two was from Dallas to Houston. That wasn't happening because of thunderstorms coming in from the gulf, so they rerouted me to San Antonio. A little irritation, but nothing major. From San Antonio, I was supposed to be on a puddle jumper to Brownsville. That wasn't happening, either, so I sat there for a few hours while they tried to come up with a good excuse to explain why they were screwing the ten or so of us, and also to try and figure out a Plan B.

They finally put me on a small plane owned by some crop dusting outfit called Conquest Air, who happened to have a plane going to Brownsville via McAllen, Texas, another small border town west of my destination. Once we were in the air for this leg of the journey, we were told the reason we had to stop in McAllen was to drop off a spare tire for another aircraft that was grounded because of a flat one.

The goofy thing was the spare tire was in the cockpit with the pilots. When we landed in McAllen, we taxied along this tiny little tarmac to the plane in need, which was obvious since it was the only other plane there and it was tilted to one side. Our plane stops and the co-pilot jumps out with tire in hand and runs it over to a maintenance guy on the ground. The exchange was made and back comes our guy. A small round of applause and off we go.

After we landed in Brownsville, I'm waiting for my Samsonite in this little airport baggage claim area. It has now been about eleven hours since I left Pittsburgh and I'm tired as hell and getting a little chippy at the goings-on of the day. As I'm standing there, I can see out to the plane, where the handlers are unloading the bags. I see the guy take my bag off the plane and set it down next to him. He repeats this simple procedure as he'd obviously been well-trained to do. I keep watching as another guy comes along with a load of bags to be loaded for the next flight. The original guy is putting the off-loaded bags onto a cart, as the new guy is taking bags off his cart and setting them on the ground to be put in the plane.

Guess what happens?

Yep, guy number two sees my blue suitcase on the ground, and since guy number one isn't watching, he puts my bag back on the plane. *Son of a bitch! Not today! Not to me!*

I try telling the gate agent next to the door what I just saw, and she smiles at me like I'm the one who doesn't speak the language. I repeat myself and earn another smile. I see this is going nowhere, and they're getting ready to close the cargo hatch on the plane. With eleven hours of attitude built up, I take matters into my own hands and sprint to the doors leading out to the tarmac, bursting past the agent (who is no longer smiling at me) and out to the tarmac and run toward the plane.

I hear the alarms going off and the yelling from a bunch of security guards, but I keep running to the plane, screaming things like, "Stop!" and "Don't close that door!" Possibly a rogue f-bomb or two, and other arbitrary phrases. I'm really hustling, now about five feet from the plane when I get jumped from behind and thrown to the ground by two very large security guards. Apparently they had been really hustling, too. One of them sits on my back as the other starts yelling into his walkie-talkie. I respond with a respectable amount of vulgarities, now aimed at everyone within earshot, which was many. I was really spewing some choice words, but I eventually figured out it wasn't helping. It's safe to say that the two baggage handlers didn't understand a single word I was saying. Well, maybe a couple. Two, three tops.

I'm being pinned to the ground when finally an American cop arrives. A real cop, with a real gun. I had calmed down, as had everyone, and I explained how the well-meaning pair of Conquest-adors were damn-near ready to send my bag off to parts unknown and I was only trying to assist them in doing their jobs properly.

As I'm lying on the ground, I recall thinking to myself I'm glad it wasn't a rainy day, but this concrete is scorching! It gets pretty hot in the bowels of Texas in late summer, especially when lying spread-eagle on an airport tarmac. Accompanied with a little bitching, I wiggle around and the guard lets me get up. Once I'm up, I see that I've stirred quite a commotion and along with the horde of security, airline workers, and supervisors, the entire length of window on the terminal building was packed with gawkers who had gotten quite a show.

The American cop talks to the rent-a-cops, supervisors, and baggage guys, and finally they open the cargo door, and there is my bag front and center. Fortunately, in all this action, I was able to keep my claim check right in my back pocket. Once I showed the cops my ticket, they matched it with the one on the bag and suddenly I was the good guy and the baggage handlers were the idiots. I'm handed my bag, and the apologies came trickling in from the supervisors. The baggage mis-handlers hung their heads in shame.

As I walked into the terminal, with the cop by my side, a huge wave of cheers and clapping erupted, and I gotta tell you the applause was impressive. I waved my arms in the air like a prize fighter, drawing more cheers. I ate it up. Score one for the little guys. Or should I say the English-speaking minority. I was so pumped up I hardly noticed all the dirt and tarmac dirt on the front of my shirt. I was taken to a little side room where I got another apology, followed by a good talking to from the airport cops because of the way I sprinted through the door and set off the alarm. I tried to explain that my English wasn't being absorbed by the staff, and I just kind of reacted after the long trip to this little Mecca. All was forgiven and I was sent on my way.

After my short-lived detainment, my suitcase and I went to the rental counter and I picked up my Town Car. My reward for successfully completing this day-long pain-in-the-ass journey was getting to my hotel and meeting up with my one-man welcome committee, the one-and-only John-Bob Waller. The job itself was in Mexico, but we were able to stay in Brownsville and cross the border twice a day. You needed to carry your passport, but it beat staying in Matamoras.

I was dead tired, but I needed to get an update on the job since the Mexicans were installing the equipment and were pressing the management in Pittsburgh for me to get down there and get the system started. I met John-Bob at the hotel bar and we talked for a while about the job, the town, the plant people. He assured me they were "ready to go," but I didn't trust his opinion.

The next morning we headed off in his car (not a Town Car), and he declared he would be the driver from now on. We made the trip into the plant, driving through small, dirt poor towns where the houses were literally shacks and barefoot kids ran in the streets. Occasionally, livestock (by the looks of them they should have been called damn-near-dead stock) and scrawny, feathered critters were in the road and had to be avoided.

I was slightly impressed with my driver for finding his way to the plant, especially with the lit cigarette constantly hanging out of his mouth. He had a few days to practice, and it seemed to have paid off. When I commended him on this, he didn't hesitate to tell me what a catastrophe it was his first couple of days, which really didn't surprise me a bit. Fact was, I received some serious laughing-at from the guys in the office, especially Shawn, when my project-partner assignment became public.

We got to the plant, and I was introduced to the plant engineer, who spoke a good bit of English, which is always a plus. We did a walk-through of the equipment, and the immediate thing that stuck out to me was the horde of Mexicans still working on the equipment. I couldn't count that high in Spanish so I counted to *uno* fourteen times. Fourteen of them still working, and they were all busy. I could feel my face getting red as I walked around and saw they were still at least five days from finishing, which meant I had no business being there. I politely excused myself from my host and went storming off to find John-Bob. When I caught up with my partner, I wasn't a happy camper.

"Hi, Barr—what's the word?"

"The word is they ain't fuckin' ready for me. That's the word. Why did you tell us they were done and ready for me?"

"Well, they told me they were just about done. You mean they aren't?"

"John-Bob, look out there. There's fourteen guys still working and half the wiring isn't even pulled. They still have four conveyors to set in."

It became obvious he didn't get it, so I was screwed. Too long of a trip to go back, and nothing for me to do here. We went to find the engineer and I was going to make damn sure they all knew I was pissed at their lying to us in Pittsburgh.

I sat down with the engineer and plant manager, telling John-Bob to get lost. He went into a nearby conference room to call his boss.

As I talked to the Mexicans, I let them know I wasn't too happy. I was in command of this little sit-down. I was in the middle of telling them they would most likely be back charged for these wasted days, when out of know where I—I mean we—could hear that asshole part-ner of mine bellowing into the phone.

"YEAH. IT'S ME. YEAH, DOWN IN MEXICO. HA HA...YEAH...THEY ACTUALLY HAVE WORKING PHONES! HA HA HA...YEAH, GO FIGURE. YEP! ELECTRICITY AND RUNNING WATER! HELL, NO, I'M NOT GOING TO DRINK ANY! HEY, THERE'S ACTUALLY TOILETS IN THE BATH-ROOMS TOO! HA HA."

We stopped talking as he insulted the entire country and its citi-zenry right before our very ears. I was so fucking embarrassed I was speechless. The tables had just turned on this little meeting. I was now the bad guy—not them. John-Bob's insulting phone call continued until I got up and went to the room he was in. Without a word, I calmly took the phone out of his hand and hung it up. He just looked at me all stupid until I told him we all heard his conversation and insults of Mexico. Me and the twenty or so Mexicans sitting in the outer room.

I spent the rest of the day on the shop floor, hiding from the plant manager, watching the workers and trying to help them. At the end of the day, I found Sluggo and we left for the day.

Driving home the exact way we came in, not much was said. I was still pissed at just about everything that had happened the last two days. We got back into the States, and I was hardly surprised when John-Bob missed the turn onto the highway ramp that led back to hotel, and I had to point it out to him.

The second day wasn't much different than the first, with the Mexicans trying to tell me they were almost done and me telling them they weren't. But I tried to help them as much as I could, with John-Bob basically staying out of the way. Even the drive back was the same. We get back on US soil and John-Bob misses the entrance ramp to the freeway. Only now I was smart enough to study and hold onto the hand-written directions and make sure he made the turns. Someone in the plant had given him a map to and from the plant that took us through little villages and dirt alleys, and that was the only route we had.

After a few days of putting up with the irritating bullshit of the customers and my partner, I was ready to blow. We were driving in one morning, and just as we get to the Mexican border, John-Bob cheers me up with this little proclamation: "Oh, shit. I forgot my passport."

"You gotta be shittin' me, John-Bob! Jesus Christ, how could you forget your passport?"

"I don't know, I just forgot it."

"Well too fuckin' bad. We're in a half-mile line of traffic and we can't turn around. Good luck, Keemo-slobbie."

There was a fifty-fifty chance of the border patrol asking you for a passport, either on the comin' in to Mexico side or the getting back in the US side. Either way, if they ask for it and you don't have one, you were in a heap of shit. He should have known better and now I was Temperous Eruptous. I was fuming, which became a regularity on this trip.

We get to the front of the line and the agent looks in the car, asks us where we're going and then looks in the back window. It must have been Have Pity on the Assholes day, because he waved us through without any problems. I told John-Bob he had one down and one to go. He must have started getting pissed at me because he didn't answer and started driving a little faster and a little more angry. Never a good idea, especially not in the back alleys of a Mexican border town.

We were making our way through one of the little villages on the only route we knew, when knucklehead goes around a bend without stopping, and actually accelerating as he made the right turn. Unfortunately, there was a flock (gaggle? herd? pack?) of chickens minding their own morning business. John-Bob Andretti makes the radical right turn and barrels through these chickens.

"John-Bob, stop!" I shouted.

He never flinched as the chickens suffered bloody and violent vehicular homicide. "Whoa!" was all he could muster.

Meanwhile, the feathers were flying and blood was spewing all over the place. The car was now covered with blood, chicken guts, and feathers. And the cackling. Oh, my god, the cackling. It was loud and piercing. This was officially the goddamndest thing I ever saw.

Hold on, though; Mr. Asshole wasn't done. He actually stopped the fucking car to look back at his handiwork. Bad idea. The townsfolk were now out in the street, en masse, and they were extremely angry. I mean wanting-to-kill-us angry. They started running toward us, throwing rocks and sticks at the car. Screaming, too, something that I couldn't quite understand but probably was not too friendly.

"Move it! Take off!" I yelled, and he put it in gear and hit the gas pedal. We tear out of there, with more feathers flying, except now they're mixed with rocks and sticks. John-Bob puts the windshield wipers on, cleaning the bloody feather-muck off the window enough so we could see out a little bit. He calms down enough to get his bearings, and we get back on the beaten path. We lose the angry mob, and make it to the plant alive.

At the plant, as we look over the damage to his rental car, it dawns on me we have no other way home. That route, through that town, was the only way we knew. There was absolutely no way we could drive through that town again. Ever. The one thing that was helping calm my nerves at this point was that the damage was done to his car, not mine.

Oh my god, it was priceless. How was he going to explain this to the rental agency? I'm laughing out loud as I look at all the dings, scratches, and dents. Absolutely priceless. Well, maybe priceless to me, but I'm sure Budget had a price for it. I made it clear it was his responsibility to get another map and/or directions so we could get home without going through that town. I thought about that for a minute and wised-up. I better take care of that task myself.

Getting back to the hotel that evening was a little nerve-wracking, with our new route and all. But we made it back to the US in one piece even without his passport. And, as usual, as we approached the on-ramp to highway, John-Bob missed the turn. This time I didn't say a word. I sat there totally silent, waiting to see how long it took him to figure it out.

About ten minutes later, he asks me, "Did I miss the turn?"

"Yes, you did. Just like every other fucking day this week."

"Why didn't you tell me?"

"I told you every single day since I got here. If you can't remember how the fuck to get back after what, nine days, I'm not telling you any more. Use your head."

And that was the last time he forgot the turn, but not necessarily because of my tough love.

§ § § § §

I vowed to get through this job without getting fired, jailed, or wrapped in a straight jacket. The weekend came, and since we couldn't get into the plant, we decided to relax by going to South Padre Island, a beach town on the Gulf of Mexico and not too far away. We got up and had breakfast, then took the drive over after stopping for a cooler and the usual necessities to put in it.

We get to the beach area and I go into a small shop and buy a fishing rod set-up. John-Bob buys a raft. The $1.98 version that you used to get your dad to blow up for you in the backyard pool. We head to the beach, and we set up our spot. I rig my rod and get fishing on the surf, which put me in heaven. About an hour passes, and as I'm fishing, I keep glancing over at John-Bob as he attempts to put air into his raft. At one point, he actually has a lit cigarette in his hand and was alternating between blowing into the raft and puffing on his smoke. I just keep fishing, totally relaxed, with a watchful eye on my partner.

God must have smiled down on him again, because some local guy stops by, probably after watching him suffer, and offered him a foot pump. Viola! He's now ready to raft. I had sort of worked my way up the shore, following the surf. He came over just as proud as punch of his new yellow raft. He walks out into the surf, lies down on his raft, and kind of just floats around. A big man on a big yellow raft.

I resumed my fishing, looking over every now and again at the yellow raft. It looked like it was in the current, slowly being pulled out and away from the shore. I figured the grown man on the raft understood the whole ocean current thing, so I kept fishing. I look out again, and the yellow raft appears to be getting smaller, but, hey, the fish are biting. I'm busy. Then another fisherman walks by, and he gives me a few good tips on lures and tide times. We share a couple of beers as we walk the shore catching fish.

Suddenly, I remember raft man and look out for him. Nothing. I run over to our little spot and thankfully find the car keys. At least I'm not stranded. I spotted his wallet and his smokes in the bag, and I kind of chuckled. No smokes or money; he's going to be jones-ing bad.

I go back over to the surf, scanning the water for the SS John-Bob, when I spot what looks like a yellow something or other way, way out. My immediate reaction was, *What an idiot. What's he doing? Why does everything have to happen to me?*

I filled my new friend in on the goings-on, and he thought I was pulling his chain at first. He looked out and thought, yeah, that could be a yellow raft. It was getting smaller, though. That much we agreed on. I continued fishing for a while, and after my new buddy left me, I left the beach for a few minutes to get a sandwich up on the roadway. I kept glancing out over the gulf, but I couldn't see the yellow dot anymore. I started wondering who I would have to call and about what time I should start thinking about making some calls. Seriously, though, who would I call? The Coast Guard? The local cops? His boss? The *National Enquirer?*

I went down to the beach, put my line back in the water and sat around waiting and fishing some more. Man, these fish were really biting.

I finally called it a day somewhere around four o'clock. I put our belongings in the car, and just hung around a while, waiting for you-know-who. He'd been gone for over five hours now when a sheriff's car pulls up next to his dinged up Taurus and out steps the sea farer himself. He gets out, as does the cop, and they walk over to me.

I can immediately see that he's sunburned to a crisp, but I couldn't resist. In my best pirate-like voice, I greeted the seaman. "Ahoy, matey. Welcome ashore. Where ya been, ya old salt?"

He wasn't amused, but the cop couldn't contain his snickering.

"Seriously, where's your watercraft, JB? Did the Coast Guard find you? You probably don't have your passport again, huh? I'm surprised you weren't mistaken for a Cuban out there."

At this point, the officer excused himself to turn and laugh out loud. He came back to make sure everything was okay, and we assured him it was. I thanked him for doing his good deed for the day, and he left the scene as a hero.

John-Bob started speaking. "Oh, man, I fell sound asleep on that thing. When I woke up, I could barely see the shoreline. I had no idea where I was. It was scary. A couple of guys on a fishing boat came and got me after I waved like crazy at them. Look at me. I'm shaking, and red as a lobster."

I actually started to feel sympathy for the guy. I handed him a beer, but he couldn't drink it. We got in the car and headed back to the hotel. His sunburn was going to a big problem the next few days, which would mean he would be even more useless than usual.

That evening, back at the hotel, I called his room to check on him, and he didn't sound too good at all. I told him to call the airline and get a flight home the next day. I would explain to Pittsburgh that he was finished and there was no sense to pay for both of us to stay on this job. He was totally agreeable to this and thanked me profusely.

I did feel bad for the guy, but how much could I take? First the loud insult of an entire people, then the passport thing, the slaughtered chickens, then passing out on a raft and drifting out to sea. That was it.

I ended up finishing the job in a week or so, alone. Upon my return, I got a lot of questions about the start-up and, "What happened to John-Bob?" Apparently Gilligan was unable to hide the full body scorching he acquired during his maritime theatrics. He tried to blame it on grass cutting, but that fooled no one, especially his closest buddies.

GROUNDED, PART 2

I was given another of those "Get Off the Road Free" cards, in the form of my wife getting close to her due date for our second child. This time, it was 1993 and she was due at the end of December. They gave me desk duty starting the first week of December, and when our son Matthew was born on December 30, I was able to stay home for another few weeks after that and get the family settled. Cindy likes me being home for a while, but methinks she's figuring out that I'm the one skating through these things. I'm not claiming to be a barrier-breaker, but I thought of it as the earliest form of paternity leave.

NORTH OF THE BORDER

We did another job in the Hamilton, Ontario, area for a company that was making windshields. We had a few presses and chemical systems to start up, but it really wasn't anything out of the ordinary. The good thing was I showed up for the start-up and met up with my old buddies Paul, Alley, and Jack. They had a good handle on things before I arrived, which was typical, so we didn't have to work sixteen hour days. (At the plant, that is.)

We did know a thing or two about the Canadian night life, and that's where the men got separated from the boys. We figured out that the bars up there closed at one A.M. because the beer was so potent, most of the Canucks could party more by midnight than most of the world does by three A.M. The Canadian hangover was unique, too, in that it basically started with a bad headache and stayed a bad headache all day. Made you miserable as hell until lunch.

One particular morning, we all seemed a little pissy and were a tad ignorant to each other when we met for breakfast. Jack and I rode in my (Town) car, and Paul and Alley rode together in theirs. Jack and I arrived first, pulling into the parking lot and heading for the security office where we would have to sign in and out each day. As we walked up to the gate, Paul and Alley were getting out of their car a few feet away. We could hear them barking at each other about something, or nothing, but we didn't pay much attention. The two of us were miserable, too. As we enter the gate, I'm carrying a cup of coffee in my left hand, with my computer strapped over my right shoulder. As I'm shifting to sign the book, the strap lets go, making me twist awkwardly, and I make a desperate grab while I tried to save...the coffee. The computer flung off and thudded to the floor, making a nice *bang* sound.

The case was padded, but I wasn't sure how well. As we all stood there, the first guard looked at me holding my coffee and said, "Nice save."

I was not in the mood. "Yeah, nice save. I saved the coffee but the two thousand fuckin' dollar computer hit the floor. Good save, indeed."

They just looked at me, a little afraid, and at Jack, who didn't flinch or say a word.

Suddenly, one of the guards yells out, "Hey! Look at those guys! Go stop them!" I guess he was talking to us. We looked out the window, and there was Alley and Paul in a full fist fight, throwing punches at each other, pushing, and finally wrestling each other to the ground while spewing obscenities. The guards ran out to break it up, but Jack and I stayed put. I was fixing the strap on the computer, hoping it was still a working computer, and Jack just kind of stood there and looked out the window with his hands in his pockets.

Those guys kept fighting and insulting each other, rolling around the parking lot throwing the occasional jab. After a few minutes, they let go and the guards separated them. They brought them into the shack and were getting ready to call the cops and have them thrown into jail. Apparently there was a zero tolerance policy on fighting at the plant.

Jack finally spoke up, and his calm voice and laid-back demeanor calmed the guards down, and they agreed to let the guys go, since they were only "jagging around." That was their story, anyway. We knew it was real enough, though. It was a direct result of the Labatt's Blue the night before. They eventually calmed down and made nice with each other, and the day went on as usual.

We were busting their balls most of the day, wondering what the hell they were fighting about. What could have been so personal and enraging that these two long-time friends got into a knock-down drag-out battle in a Canadian factory parking lot? It took a while, but they finally spilled the beans. The argument started on the drive in, when they were listening to the car radio. Apparently Paul is of the opinion that Skynyrd's "Freebird" is the greatest guitar jam in rock and roll, but Alley, on the other hand, feels strongly that it's "Green Grass and High Tides" by the Outlaws. That's worth fighting for, right? Everyone knows it's the Outlaws.

§ § § § § §

One night we were returning from a typical OT shift at the local pub and grub, when bestowed upon us was a sight none of could have ever been prepared for. We had just gotten out of the car and were walking toward the hotel with no particular purpose, just kind of BS'ing as we made our way to the doors.

Out of the blue, Paul lets out a distinctive, "Holy shit, Barr! Look!"

I looked over at him, and he was pointing up at the hotel, about midway up the building. I squinted, trying to focus in on whatever he was looking at. "What? Where?" I asked.

"Look at the one, two...around the sixth floor, on the left side. Look in the window, Barr!"

And there it was. A sight we'll never forget. There, in all his glory, was a lonely traveler who was feverishly testing the You'll Go Blind theory. Yes, indeed, a pot-bellied guy getting busy spanking his monkey in front of god and everybody. Apparently he was unaware of back-lighting and how it works when you're in front of the window.

Paul was going ballistic. "Look at him go! Holy shit, he's gonna hurt himself. Look at him! Let's go." He stopped and counted rooms and floors, so he could figure out what room Lance Romance was in.

We went to the front desk, where Paul asked for a house phone. The clerk, a middle-aged woman, asked if there was anything he needed help with.

"Not me," he said. "But your guest in 610 needs a date."

I was howling with laughter. This was Paul's show now. He dials the phone, and after a few seconds, the abuse begins. "Good evening, sir, this is the front desk calling. We know what you're doing in there, and you better knock it off or you'll go blind."

I keep listening.

"Yes, sir, you certainly were doing SOMETHING. You see, sir, when you choke your chicken with such ferocity, you put yourself in danger, and we don't want that. Sir, wait a minute, sir, yes, you were. If you like we can have room service bring up a bottle of wine and maybe put on some Sinatra…or perhaps we'll send up some self control." A slight pause. "We saw you through the window, asshole. My god, you were beating little Joey like he owed you money. Come on, now."

At this point, we are all in tears, laughing out loud. Even the lady at the desk; she was bent over, wanting to hear but not wanting to be a part of it.

"Listen, pal, if you're gonna run one off, close the goddamn curtains. Better yet, take a cold shower. This is a family hotel, not a truck stop peepshow. And no porno movies. Holy hell, you'll be swinging from the rafters." And he hung up.

Paul wanted to walk to the guy's room and bang on the door, but I convinced him the damage was done and to just let it go. I guarantee that was the last time Loverboy stayed at the Sheraton Hotel in Hamilton.

ST. LOUIS BLUES

The service department hired yet another body, this time a guy about our age, from the general area. His name was Mickey

Zombeck, but we all called him Mick. He had short brown hair combed straight back, basically average size and height. And he was single. One hundred percent single and proud of it. Mick was always sniffing around for a date, in the plant, the airports, the rental car counters, and even the rental car shuttle busses. Which for us married guys was fun to watch. He was a good fit to the group, not just for the entertainment value, but he was a damn good technician. He knew how to get things done, and he actually made my life easier because he didn't need his hand held. If he called in and said "we're ready," I knew the job was ready for the software.

One of Mick's first assignments was to our old friends in Missouri. I knew a lot of the staff in the plant, but by the time I arrived on this particular job, Mick could have been elected mayor. I flew in on a Thursday night, hoping to get started and finished within a week or so. I arrived at the St. Louis airport in the early evening, with the intent to rent my Town Car and make the two-hour-plus drive south to the hotel and/or Back Door Lounge, where Mick and friends would be waiting for me.

I went to the Budget counter and discovered I did not have my Pennsylvania driver's license on me. They wouldn't rent me a car, even though I pleaded with them, knowing my license was on file, as I rented cars from them almost weekly. No good. They did tell me I could walk over to the Missouri State Police's satellite office in the airport, and a temporary license would be issued to me. All they had to do was look up my PA info and that was it. Sounded easy enough, except for one slight problem.

One of the things that goes along with a lot of travel is the occasional out of state traffic ticket. It was just an inherent part of the job, especially when zipping around in a forty-thousand-dollar rent-a-car. At the time of this particular trip, I had two outstanding speeding tickets in the state of Missouri that required my immediate attention, but I always figured there was a slim chance I would get caught again, so I blew them off. When the rental agent suggested I walk in to the State Police office and get a T-License, well, I knew that would be an incredibly stupid thing to do. My license was in Pittsburgh, sitting on my dresser exactly where I left it. I was officially screwed. And stranded. At that point, I figured I better go home and get it.

I went to a pay phone and called the plant to talk to our guy Mick. (This is still pre-cell phone era.) I get him on the phone and deliver the bad news. "Mick, I'm in the airport but there's a slight problem. I don't have my license, and I can't go to the state cops to get a temporary one issued 'cause they'll probably throw me in jail."

"What the hell are you going to do? Take a cab?" He was kidding, I hoped.

"No. I'm going to get a flight back to Pittsburgh, get my license, and fly back here on the next one out. Maybe later tonight, or tomorrow sometime. I'll let you know when I find a flight schedule." I was dead serious. This was back in the day when flying was like taking a bus, only more expensive.

His response was quick and direct. "No fucking way! If you fly back home tonight there's no way you're coming back and we both know it. You stay right there. I'm coming to get you." He, too, was dead serious.

"Mick, come on. I can get a flight back to Pittsburgh in thirty minutes. I'll come back, I promise."

He wasn't interested. "Barr, no fucking way. You stay there. Go to the sports bar next to the ticket counter. I'll meet you there as soon as I can get up there. Find something to do while you wait."

I tried to explain to him he would be looking at a solid four hours of travel to the airport and back, but he didn't care. So I went to the bar, ordered a burger and a beer, and waited for him to show up. A couple hours later, he walks in with a couple of the plant guys, and it was like a big happy reunion. We all had a beer and off we went, like it was nothing.

He did scold me for the unpaid tickets, but I knew damn well he had a few of his own floating around out there. It actually worked out well because I had a personal chauffeur, a competent one who wasn't named John-Bob. The plant guys were having fun as well, seeing as how they drank half a case of free beer on the way up, and the other half on the way back. But that was part of the code of road—you helped each other out without even thinking about it.

He was probably right, though. If I turned around and flew back home, it would have been a few days 'til my return, if at all.

I ♥ NY

Long Island, New York, was the home of yet another steering wheel manufacturer that we did business with. The company was called Muzimi, and no, it wasn't owned by some Irish conglomerate. It was a Japanese company, with Japanese senior management with an American mid-management team and general workforce of illegal immigrant line workers and press operators. This had become the norm for a lot of the automotive business we had been doing.

We had done a few projects there, and had become friends with the maintenance and engineering departments, which was typical. I arrived on the job to meet up with Jake and another guy we had hired, named Jerry. This job was late, as usual, and the Japanese managers were a bit pissy with us. The maintenance staff was managed by a guy named Steve Stipe, and he was about our age, with a New York accent and a New York attitude. He did a nice job of buffering us from the Japanese management, mainly because he knew that whenever they pulled us away to talk about the schedule in various forms of English, it was usually his department that suffered.

After a couple of weeks of late nights and on-the-fly engineering changes, we were ready to make some test parts. Our first step was usually to run the system with mineral oil before the chemicals, mainly for safety, then drain the oil and put in the first batch of chemicals to use as a flush. This step meant running the chemicals through the pumps for an hour or so, then draining it, as it was contaminated with the oil residue, which was kind of significant to most customers.

Our man Steve had a different idea. One evening around seven, we were all dragging ass, but we finally had chemicals pumping. We had made a few test parts, and even I could tell they looked like shit. They were round, yes, but made of a colored foam that was a god-awful mixture of polyurethane and oil. Steve grabbed one right out of the press, and we all looked at.

"We'll drain and flush one more time, Steve, then these should look a lot better," I said to him.

Our guys all kind of nodded their heads in agreement. He looked really hard at it, squeezed it a few times and looked at us with a twinkle in his eye. "Ship them," he said, then looked at the Latino kids. "Start production."

They scurried to their stations and started making parts. The rest of us, including his maintenance guys, stood there in shock. I went over to him, and said, "Steve, you can't ship these; they're scrap."

He was the boss, though. "Fuck it. We'll ship 'em. Let the customer tell me if they're scrap."

And that was it. I looked over at Jake and Jerry. I shrugged, and Jake looked over at me and said "We're done. Sign this, Steve."

And with that, he handed Steve our standard, "We're Outta Here" form and he signed it. Project completed. Party time.

We all headed to the local hangout for a little party to commemorate our fine work. We hung out for a while, had some music going on, and ordered typical bar food. We went on for a few hours, and eventually the long hours caught up to a couple of us "old" guys. We were calling it a night, meaning Jake and myself, but the rest of the group was pretty wound up and decided to hit the city, meaning New York, of course. Jake and I decided to stay put, wise enough to know that not one good thing could come from going to the Big Apple after midnight on a school night.

To this day, we're still not sure what really happened, but I got a call from the NYPD at about three in the morning, telling me they had six drunken men in custody, and one of them belonged to Kanton. *Son of a bitch...Jerry.* I thought to myself. Why'd they call me? I just met the guy. I didn't even know his last name and I still don't.

Apparently they got arrested for urinating in public near the river. One of the locals knew a guy with a boat, so they went to the city, and I'm not sure of the rest of the story. Our guy and one other was allowed to leave, if someone sober came and got them. It turns out a couple of the locals had drugs on them, and it's neither cool nor legal to have them in your pocket while peeing outside at three A.M. in New York City. Sounds like an Elton John tune. But I had to call Jake, because I really didn't know Jerry, and he also had customer Steve's home number. I woke him up and explained the goings-on as they were explained to me and gave him the precinct phone number.

He said he could handle it, "Just like last time."

That was comforting to hear, in a twisted kind of way. Jake and Steve went to the city and liberated those who were liberate-able. We got our guy back, and the next day I got on a plane and headed home. Never heard what really happened and mostly didn't care. A bunch of guys got arrested, and a couple got kicked loose. Just another day on the road.

THE GREASY WOG

Kanton had introduced a new technology for machine control using a new thing called *fiber optics*. It's not new now, of course, but at the time it was very new, and unproven. Our Italian design department incorporated this new way of transferring computer data on our machines. Our first experience with it came with a project we had for a Tier 1 automaker. Not one of the big three, but what we called a Japanese transplant, a major facility in middle Ohio where we supplied this first-of-a-kind machine technology. My buddy, Shawn, and I were assigned to handle this start-up. Since it was a new experience for us, our leaders in Italy sent one of their young service engineers over to give us a hand and basically train us on this machine. This young Italian's name was Marco Galliardi, and he was a pretty knowledgeable guy in his late twenties. He stayed in Pittsburgh with us for a couple weeks and then went to the field with us for the start-up. He loved the United States, and especially the American nightlife. When we took him to Ohio, we worked some funky hours because we had to install the system and get it running, but we also were required to train each shift for two days each. Marco loved it, and Shawn and I decided to train the second shift first, so we could get them out of the way and use that time slot for showing Marco a good time the rest of the week.

This plan went well, and Shawn and I enjoyed watching Marco try to get Americanized. We took him to a lounge in the area that was truly mid-America—a quiet bar in front with a dance floor and loud music in the back. One evening, as Shawn and I were at the bar watching TV and relaxing, Marco was having at it on the dance floor. After a while, he came to the bar and sat with us. He was looking at us like something was on his mind.

"Hey, guys," he said, "I have question for you. I think I miss something in English. Maybe is only from local talk?"

Shawn took the lead. "What is it, Marco?"

"What means greezy wog?"

"What was that?"

"I think, what is greezy wog?"

We looked at each other, Shawn and I, trying to figure out what he was talking about. We kind of said it over a few times…greezy wog…greezy wog…

"Oh shit!" Shawn had it. "Marco, where did you hear this?"

"The girl over there say to me. She say 'go away greezy wog.'"

"No, no. Not greezy wog. It's greasy wop. Not greezy wog. Greasy wop."

We were both laughing now, since some local chick just dusted Marco and called him a greasy wop.

"Shawn, what is greasy wop?"

"Greasy wop is a derogatory term for Italians, Marco. It's not very nice, so let that one go."

He laughed it off, which was cool, and back to the dance floor he went. We figured that since he was hitting on basically every woman in the bar, his reject rate was still way above average.

§ § § § §

A few weeks after we left the plant, we got a call from the plant management that the data collection system wasn't right, and they were pissed. Apparently the system would collect data all day and then mysteriously stop in the middle of the third shift. They demanded I get back out there and fix it, putting a lot of heat on our management.

Since it was a new design, I was actually kind of worried about this. The machine used a personal computer to collect data with a special program using fiber optic cable that we had never used before. I scoured through the program to see if there was a bug to cause this, but didn't find anything. I just didn't know, but now the customer's management had complained very loudly to our management all the way across the Atlantic to Italy. I spent hours looking into the computer code, but everything looked normal. Time for yet another unplanned road trip.

I went to the plant and watched the system run during the day. No problems here. The plant manager was a little pissy with me, and he was sure it was a computer glitch. And he had no problem mentioning this to me over and over. For a guy like me who was only there to help, he sure gave me a lot of shit over this.

I went back into the plant at about two A.M., the approximate time when the problems seemed to be starting. I made my way through the plant into the control room where the computer was. I was surprised to find four maintenance guys all huddled around the computer screen. They recognized me from the training, and they all gave me a friendly hello. I looked on the screen and saw a nice green fairway with a couple of trees and a little cartoon golfer-guy.

"What'cha doing, guys?" I asked gingerly.

"Well, when we found out this was a regular PC, we put a golf game on here. We have a tournament going on."

"A golf tournament? Really?" I asked them. "You play this every night about this time?"

"Yeah. It breaks up our shift."

"Oh, okay. So you take the computer offline so you can play golf. That would explain why we're not collecting data every night."

They looked at me kind of funny, as, one by one, they all figured out why I was there and who ordered me there.

"Is this a problem?" one of them asked me.

"Well, yeah. It is. When you start playing golf, the data doesn't get collected. Your bosses called my bosses and bitched all the way to Italy that the system wasn't working."

This match was now over, and they looked at me for forgiveness. "Are you going to tell our boss? Can you tell them you fixed something and it's all working good now? We could get in a lot of trouble, you know."

"Don't worry about it, guys," I told them. "It's cool. I won't tell." They all smiled and skipped back to work.

That was horseshit, of course, because their management had made such a racket over it and made my life so miserable, blaming me personally for a computer program fault. These guys were using a million dollar production system to play computer golf.

I was so giddy I wrote the full report that night and had the overnight girl at the hotel fax it to my home office, so my bosses had it in their hands first thing in the morning.

Mission accomplished when I received a quasi-apology from the customer, but I never heard from anything from the Midnight Duffers.

OUR BUD

Kanton had a CFO/VP who was quite a character. Bud McKenzie had grown up on the rough side of town, as they say, and he was a big guy with an attitude. He was great to work for, though, and as long as you did your job, Bud would always have your back.

One of the dearest memories we all have of Bud, and the one that sums up his background and disposition, was the day a few guys were standing around in our fabrication shop together. One of our high-ranking colleagues had just walked past, giving a pseudo-wave and the obligatory nod. Without looking at anyone directly, Bud simply said, "I'd kick his fuckin' teeth in for a cheese sandwich."

How about that from the CFO? I'm glad he's on my team.

He could give and take a joke, too. One of the things I liked to do was call him occasionally, usually from around thirty thousand feet. The phones installed in the airplanes were a novelty, and at a hundred bucks a minute or whatever it was they charged, should have been a rarity.

I liked to call the office and ask for Bud. "Bud? Hey, it's me, Barry. What's going on?"

He would chat for a little bit, then ask what I wanted.

"Hey, guess where I'm calling from? I'm flying across Missouri right now. I'm in the airplane, Bud? How do I sound?"

"Goddamit, quit this shit!" was his usual reply, followed by a quick hang-up.

CHECK, PLEASE!

They hired yet another new technician and sent him with Paul and Jack to Missouri. I met up with them for the usual start-up. This particular new guy was unlike the others, though. He seemed like a decent guy, but he was a lot older than us, in his mid-fifties, so he was given the obvious nickname of Pops, and he apparently liked it.

We had completed a couple of long days, and as usual we were making good time. Friday night came along, and after the work day, we all headed to the Back Door and started getting busy. Paul had informed Pops of the tradition that the newest guy bought the first round. Pops gladly handed over his corporate credit card to our man, Clark the bartender, and he logged it in. Being the good guy that he is, Paul had invited about eight of the folks from the plant to join us at the only bar in town.

We had quite the time, including Pops, and the drinks were flowing. We ended up there until closing time, and that's when Clark did his thing. He tallied up the bill, and handed it to our dear Pops, thanking him in advance for his patronage. Pops looked like he saw a ghost. Either that or a $300 bar tab.

Ouch. New guy should have known better, but hey, we had fun. He tried to wiggle out of it, but Paul was having none of that. He made Pops sign it and we called it a night.

The next morning, we're all sitting around at the hotel breakfast tables and there was Pops lamenting his predicament and wondering out loud what the hell happened. "Will I get in trouble for this?" he asked Paul.

"Don't know, man. Can't be good, though. I mean three hundred bucks on your first expense report? Bud McKenzie is going to go postal when he sees that receipt."

Pops just groaned. He was worried about losing his job, not knowing that it was really no big deal as long as the rest of us didn't turn in any expense for the evening, which we wouldn't. But he didn't know that.

After twenty minutes of listening to him whine, Paul was going to make him feel better and had some advice to dispense. "Listen, Pops, there's really no problem; here's all you have to do."

Pops leaned forward and listened very carefully for some sound advice. He instantly perked up, ready to absorb some job-saving advice. "What, Paul? Please…tell me."

"When we get back to Pittsburgh, just go in and talk to Bud, man to man. He'll listen."

"Really? Do you think he'll hear me out?"

"You betcha he will. Just look him straight in the eye and say to him, 'Bud, listen. I have a drinking problem.' He'll probably understand."

Pops looked like he was going to faint, but Paul continued. "You'll still have to pay it back, but he might not fire you."

I think the sound we heard at that point was Pops shitting his pants. He looked like he was going to puke, but Paul just kind of smirked like, "oh well," and Pops truly thought he was in deep shit. None of us made a sound even though we were choking trying not to laugh out loud. THAT was his advice. Tell the VP of finance you have a drinking problem.

We went into the plant, and with Pops moping around all day, Paul made sure all the plant people thanked him for their free Friday night. We let the poor old guy consume his day with worry, kind of an initiation. Paul finally told him later that day that we would cover him by not turning in any other expenses for the night and nobody would give it another look. From that point on, though, Pops was pretty shy with his company Visa card. I think he hid it under his mattress with his communion money.

YAK-DONALD'S

One of the maintenance guys who worked in the plant liked to hang around us as we were working every day, which wasn't unusual. Alan Kinter was his name, or Big Al, as he was more commonly known. Al was a big guy in his mid-twenties, with decent technical skills and a great sense of humor. He was a typical Midwestern single guy, who lived in an apartment and sucked up as much overtime as he could.

It was also common knowledge that Big Al had at least one meal a day at the local McDonald's. His co-workers would bust his balls constantly about this, but it didn't faze him in the least. He *relished* it.

Anyway, as we were working one day, the McDonald's thing came up, and I innocently asked Al what he liked best on the McMenu.

"Everything. I love everything on the menu. Breakfast, lunch, or dinner; it don't matter."

And we knew he meant it.

Throughout the day, we kept banging Big Al on his McJones and his piss-poor eating habits but he didn't flinch. His buddies stoked the flames and we kept it coming. After some trash talking, Big Al threw down a gauntlet that he could eat everything on the menu at one sitting. One of everything on the board at one sitting.

One sitting? Game on.

The rest of us accepted the challenge, and the next day we would make it happen by all pitching in and taking Big Al to McDonald's, where he would show us his appetite and blatant disrespect for his body. We would also pitch in to make a fifty dollar pot for Big Al to walk away with should he win this challenge.

Lunchtime came and we all headed to the Mickey D's. Yes, the same McDonald's of the aforementioned bin burger incident. There was about eight of us all told, and we all pitched in to buy the food. We needed to lay down some ground rules, though:

- Only one drink was required.
- Milkshakes counted for food, but only one flavor was required.
- Lunch menu only—no breakfast items required.
- Only one order of fries required, but it had to be the large size.

With these rules agreed upon and written in stone, we entered the store ready for the challenge. As we sauntered to the counter, we made sure we told the manager what we were doing. He ate it up. He didn't offer any discounts or freebies, but he was excited to see this go down, as was the rest of the McStaff.

When Big Al went to order, we all made sure it was complete. It was one each of the following:

- Hamburger
- Cheeseburger
- Quarter Pounder
- Quarter Pounder with Cheese
- Big Mac
- McChicken
- McRibb
- Large Fries

- Chocolate Milkshake
- One Regular Coke
- Apple Pie
- Cherry Pie
- Ice Cream Cone (delayed purchase allowable)

With the order placed, we all got our own "little" meals, Big Al got his (on two trays), and away we went. We took up in the dining room, and it seemed to start off smoothly enough. The hamburger and cheeseburger went first, as expected, and he made quick work of those. In a bold strategic move, he piled fries on each of them. Double duty and good gamesmanship. Next was the QPs, and they went a little slower, with intermittent sips on the shake and pop. The Big Mac was next, and went a little slower.

The rest of us had all finished eating by now, so we sat around cheering and watched, with a little bit of wagering even going on. A bunch of other diners also came over to watch this challenge, and a few of them also took part in the betting. By the time Big Al committed to the Big Mac, he was clearly slowing down, maybe even looking a little uneasy, for lack of a better word. He slowly chewed away on the Big Mac, with the occasional French fry accompanying a bite, until the fries were history. He took a pie break, shoving the apple-filled tube down his throat in two bites.

He finally made it through almost the entire table of food; now down to his last serious obstacle. It was the dreaded McRibb. Yes, the lowly McRibb, Ray Kroc's personal insult to swine everywhere, sat there as the only obstacle between Big Al and victory. He sat there for a few minutes, collecting his composure and looking, well, concerned. By now he looked bad, as sweat was forming on his forehead, his arms were straight down at his side, and he wasn't talking.

We tried to cheer him on, at least those of us who bet on him to win. The others were trying to get him to puke. At this point, it was really touch and go and could have gone either way. Al took the McRibb in hand and took a little bite and set the sandwich down. The first bite slowly worked its way down. Now another bite. He chewed a couple slow ones, and tried to swallow. He tried again, but it wasn't going down. Finally, he spit the half chewed mouthful on the table and got up, waving his arms in front of him signaling, "No more."

Half the crowd groaned and the other half cheered. The manager looked away. Silently, Big Al just got up and headed for the door, slowly, and a couple of us went with him. As he got outside, he stopped dead in his tracks, just standing there with his hands on his hips, unable to move.

What came next was not only predictable but probably avoidable, if any of us acted our age. Big Al, in obvious need of immediate gastrointestinal relief, groaned in a tone I don't think I've ever heard from a grown man. In a single motion, he turned away as his free lunch came spewing out. Problem was, when he turned away from us he actually turned toward the building. He started hurling in uncontrollable spasms, each one projecting the McLava like a human volcano. Right onto the building.

But not just the building; I mean the full glass windows that went from floor to ceiling, which had a lunch-time crowd sitting on the other side having lunch. These people must have had the view of a lifetime, with a two hundred and twenty pound man violently throwing up on the full glass windows right in front of them. As an added touch, he was actually leaning on the glass with both hands as he yakked over and over again. We all headed to the cars in a trot, the thinking being that if we were in our cars, we would not be involved anymore.

The manager came running out yelling, "No! No! Al, No!" He was absolutely a frantic mess.

What a sight to behold. We could see the people inside as they were all getting up and holding their eyes and or mouths. Finally, Big Al finished his second taste of lunch, regrouped himself for a few minutes, and quietly got in the car with Mick and me, and we headed back to the plant.

We didn't have the heart to bust his balls about the whole thing since he was obviously shamed enough, as he just sat in silence. We tried to ease his mind a little, cheer him up even, but he wasn't talking.

The only thing he finally said was, "That goddam McRibb. I tell you now, I would have made it if it wasn't for the fuckin' McRibb."

I still don't know if he was upset about losing the $50 challenge or puking on a restaurant storefront in front of fifty or sixty people, most of whom he probably knew. I chuckled to myself, though, as I couldn't help thinking that this was the second time I was involved in a not-so-pretty incident at this little McDonald's recalling the 'bin burger incident.' It's not like I came seven hundred miles, twice, to intentionally rag on the place, but it's strange how things work out. A lot of us will never eat a McRibb, either.

NEW YORK STATE OF MIND

Another project had me meeting up with my buddies Shawn and Kenny back on Long Island, where the install was running the customary two weeks behind schedule. Our customer, Steve Stipe, had told us the Japanese were furious over the delay, but he would run interference for us.

The hotel we stayed at was a nice little place, with a couple of floors, a bar, and a decent staff. Being a smaller place, we, of course, became quick friends with the manager. One of the features of this hotel was selecting a Guest of the Day. The winner would receive a gift basket with a bottle of wine, some cheese and crackers, candy, and even a corkscrew. The day I arrived and went to check in, the sign in the lobby was congratulating, "Kenny Toll—Guest of the Day."

Kenny saw this and it made his year. He was a happy, happy boy. The manager gave him his gift basket and he carried it to his room like a pot of gold. What we didn't know or expect was that he was going to rub this in our faces all night and all the next day. We were both happy for the guy, but he just wouldn't shut up about it. He was convinced it was a real honor and rare chance to be selected top dog at the Medford Inn.

The next afternoon, after our workday, we all headed back into the hotel to hit the bar for a cold one. We walk through the front doors into the lobby, and there it is...the sign. And in bold, white letters, it pronounced, "Congratulations Barry Metzler—Guest of the Day."

I laughed at the irony, as Kenny looked like he just lost his best friend. I looked at him. "AH HAH! It's me! It's a major award! I won, I won, I won!"

And as an added touch, I did a little dance, a la Darren McGavin in the movie *A Christmas Story.* I made a mockery of it, and of Kenny, of course. The front desk manager laughed pretty good, though, knowing we were a fun bunch. So I collected my basket and up we went to my room to have some wine and cheese.

Kenny was still trying to rub it in that he was first. The first winner among us. We all argued about it until the wine ran out, and we went to the bar for the rest of the happy hour.

While we were down there, I walked out to the front desk, and when I saw the manager was still there, I asked him for a small favor. I asked him if he could select our Kenny for the Guest of the Day for the rest of the week or so. Not necessarily every day, but most every day. With a twenty dollar bill as incentive, he had no problem with it. None at all.

So the next day, we came back from the plant and there it was again. "Congratulations Kenny Toll—Guest of the Day." He won again and was back in our face with it. No clue. He was telling anybody who would listen how lucky he was.

Next day, same thing. "Congratulations Kenny Toll—Guest of the Day."

Now you would think he might have smelled a rat at that point, but not our boy. He won that stupid prize four days in a row, and something like nine out of twelve days. He really didn't like the wine, and he actually started bitching about winning so much because he had these bottles of wine, packs of cheese, and other foodstuffs piling up in his room.

When he figured out Shawn and I had set him up, like day fourteen or so, he actually begged us to have them stop. We walked in one late afternoon, when he saw the sign he just groaned. "Oh my god. Not again."

Shawn and I laughed out loud, as did the manager as he shouted, "We have a winner!"

Game. Set. Match.

Kenny conceded to the true professionals and we all agreed he would never again be the 'guest of the day.'

Poor ol' gullible Kenny. Watch what you ask for, bucko, because you just might get it.

§ § § § §

The mood at the plant was getting a bit strained, to say the least. We were behind schedule, but we were getting close. We were constantly being told that the Japanese plant director, Mr. Fujiyama, was on the warpath. Our customer, Steve, would tell us when Fuji, (as he was called behind his back), was snooping around our area or just in a foul mood in general. He was one ornery son of a bitch, and he had the look to match. Hairy eyebrows over his slanted eyes formed grayish-black horns, and he was always scowling. He didn't speak much English and was always mumbling something. The rumor was he was assigned to a five-year stint in the States and his only companionship came from Johnny Walker.

Shawn and I figured we only needed a couple more days, so we gave Kenny his Get Out of Jail Free card and sent him home on a Thursday. I remember that day because of the goings on that I'll never forget. About mid-morning, Steve came out to our install area and told us, "Fuji wants a meeting right now to go over the schedule."

I kind of expected it, so I told our Shawn to keep working, that I'd go to the meeting. On the way there, customer Steve filled me in a little more. "Fuji got slammed by our customer for being late so he's taking it out on all of us, but it'll be mostly you today. Just want to prepare you for it."

"Thanks. We're pretty close, though, so I may have a little good news to tell him."

We went to the conference room, where I followed him in through the doorway. Inside was a huge oval table that already had at least seven people sitting around it very quietly, and each one of them looked as nervous as a virgin at a prison rodeo. I followed Steve to the back of the room, making our way behind the occupied chairs. He took the first empty one, and I naturally sat down next to him.

We all sat there quietly for a couple minutes when Fuji himself stepped into the room. He stopped in the doorway, took a look around the room and scowled.

He started stammering something in an unidentifiable language that seemed to have morphed from Japanese and English. It was hard to tell. He was furious about something. He started stomping his little feet on the floor and pounding his fist into his hand. His head was rocking back and forth as he stomped. Ranting and raving, stomping and pounding liked a raped ape.

What was he saying? Holy hell, this guy was having a fit right in the doorway. Nobody in the room looked up or even made eye contact with him. He went on for what seemed like forever, in this violent rage, when I finally leaned over to Steve, and in a little whisper, I asked him the obvious question.

"What's up with him?"

"You're in his chair."

I thought I was going to faint. I became flushed and my stomach dropped to my ankles. *You gotta be shitting me.* This epileptic fit was happening because I was in his chair? Surely Steve was joking. "Are ya fucking kidding me?" I asked him in a low voice that was now a desperate, frightened whisper.

"No. You should really think about moving."

I was now officially in a panic. Nobody in the room had the balls to say anything to me, so I just pissed off a customer like nothing I've ever seen before. My mind was racing. *What to do? What to do?*

Realizing my total lack of choices, I got up from my ill-gotten seat, and with bowed head, I silently and shamefully made my way around the table to the next empty seat. I sat my sorry ass down and Fuji silently made his way to the seat I had warmed up for him.

That prick never even said thank you, go to hell, or sorry for being such a dick. Nothing. Nobody else spoke, either, until Fuji's number one lackey started talking about the time schedule and other issues.

I made it a point to make eye contact with every sorry son of a bitch at that table and at least let them know I wasn't happy about the *chair incident,* as I came to call it. When it was finally my turn to speak, I told them, "Two days," and left the room.

Steve later came out to apologize for not realizing when I sat down where I was actually sitting. Apparently it's a Japanese custom for the senior or top ranking official to sit furthest from the door, which I hadn't known. Oh, I fucking know it now, that was for goddam sure. Hell of a way to learn Asian business etiquette, I must admit.

I tried to relate the story to Shawn, but it didn't come out right because I was in such a funk over it. I'll never forget the sight of that little fuck having his seizure in the doorway because I was in his hallowed spot. Nor will I forget the nutless wonders around the table who started admiring their pencils the minute Fuji went postal. It took me a day or two to get over it and really laugh my ass off over it.

§ § § § §

The Fuji incident provided some serious motivation to get the hell out of there, and, that, we did. We finished up the job on Saturday afternoon, and we got our guy Steve to sign off on the completion form. We went out for a quiet night that evening, and on Sunday morning, we headed to the airport, albeit way late.

The Long Island airport had their rental return lot far away from the terminal, and this presented a little problem for us.

We were really running late, so when we pulled into the airport, Shawn headed right for the main entrance, where he conveniently pulled the car over in the unloading zone and put it in park. "Let's go," were his words of advice, so I went.

We grabbed our bags and ran the six feet or so to the main doors to the terminal, and he went right over to the Budget counter. Bypassing the line, he walked right up to the counter and threw the keys and the little folder onto the counter and told the girl, "Here's the keys. We gotta run."

As we walked away, she yelled back to him, "Where's the car?"

Without breaking stride, he pointed out the front window and said, "Right there!"

She (and the other ten people in the line) looked out the window to the front curb where there sat a pearl white, brand-spanking new Lincoln Town Car. We ran toward the airline ticket counter with her yelling something like, "You can't park there," or "You can't do that." I remember the word *illegal* being tossed out there, too.

A few minutes later, as we were heading up the escalator to the gate, we heard the announcement over the loudspeakers: "Will the owner of a white Lincoln Town Car with New York license plate please return to your car or it will be towed." We both laughed out loud as we went right to the plane and got on about ten seconds before they closed the door.

Shawn did get a parking ticket in the mail, which he immediately shit-canned. A few more came, and they were dealt with in the same fashion. They were followed up by a few nasty letters from Budget, the DMV, and the New York State Police, and the whole thing got kind of ugly, but the Kanton legal and accounting departments did something with it and the whole thing disappeared like a fart in the wind.

BLOOMINGTON BEAUTIES

Next stop was a summertime start-up in exotic Bloomington, Indiana. We were working in a plant that made a well known line of refrigerators. Not much going on in this neck of the woods, but apparently the men-folk had a place to sow their oats, one dollar bill at a time.

Driving from the airport to the plant, we passed a billboard for a strip club that I always thought was kind of funny. We all saw it and laughed. Whoever thought of it had a good thing there. It went something like this:

DIAMONDS

A GENTLEMEN'S CLUB

EIGHTEEN BEAUTIFUL WOMAN AND TWO UGLY ONES

§ § § § § §

Working in the plant was brutal with the Midwestern summer heating up the plant like an oven. I was working in the control room, and one day the customer's program manager, Terry, declared he was getting an air conditioner for us. He had started spending some time in there with us, and we convinced him the electronic control panels in the room needed to be kept cool. This was true for the most part, but it wasn't absolutely necessary. He was on it, though, and as a young up and coming engineer, we knew he would succeed.

He showed up one morning with a huge window air conditioner, and he had his maintenance department get it installed in the side window of this control room. With he and I the only guys there at this time, he was proud of his contribution to the start-up effort. "What do you think, Barr? This is nice, huh? Nice and cool."

I looked at the AC unit and saw something that was amiss. "Yeah, Terry this is nice. Good job."

He smiled unassumingly as I readied for the sucker punch.

"I'm wondering what your bosses are going to say when they see you put a Whirlpool air conditioner in this plant? You must have a lot of weight to pull this one off. I mean, putting your biggest competitor's equipment in your plant? Sa-lute, brother."

This look on his face made me think today was the day. Yes, today is the day when I see a grown man cry in a refrigerator factory.

Poor Terry turned white as a ghost, and actually looked ill. He let out a little "Ah!" and just kind of stood there looking stupid. He didn't actually cry, but the term "extremely puckered" definitely fit.

"I'll lose my job if the plant manager sees this." His first action was a desperate move, but in his panic I guess he thought it was a good one. He grabbed a black marker from the desk and tried to rub out the Whirlpool name on the AC unit. Didn't work, though—the logo had raised letters. And now it couldn't be returned to the store because it obviously had black marker smeared all over the front. He ended up getting his company's logo on a stick-on pad from the production line, and stuck it over the competitor's name. This was a temporary move and a desperate cover-up until he ordered a new unit made by his own company.

When it finally came in, he gave the old one to the maintenance guy who swapped them out, as a form a hush payment. This guy was a smart engineer and a good guy to work with, but he almost lost his job over something so stupid. What a knucklehead. Just goes to show you they don't teach common sense.

IOWA AWAITS

Kanton landed a huge project in another Vegas-like metropolis we know as Cedar Rapids, Iowa. Actually, the plant itself was about twenty miles outside of Cedar, in a little Amish-like town called the Amana Colonies. The Colonies, as they were known, was home to an old order settlement of farms, weaving mills, family style restaurants, and a big-ass refrigerator factory that made, obviously, refrigerators. It was a nice plant, though, and they were really good people to work with. With no real signs of life in the immediate area, we stayed near the city and drove forty miles round trip to work every day.

I arrived when the install was about half finished. The electrical job was being run by my man Kenny, with Paul and Alley there to do their thing. The equipment was in a new building, and it wasn't even completed when we were installing our system. When I got on site, I got the nickel tour from Kenny. This included meeting up with our project manager, my ol' buddy Douglas.

We went toward the smoking area, and there he was. "Hi, Barry!"

He was actually glad to see me. And I was glad to see him, too. He was doing a good job, and we had actually already worked a few months on this project back in Pittsburgh. But, as usual, there he was, enjoying his Marlboro Red, and as usual, he was wearing a white, long sleeve, button-down shirt, faded straight leg blue jeans, and worn-in cowboy-like boots. Douglas was in uniform.

As we made our way through the plant, I noticed some contractors working in the building. I noticed one guy in particular, and it almost looked like he was following us. Or leading us. I couldn't tell if he was behind us or in front of us. I pointed him out to Kenny, and my impression was right on. This guy was a strange dude. He was kind of short, maybe five and a half feet tall. He wore a blue flannel shirt, buttoned all the way up, and had a face full of black hair, big bushy sideburns, and a humongous hairy una-brow that would make an Iranian jealous. To top it all off, he had thick, Elvis Costello glasses and a beige baseball cap pulled down low. And his teeth were always showing. No words, just slick movements and sudden appearances.

Kenny enlightened me. "That dude is strange. He's a local electrical contractor and I think he thinks we're taking his work. He just shows up out of nowhere, and then he's gone. Walk away somewhere else and there he is. We call him the Lurker. He's always lurking around somewhere. He gives me the creeps."

The Lurker. Yet another local to hack on.

A few days into the start-up, Douglas and I were taking a smoke break and making small talk. The smoking area was a fenced-in area with benches just outside the restrooms. He was starting to tell me about the customers, Jerry and Ben. Jerry was an older guy, very reserved and quiet. Ben was middle-aged and very knowledgeable, but Doug made it clear I shouldn't go out drinking with him. Apparently, Ben likes his sauce and gets pretty wasted.

As he was telling me a story from of couple weeks earlier, he suddenly stopped talking mid-sentence. He'd spotted the Lurker off to his left, and he walked past us, into the men's room behind us. He was gone as quick as he appeared.

Anyway, Douglas proceeded to tell me about a nice little dinner that turned into an all-nighter with Ben getting rip-snortin' drunk right before his very eyes. After dinner, he decided to have dessert at the bar, and that had consisted of ten or eleven beers with a half dozen shots of whiskey. The night ended when Ben fell off his bar stool and landed on the floor with a thud. Doug ended up taking him home. I listened with wide eyes and barely noticed the Lurker doing his thing.

Crazy story from Doug, and Kenny was absolutely right about the Lurker. He gave me the creeps, too.

§ § § § § §

One night during the second week or so, Ben was hanging around in the evening when we were finishing up for the day. We got to chatting a little, and Kenny blurts out, "Hey, Ben, how about joining us for dinner?"

I couldn't stop him in time, and Ben accepted in a New York minute. As the plans were being made, I got Douglas and made sure he was joining us. I didn't stutter or give him a choice. He was coming.

We get to this little lounge outside of the city, and we all go in. Lo and behold, they all know Ben. We sat down and ordered some beers, and we basically all ordered burgers or some other sort of bar food. It was a good time, relaxing, and we all just BS'ed for a while. After a few hours, we tried to leave but Ben wasn't hearing any of that. He was fun to watch, but it was a little uncomfortable being with a customer getting ass-faced.

We ran into one of the plant guys we knew, a guy named Tucker, but everybody called him Mother, for the obvious reason. With him as my wing man, I let Douglas and the others go, and we stayed with Ben. Eventually he started staggering around and back-slapping anybody who would listen to him. As annoying as he seemed to be getting, the bartender actually told me this was a typical Ben night.

Just before closing time, Ben stumbled around enough to give us our window to leave. Mother and I each grabbed an arm and drug him out of there and chucked him into the back Mother's car. We made our way to his house, as he slurred and babbled in the back seat until he finally just passed out. We made it to his house, and after we stopped in front, we kind of just looked at each other like "Now what?"

Drawing from a similar situation way back in my youth, I took charge and told Mother, "Let's just get him to the door."

And that's what we did. We dragged him to the front door, and I plopped him down on the porch, leaning his back against his front door. I told Mother to get in the car and start it up. When he did, I made sure Ben was firmly leaning his back against the door, and then rang the doorbell three or four time in a row. I then turned and ran like hell to the car, jumped in, and told him to get moving. And away we went. The basic plan was to lean him on the door so when his wife opened it, he would fall right in, like a drunken gift from heaven.

The next day, we were all doing our thing, and Ben shows up, fresh and spry as a new puppy. Not a word about the night, the ride home, the grand entrance, nothing. Just another typical day with us working, the Lurker lurking, and Ben making his rounds. As goofy as it was, it was a fun night. The burger wasn't bad, either.

§ § § § § §

After a few weeks, the days were getting long and, as usual, we were all getting a little chippy. Kenny was especially fed up with the Lurker. He just couldn't stand him. For some reason, he was really eating at him, and this wasn't normal for Kenny.

One night, around seven-thirty or so, we were leaving the plant heading out the back door to the parking lot as we usually did. As we got to the plant doors, we saw a ladder leaning against the interior sheet metal wall, and guess who is on the ladder about ten feet off the ground. The Lurker.

Only now, and this was unusual, he appeared to be actually working. He appeared to be installing some wiring for the plant lighting. We all saw him but nobody said a word. We kept walking and talking to each other as we made our way through the parking lot.

As we walked along, Kenny just stops, bends over, and picks up a rock about the size of a tennis ball. Without saying a word, he turns toward the building and aims a little left of the doors we just exited. He holds his arm straight out at the building to take his aim for a second or two, then winds up and throws that freakin' rock full force against the sheet metal wall, hitting the spot where he judged the Lurker to be, well, lurking. BOOM! The sheet metal wall let out a humungous thud. A direct hit. We all stood there in silence, just kind of looking at Kenny.

Without a word, he smiled and walked to the car. We were all stunned and it showed. We were literally too shocked to speak. Was this Kenny? Our Kenny? Who knew? I mean, really, who would have thought this about Kenny? We just couldn't believe it.

Not a single one of us ever dreamed he had such a good arm.

We all then got into our vehicles and headed to the hotel. We never said a word about it. The Lurker never said a word, either. Not ever, as a matter of fact. It didn't stop him from lurking or giving us the creeps, but I know he had to shit his pants that one particular evening. Workin' when he should been lurkin.' The irony of this was hilarious.

GROUNDED, PART 3

It was time for another moratorium on travel for this guy. Our third child was due in February, so from about Valentine's Day on, I was grounded. This was the honorable thing to do, but I was actually supposed to be on a big installation job and the customers wanted me on-site. Of course, it was my friends from Iowa, Ben and company, so they gave me a little bit of good-natured abuse over it. Cindy was due somewhere around February 22 or 23, and the yet unnamed bundle of joy was late.

On a conference call one day, they asked out loud why I was still there. "The baby's late," I told them.

"Doesn't surprise us a bit, Barr. Everything you guys do is late."

Ouch. They were kidding, I think, but it didn't matter. I wasn't traveling. On March 3, our third child was born as our daughter, Shannon, joined the team, which was now enough for an official basketball team. I stayed in town until after April, milking this baby thing like an Amish dairy farmer.

Chapter 5

TIME TO BUY NEW SHOES

Getting a promotion to project manager meant less travel. At least that's what I told my wife. It actually meant less time on start-ups, but only because now I had the whole project to worry about, not just the software and controls. It meant I had to deal with the customers a lot more, both in good times and in bad. It also meant I would have to wear a tie and get a little dressed up. It seemed like the right thing to do, plus I got to work a lot more with my buddy Jake, who was now one of the sales engineers.

We became a pretty good team, since I was one of the few people that could deal with his Italian temper. The cool thing was I would work on multiple projects simultaneously, so I really wouldn't get dragged into months-long start-ups. I had to be more mobile, pick up a golfing habit, and learn to drink red wine. Can do.

ONE MISSISSIPPI, TWO MISSISSIPPI…

We had a project with an automotive supplier that was located in the deep south, in a remote town in Mississippi. I had to travel there for project meetings as well as have them travel to Pittsburgh for the same. The plant manager for this company was a nice southerner named Red Layman. Red was a real good ol' boy, very knowledgeable and easy going. He made it a point to have his maintenance manager with him at most of the plant meetings. This guy's name was

Ruben, and he was a tall, very black guy that talked with the full southern twang and was just as easy-going as Red.

I had a lead engineer working with me, a guy who had transplanted from our division in England. Barton was a good engineer, and a good guy to hang out with. One evening in Mississippi, we were having a group dinner with Red and Ruben. It turned out that Red was a dog breeder on the side, raising hunting dogs, and it sounded like he made a nice buck doing it. He told us the way it worked this particular evening, and Barton was mesmerized as he soaked it all in. Red told the story in the full southern twang like only he could.

"Ya see, when we have these pups, I'll know within a week if they's a good dog or a bad dog. I'll go through the basic teachin' for 'bout three days, and if they ain't getttin' it, I goes through the litter and I'll just shoot the bad dogs and keep the good ones."

Barton was shocked. "Why do you shoot the bad ones? That's not very humane," he asked in his British accent.

"Cause a bad dog eats as much as a good dog," he quickly countered.

Barton just looked at him for a minute, then agreed. "Wow, that's pretty tough, but good business, I guess."

A couple days later, in the same setting, another discussion took place and Red explained the whole hunting thing to Barton.

"These are coon dogs. They're specially bred to find coons. They's trained to go huntin' at night, with a group, and they'll go into the woods and spook out a coon and get him on the run. When they's chasin' the coon, they'll git him a runnin' and they force him to a tree, and he ain't gonna have no choice but to climb up that rascal. When he climbs the tree, ain't nowhere for him to go no more and we get him. That's called 'tree'n the coon.' The dog treed him and then we catch up and shoot that bastard."

Barton was speechless and absolutely mortified. He sat silently with his hands out like he had a major question to ask but couldn't get the words to cross his lips.

Finally, I asked him what was on his mind. "Barton, what's the matter?"

"Well," he started, and then slouched forward, looked sheepishly at Ruben, and tried to whisper. "Isn't it illegal to hunt them anymore? I mean, don't they object? I know it's the south and everything, but surely someone must know you're still hunting these people and chasing them up a tree to shoot them. It's really not right."

We looked at him in silence for a minute or two, and finally our rebel friends just started laughing. Especially Ruben. I was a little embarrassed at first, on two separate fronts. First, as a project manager because this cement-head worked for me, and second, as an American. This asshole actually thought they were hunting African Americans. At night, with dogs and guns.

Red spoke up first. "Jesus Christ, Barton. I'm talking about raccoons. Not people. Raccoons, and yes, it's very legal."

We all chuckled about it, but this guy must have been horrified when he heard the story of chasing a coon up a tree with a pack of dogs so you could shoot the bastard. Especially hearing this with Ruben sitting at the table taking it in like everyday happenstance, which apparently it was.

We had these guys in Pittsburgh for a couple of days for more meetings. It was Red and another guy, not Ruben. I was taking care of them, meaning dinner and whatever in the evening. Being a huge Penguins hockey fan, it was a no-brainer to take these guys to their first hockey game. Of course, being on the expense account, I wanted the best seats and the full experience. We had dinner at the Igloo Club, the nice restaurant inside the Pens arena. Afterward, I took them down to our seats, a mere four rows off the ice. I was in heaven, almost forgetting I was with clients. When we sat down, I got us each a beer and asked them how they liked it.

Red looked at me in amazement. "I can't believe it ain't freezin' in here."

Turns out it was their first time at an ice rink, and probably just seeing ice, and not just their first hockey game. Forget about Lemieux, Jagr, Stevens, and the whole NHL thing. I knew right then and there that for me to really watch the game I needed to keep the beers and nachos flowing. And that I did. When Mario buried a breakaway goal, I asked them if they knew that they just saw the greatest hockey player in the world do his thing.

The reply was not unexpected, albeit a little slurred. "I still can't believe it ain't freezin' in here."

I must have heard that six times that night, but it never bothered me because the seats were excellent and Pens beat the Rangers again.

§ § § § §

Another lunch meeting in Mississippi and another southern gem from Red. We had been talking a lot about going golfing together, and he really wanted to take me to his country club. He brought it up many times, and it looked like we were finally going to go. During our lunch, about six of us were sitting around the table making plans to go later that afternoon, and Ruben decided to chime in.

"Mr. Red, when y'all gonna take me to that nice country club and take me golfin' with y'all?"

"Ruben, the only way your black ass will ever get on my golf course is pushin' a lawn mower."

I almost choked on my lunch but everybody else was laughing like they were watching the Bob Newhart Show. This would be an instant lawsuit in the north, and I was afraid to look up. Fortunately, Ruben must have expected this answer and he just laughed it off and made a joke of it.

God bless him for that, I guess.

IOWA, AGAIN

Jake Otum was trying to sell a big project to our old buddies in Cedar Rapids, and he asked me to help him out in the proposal stage. Basically, this meant traveling to the plant with him to review the design details and help explain the technical features. We made our way to the great Midwest with a half day of travel and a couple of uneventful flights. We got into Jake's rental and headed to the factory, but when we got to the plant gates, we were met with a totally unexpected situation.

The union workers were on strike. We had heard this might happen, but they had walked out as we traveled from Pittsburgh. So we pulled up to the entrance and stopped to check things out. The workers were walking in a quasi-picket line, with a few signs here and there, and a TV news truck covering the strike. As we sat in the car, I saw a couple of guys I knew kind of standing around, doing nothing. Jake and I called them over to our car, trying to get a heads-up on what was going on. We needed to get inside and have our meeting, but I wasn't in the mood to cross a nasty picket line to do it.

Except, this didn't appear to be a nasty picket line; in fact, it was probably the most polite picket line I ever saw. I'm telling you, these folks are genuinely nice people. When they came over, they stuck their heads in the windows, and we had a little talk.

The lead guy, Pete, did the talking. "Hey, guys; how's it going?"

"Pete, what's this? You're killing us, man. We came all this way to see Ben and the engineers. Can we get in?" I asked him.

"Yeah, you guys can go in. It won't look good for us, though. We'd really like to look tough for the TV cameras."

Jake spoke up with a great idea. "Tell you what, Pete, we'll inch the car across the gate and you guys pound the shit out of it. Get good and mean and everybody start yelling at us."

"Are you sure? We don't want to damage the car. And we're not mad at you guys. We all like working with you. Plus you install new equipment and it creates more jobs for us."

"Pete, this is a rental car. C'mon now. It's a win-win situation for all of us. We'll get in and have our meeting, and you guys get on TV and prove to management that you're pissed off and that you really mean business."

Pete finally got it. "Wow…what a great idea. Give me two minutes to tell everybody what we're doing. I appreciate this, guys. Really, this means a lot to us."

So in two minutes, with cameras rolling, Jake slowly drives the car across the entrance, and the workers let loose. They were rocking the car, pounding on the roof and hood, and screaming and yelling in a truly award winning performance. Jake and I were amazed.

We made it to the parking lot, and the TV cameras were still zoomed in on us. We laughed all the way into the plant and did our business.

Leaving the plant, same thing. When we got close to the gate, we gave Pete a wink and the strikers went at us again.

As we made it off the plant property, we turned onto the road leaving the plant, and who did I see? The Lurker! Sitting in his pickup truck because he couldn't go in. Huh! Wait until I tell Kenny.

What a day. The rental car took a little beating, nothing noticeable, but what the hell did we care, anyway?

The actions of this day gained us the respect of the entire plant. I did a lot of work over the years in this place, and if there was ever anything I needed, I got it.

§ § § § §

Another addition to my job description was golfing with the customers whenever needed. Jake had turned me on to it, and we would sneak away and hit the local course once in a while and he would give me some lessons. I got the clubs and shoes and all, so I was now a *golfer.*

Now that I had the new shoes, we took our clients out to the links one sunny afternoon. I was paired up with quiet little Jerry, and Jake was with Ben. I was shanking them all day, but so was my cart partner. Except Jerry never said much, and we were having a good time, or so I thought.

I had a tendency to hit a ball into the woods, get really pissed off about it, and follow it up with a shouted obscenity. This, too, I learned from Jake, and assumed it was a normal part of the game. But after a few hours of hacking the little white ball and swearing at elevated decibels, Jerry and I were approached by a pair of older guys who were golfing behind us. As we waited for the green to open up so we could hit, I was in the tree line, as usual, when their cart drove up next to me.

The kindly older gentleman offered me a piece of perpetual wisdom. "Hello," he said.

"Hello backatcha," I said.

"Son, I've been watching you golf today and hearing you cussing, as well. And after watching you golf, I can tell you, that, ah, well, son, you just aren't good enough to be swearing like that. How 'bout you knock it off now, okay?"

I was a bit stunned, I have to admit. But then I just started laughing 'cause the old dude was absolutely right. The wise old guy from Iowa doling out some words of wisdom to me. I was so impressed I felt like asking him how many licks to the center of a Tootsie Pop.

From that point on, I decided to lighten up and try to have fun.

MEXICAN METER MAIDS

We had a project being installed in Mexico, in a city called Queretero. I made a trip down there toward the end, meeting up with my buddy, Mick. When we did these jobs in Mexico, we had a sales/technical guy who lived there named Ricardo. Ricky, as we all called him, was a sly one. He knew all the ins and outs of the Mexican culture and this usually came in handy.

One evening, Ricky took us out to dinner, and when we got to the restaurant, he pulled up on the street in front and parked. We were walking into the place when Ricky turns and says something to a young kid standing out front. He reached in his pocket and gave him some pesos. Apparently, this was to watch the car and/or move it if the cops came. Out of nowhere, two cops jump out, grab Ricky and the young kid, and start screaming at them. Mick and I quickly slid into the restaurant and peeked out the windows like Gladys Kravitz on *Bewitched*. Right before our eyes, our escort/guardian/tour guide was taken away by the cops, thrown into the back of their car, and hauled off. The two of us were horrified. And stranded.

We figured since we were already here, we might as well eat something and drink some tequila. After a couple of belts, we found a waiter who spoke pretty decent English, and he explained to us that what happened was a form of *car-hopping,* an illegal practice of parking illegally and having a team of spies watch out for the cops. We only saw one guy, but apparently there were a few of them out on the streets. We were also told that our friend would have to pay a hefty fine before he could get out of jail.

Mick and I were glad to know what was going on, but it confirmed our suspicions in that we were now officially fucked. And stranded. We stayed there and drank for a while, and it dawned on us that cash was the international language spoken by all. We threw some US dollars at our waiter, and after hearing our plight, he arranged for us to get a secure ride to the hotel. It ended up being no big deal. At least for us. We didn't really know or give a shit about Ricky. He'd figure something out.

CALIFORNIA DREAMIN'

Mick and I had another one together, this time in Los Angeles, California. It was a small project, but this particular client didn't know a lot about the equipment, or machinery in general for that matter. His name was Frank something or other, and he made it a point to call and bitch almost every day, so he finally garnered the attention of our management who made me go out and talk to him.

Mick had already been working out there for a couple of weeks putting up with his crap, so he coerced me into going out there and talk to Frank with him. Mick had told me that the machinery was doing what it was supposed to, but there were a lot of issues with chemicals and other things we didn't have any control over. I talked to Frank for some time, told him our plan to visit, and he seemed genuinely pleased to hear it. I set up appointments and travel plans so Frank knew exactly when I would be there.

The travel day arrived and Mick and I were booked on a flight to LA from Pittsburgh. We made it to the plane, and as we were both very frequent fliers, we had first class seats right next to each other. We got on the plane, sat down, and the stewardess came over to take our order, just like any other flight. We were sitting there, reading, relaxing, and having our cocktails as the other passengers were boarding.

I was looking over the newspaper, quietly minding my own business when Mick erupted and got my attention. "Who's this Dash Riprock-looking motherfucker?"

Looking up at the door, I spotted the character in question. An older man is standing there, wearing a long black overcoat, a black, newsboy cap, and the obligatory, oversized, black, wrap-around sun glasses. The real topper was the man-servant who accompanied him, gently guiding him by the arm like he was some kind of royalty. They made a semi-scene getting to their seats, which were directly in front of us. Before the mystery man sat down, though, he took off his coat, hat, and glasses, and gave it to his assistant, and revealed his true identity.

I looked at him for a minute or two trying to put my finger on who this guy was. Then it came to me, and we were both shocked to see that this "Dash Riprock-looking motherfucker" was in fact none other than Don Knotts, aka Barney Fife.

We made a big to-do over him, and he was smiling from ear to ear. We toasted him with our drinks and started making him feel like a rock star. He and his sidekick ate it up, for a little while, at least.

As we all know, all good things come to an end. Over the next couple of hours, we basically bugged the shit out of the guy, like Mick repeatedly referring to him as Barney and asking him if he ever tagged Aunt Bea. His mood swung hard when we started on the Incredible Mr. Limpet thing. Looking back, I really think that was the turning point for us and that we had worn out our welcome. For the life of us, we couldn't remember his name on *Three's Company,* but he finally clammed up and wouldn't tell us. We asked him if he still had the bullet, the one he had in Mayberry but never did get a chance to shoot. That, too, got old because about the fourth time we asked him, he got really pissed off at us and yelled for the stewardess, demanding we leave him alone. He played the *famous guy* card and we ended up getting a good talking to, agreed that we would behave, and left him alone for the rest of the flight.

Yet another brush with celebrity and yet another let down.

We arrived in LA without any problems, other than the Don Knotts incident. The next day, we got to the plant where the secretary tells me Frank will be right out to see me. I went out to the factory floor with Mick, wanting to get a good look at things, and, as expected, the machine was plugging away over a conveyor system they had supplied on their own. The thing was just dumping liquid foam into these molds that were flying by faster than the machine could track.

After an hour or so, I went back to the receptionist and again ask for Frank. Mick had filled me in on a couple of things about our Frank. Number one, he's a strange guy who rarely finishes a thought, and number two, he probably weighed in at about four hundred pounds.

Okay, I thought. *I've dealt with strange before, and as far as the* big *part, who cares, really.*

Another forty-five minutes pass, and I walk back to reception area and just give the secretary a look and tap on my watch, kind of like, "Let's go."

She nods her head and holds up the "One minute," signal.

I go back out to the factory with Mick, and as I stroll past a window, by dumb luck I peek out, and what do I see but a fat slob rumbling in a fat slob trot to a car out in the parking lot. I yelled for Mick to look and asked him, "Is that him?"

"That's him. Where's he going?" He started pounding on the window.

"I don't know but I think he's bagging us. I mean me. He's bagging me!" I stood there in disbelief, with my mouth hanging open, like most bagged people do.

We went back to the reception area where the young lady made a lame attempt at telling me he didn't leave. She finally broke down and said he had an emergency at home.

Yeah, right. He had an emergency at IHOP or Denny's maybe, but I flew all the way across the country to talk to him and he just blew me off, big time.

I looked at Mick and we both knew what to do. Go directly to the airport and get on the next plane out. And that's what we did. We left on the spot, with instructions to the secretary to leave a note for her boss thanking him for blowing me off and to "absolutely do not call either one of us for anything."

We left for Pittsburgh on the next flight, and we never heard from him again.

THE AUTOMOTIVE WORLD

We had a project going for an automotive manufacturer in the Detroit, Michigan, area. I'm not naming names, but if you said "fix or repair daily," you'd know who I meant. We were installing a pretty big system to make car seat cushions. The lead engineer for this client, though, was a real piece of work. He was an immigrant from somewhere in Europe, and his name was Nick. He was a crooked as a three-dollar bill, the most corrupt customer I ever dealt with. He was smart, though, because he covered his tracks by bringing his boss into it.

During the project design and build stage, he made it clear he was fixing up his house and would need a new garage door. He got it. He was kind of bipolar, too, as he could be a good buddy one day and a total prick the next. One day, we were there to have a design review meeting, and we decided to go to lunch. I was there with one of my engineers, along with the two guys we were meeting with.

Nick wanted to go to an Italian place down the road, and as we were heading to the door, he asked us to wait for a minute, because he wanted to see if "someone could join us." I know now that what he really meant to say was he was going to walk through the plant and see how many bodies he could round up. He was like the Pied Piper, because when he came back, he had about eight more guys following him. Maintenance workers, clerks, you name it. All were very hungry and ready for a free lunch.

We got to the restaurant, an upscale place where you might go on your anniversary or your mother's birthday. Nick gets us a table, quickly, as it's pretty obvious that they know him very well. Before we even get menus, he orders five broiled seafood dinners as appetizers. He also gets himself a shot of Glenlivet, at $40 a pop, and all the other guys order beers and bourbon. Two hours later we leave, and I'm stuck with a $450 lunch bill, easily the largest one I've ever had.

Turns out that this is just a typical lunch for our friend and his wacky bunch.

We were installing the equipment a few months later, and I showed up to check on my crew. I absolutely hated coming here, as just about everyone did. It could be a beautiful sunny day, but it felt like every time I turned into this parking lot, the winds whipped up, black clouds formed out of nowhere, and the rain came down in sheets. It was like pulling into 1313 Mockingbird Lane. I never knew what hellish happening was going to rear its ugly head at any given time.

Today was no different. While I'm in the plant, Nick introduces me to a work crew that he says I need to do business with. They're doing some invisible work in the plant, but they install garage doors "on the outside." Nick still needed one, so I would need to give them a purchase order to do "'steel services" for our in-plant job, but in fact the work was the door on Nick's garage. If we didn't play the game, he would make our lives hell, withhold progress payments, and casually threaten that we would never get another order. That takes some balls, but it was the way things worked.

The really ballsy move came later that day when Nick comes out with his boss. They come over and start talking about their upcoming weekend hunting trip, but they both needed new boots. I laughed to myself as they told me their plight, because I knew what this meant.

I asked if, by chance, there was a place nearby where one could buy hunting boots, and as luck would have it, there was. And as luck would also have it, it was right near his favorite Italian restaurant. So off I went with Ali Baba and the Forty Thieves for Scotch and boots. Another $500 lunch on the expense account.

§ § § § §

There were a lot of plant workers assigned to our machinery area to basically meet the contract quota of people standing around doing nothing. Most were pretty cool, though. Lazy, but cool. A couple of the women who were chaperoning us from seven to three had taken a shine to two of my best techs. These gals had figured out that the boys had the expense accounts going on, and the boys had the out-of-town thing going on, so it kind of equaled out.

These local breeders were much older than my thirty-something electricians, but they were dumber than a box of rocks. We could see why they weren't doing anything, and it wasn't because they were lazy. They were too fucking stupid to do anything.

We were actually supposed to be training them on how to operate this machinery, but we quickly found out that this was a no-can-do. They would have seriously hurt themselves or someone else—namely one of us.

These gals were so useless that we nicknamed them the Sisters Brunswick, and not because of witchcraft. It actually came from the old Bugs Bunny cartoons. As Foghorn Leghorn used to say about his canine rival, "He's about as sharp as a bowling ball and just as useful." Thus, the Brunswick reference, as in Brunswick bowling balls. We called them this to their faces, and they assumed it was some sort of term of endearment.

Karma struck back, though, because we found out that Sisters Brunswick each cleared over forty-five grand a year.

§ § § § §

After the project wrapped up, we were trying to get our final payment from Nick, who seemed to have a hard time letting go. So I ended up in Michigan one night with my boss and our sales manager. The three of us were at a restaurant trying to discuss the list of items Nick didn't think were done correctly. One item in particular pissed me off, since I followed his exact request against my better judgment. It was a component that we used by his insistence, since it wasn't our standard component. He said he now wanted me to replace them all because they weren't working.

I leaned over the table and told him, "Nick, you had your electrician go into his stock room and get me one of these switches because I didn't want to use it. You handed it to me and said 'use this.' I objected, but I agreed. I'm not changing them, but feel free to do it yourself."

He was furious, as he apparently wasn't used to hearing the word *no* very often. He leaned toward me, and in his thick accent says, "If this was the old country, I'd take you out right now."

Holy shit! This asshole just threatened to kill me. I looked over at my two fearless leaders, and they suddenly decided to admire the artwork on the walls. I assumed they made a bee-line to their "happy place" and it was clear I was on my own here, so I looked back at Nick. "Well, big boy, we're here now, so if you want to dance, I'll dance." That was followed by a short staring contest.

My boss finally spoke up, or should I say stuttered-up, and tried to diffuse the situation. Kind of like Porky Pig coming between Bugs and Daffy. We calmed down and kind of awkwardly laughed it off. I think Nick gained some respect for me, because he backed down and smiled like the two-faced prick that he was, and said it wasn't an issue. He would pay what he owed us and sign off on the project.

When we got into our car, I was in the back seat with my heavy hitters in the front. I immediately started sounding off like Joe Pesci. "Where the fuck were you when I needed you? Jesus Christ, I was in room full of people and I never felt so alone in my life. I'm glad you guys were here, man, I'll tell you that. Now THAT'S team work." I barked at them for a little while, all in fun, though. Well, not ALL in fun. Some fun. A little bit of fun maybe. Not much fun, really.

It was pure hell but we finally finished that job. I learned something, though. Coming into this, I always wondered why cars cost so much. After dealing with these bastards, I wonder why they don't cost a hell of a lot more.

IRISH I WAS IN ITALY

One of the requirements of the job was traveling to Italy when needed. No problem there. My first trip was with Jake, as we went over to do a pre-ship test of equipment he had sold to my refrigerator buddies in Iowa. We were meeting the customers there, but we would go over a couple of days beforehand to make sure they were actually ready to do this. What they hell would the two of us do for two days in Italy?

First thing we have to do is get there. Our flight from Pittsburgh took us through JFK in New York to Milan. The New York to Milan flight was something like nine hours, but fortunately, the beer was free.

The first time I flew over there with Jake, we made like we were sitting at Fishers Bar instead of being on a TWA 747 at thirty thousand feet. The flight wasn't full, so we had room to get away from the pack, in a smoking section, no less. We sat in a four-seat row, with the two empty seats between us. After the meal was served, we settled back with a cold one. The stewardesses made their way around once in a while, and we got a fresh one whenever they were within earshot.

Problem was, after an hour or two, they disappeared. I guess they intended for us to sleep or something, but we weren't done drinking. It got to the point that we had to take matters into our own hands. We were lucky enough to be sitting near the center galley, so I went first. A nonchalant walk like I was stretching my legs turned into a sneaky slip into the galley where I made a cat-like move to get to the little drawers that had our sauce. I grabbed a few Buds and quickly made it back to our seats.

The next trip was Jake's turn. He wasn't nearly as sneaky as me, but he basically didn't give a shit. We continued drinking for a few hours while everybody else slept. We drank all the Budweiser, most of the Miller Lites, and even put a good dent in the Heinekens. Little Jack Daniels even showed up once or twice.

After pounding all these free beers, we realized we would have a problem on our hands, and that was the empty cans. There we at least a dozen empty cans shoved under the seat, in the cushions, seat pockets, you name it. Now we had to get rid of the evidence, but we handled it like men. I found an empty plastic garbage bag in the galley, and we shoved our empties in there. The can crunching sound was very hard to hide. Hard, but not impossible.

Jake took the bag somewhere and got rid of it. Not sure where, but really, there ain't many hiding places for a bag of empty beer cans in a jumbo jet. Turns out the guy in 18G had a heck of a surprise after we landed, when he stood up to open the overhead and a bag of empty beer cans came clanging down on his gourd. He made a feeble attempt at telling everyone it wasn't his, but the general consensus was, "What a boozer."

§ § § § §

We found our little hotel and figured we better get into the local time of day and act like we weren't tired. That's the secret to Euro-travel. Get right into the swing of the day, and don't sleep until their bedtime. Jake and I decided we'd venture out of our hotel, take a walk, and check out the town for a while. I followed his lead, since he had been there a few times. We left the hotel with no particular desti-nation, and no map. I brought this up, but got the kind of no-nonsense answer Jake was known for.

"Just watch the street signs, and keep track of the one you're on. Follow the street name."

I looked up, and sure enough, there was the little sign with the arrow and our street name: Senso Unica. No problem. We just had to follow our street and we won't get lost. We walked for a while, not really paying attention as we stopped for an espresso here and there. We walked a little further, and we looked up to see we were still on Senso Unica. We could easily make it back to the hotel, because hell, we really never left our street.

We actually were making fun of the locals because when they had a name they liked, they really stuck with it. We kept milling around the town, and later, after making a couple more stops, we decided to head back to the hotel. We made a left back onto Senso Unica, walking for a while, making sure we stayed the course. So we walked. And walked. And walked.

We can't figure it out, but we stayed on Senso Unica and we should have been back by now. So we ended up walking for another half hour or so until we find a guy who can speak English. He's kind enough to give us directions to our little hotel, which ended up taking another twenty minutes. We finally make it back to the place, tired, hungry, and sick of bitching and moaning at each other.

We decided to go check out the bar, and we told our tale to the bar-tender. All about how we stayed on Senso Unica but still got lost for so long. This ended up being our first lesson in the Italian language, though, because when the bartender finally stopped laughing at us, he informed us that Senso Unica means "one-way street."

§ § § § §

All throughout our trip, I kept repeating the same corny joke over and over:

Q: Why is Italy shaped like a boot?

A: Because you couldn't fit that much shit into a shoe.

I didn't make it up, but I got a kick out of it because Jake was Italian, we were in Italy, and it was funny to keep irritating him with this stupid joke. Even when the clients, Jerry and Ben, showed up, we would be sitting around the table and I would inevitably ask the same stupid joke. It was kind of expected.

I was introduced to the owner of Kanton, Mario Vilipazzi. He was a middle-aged guy, real nice to us, but a little flaky. I had been told about this and was warned to expect him to introduce himself every time he met me. And he did.

One afternoon, we were in the fabrication shop where they were building all the machinery that we actually came to inspect and hopefully test. As usual, it was late. Really late. When Mario came into the plant to meet with us, the customers voiced their displeasure at this. Mario started asking his lead engineer what it would take to finish this thing.

"We need one thousand man hours more to finish."

Mario just kind of stood there, rubbing his chin and surely wishing he was somewhere else.

The engineer spoke again. "I think the answer is easy, Mario. We need to hire one thousand men and we have them work for one hour."

I kind of chuckled to myself at this, actually proud to see they have smart asses in Italy. We looked over at Mario, supposedly the smartest guy here, and it looked like he was actually considering it!

No one spoke for a little while, until the engineer finally realized it was still his turn. "Mario, of course we are joking. We cannot do that. We need at least three more weeks to finish."

That answer went over like a fart in church by all who heard it but at least we had the truth. Later that evening, we had dinner with the Italians, including Mario and the engineers. Afterwards, we were all talking and drinking wine. A lot of wine.

We were all laughing and having a good time when Jake decided to hose me. "Hey Barr...tell them that joke."

I looked at him and gave him the *stupid* look. I pretended I didn't know what he was talking about, but he kept at it.

"Hey...tell them your joke. How does it go? Come on, tell them."

Now everybody was looking at me.

Jake kept it going. "How does it go? Why is Italy shaped like what? A boot?"

I looked at him and everybody else, shaking my head like I had no idea what the hell he was talking about. I'm sure my face was a red as the wine, but I was not playing this one. What the hell was he doing? What an asshole. The freaking owner is here, glaring at me with sinister look in his eye and a mix of shitty-ness and red wine.

I instinctively played dumb for a few minutes, waiting for the right time to quietly get up and head for the restroom. It came and I did. Fortunately when I came back, it had passed over and that was the end of it. If it took me the rest of my life, I promised Jake I'd get him back for that.

MICHIGAN LOVE STORY

Another automotive job in Michigan had me living outside of Detroit for a few weeks. The project was routine enough, with Kenny and another tech finishing it up. We were nearing the end of the last scene, and the customers were pretty happy.

I had been spending time with the lead engineer, who was a nice guy who really loved his wife. I know he loved her a bunch because he made sure I took the two of them to dinner four times in a week and a half. He knew the game, and he played it well. A mere amateur compared to his automotive brothers over on Mockingbird Lane, but he was a player nonetheless.

The first time it happened, I had actually asked him to join me for dinner, he said yes, and gave me directions to a place he liked. I showed up, and low and behold, there were the two of them at the bar waiting for me, and these lovebirds were even kind enough to start a tab for me. Isn't love fun?

From that point on, he'd make it a convenient habit to ask me what I was doing on a particular evening, obviously working me. On our fourth date, we went to dinner at a sports-bar type place that had decent food and a casual atmosphere, befitting of a fourth date. We started out with a couple cocktails, and we soon were talking like the dear friends we apparently now were. The missus was yakking on and on about her days as a party girl in her old hangouts, "back in the day."

Taking that as a cue, I started the party with some tequila shots, followed up with some more tequila. If these two wanted free booze, then that's what they'd get. The Coors Lights helped wash down the Cuervo, and we sat and sipped for a few hours. I would make eye contact with the waitress and give her the ol' swirling finger "Bring another round" signal and get more sent over.

After half a dozen or so slugs of liquid attitude, the missus accidentally got hammered. Really hammered. She was loud, obnoxious, and not very lady-like as the hubby tried to keep her in check. Later in the evening, I was trying to be courteous and offered a nightcap, which she immediately accepted, but he declined.

This sparked a barking session on her part as she slurred insults at him loud and mean. She'd had quite a snoutful and pretty much everyone in the bar knew it. He finally was able to get her upright and pinball her toward the exit, where the hostess was waiting with a wide open door, a smile, and a thank you. Party girl was still spewing drunken obscenities, but he turned to me, kind of embarrassed, and thanked me for dinner.

"No problem," I said. "Anytime." I was pretty sure he wouldn't be working me for another freebie any time soon. Jose Cuervo to the rescue.

I heard that wifey spent the night praying to the porcelain god and the next couple of days were pretty rough for my mooching customer. Mission accomplished.

TIGHTY-WHITIES

Day Four of a planned overnighter to the Midwest was taking its toll on my travel partner, the electrical engineering manager named Tim. Tim was a true engineer, a guy who would mentally dissect anything you asked. Or anything you didn't ask. He was a hands-on leader who would jump into anything and never ask for help. I guess that's why he was with me and not one of the guys who worked for him.

Anyway, we were trying to wrap-up one of my projects, and Tim and I got stuck there for some reason. Being Day Four meant clean clothes were at a premium, but a true traveler could easily overcome this and deal with it. Tim wasn't a true traveler.

I met up with him at breakfast in the hotel, and as I sat down to join him I started the usual morning chit-chat. "Morning, Tim."

"Morning," he said without looking up.

"Another day in paradise. Do anything exciting last night?"

"Did I do anything exciting last night? Well, let me think about that for a minute. Wait…Yes! I did do something exciting. I washed my goddam underwear in the sink. With hand soap, no less. Completely soaked them and scrubbed them pretty good, too. Then I stuck them on the air blower so they would dry. But guess what? They fell off the fucking blower during the night and never dried. So I'm sitting here this morning in wet fucking underwear that was washed with hand soap."

Tim was not a happy camper. He just stared at me for a minute before resuming his tirade. "So that was my fun evening. Is that exciting enough for you? Try and top that. So, how did you spend your evening?"

"I walked across the parking lot to Target and bought a pack of underwear for three bucks."

He threw down his fork and stormed off like a guy wearing wet underwear. The best part for me was that I knew that, as uncomfortable as he was now, this was as good as he would be feeling all day.

AMORÉ ITALIA

Jake and I had to make another trip to Milan, again meeting up with our guys from Iowa. Ben would be there, but now they had new engineer, a guy named Dean. Dean was a really serious guy, probably about our age. I got along fine with him, but he was dead set in his ways and wasn't interested in change.

We spent a lot of time together, walking through the streets of Milan. Ben was always walking behind, but we knew where he was because we could hear the constant scuffing of his shoes when he walked behind us, since he didn't pick up his feet. Everywhere we went, the constant scuffing behind us was always there.

After about three days of this, Dean was grumbling about how "goddam sick of this" he was. Actually we all were, but we couldn't say anything. One afternoon, as we walked and Ben shuffled down sidewalk, the three of us in front came across a respectable pile of dog shit. We all stepped over it without any problems, never breaking stride. Ben, however, shuffled right into and through it.

We could literally hear it happen. Kind of like a "scuff, scuff, squish." We turned around and looked at him and he had this goofy look on his face as he looked down at the turd that engulfed his Hush Puppy. We all kind of stood there, looking at Ben.

"Merda," was my lone comment. (*Merda* is Italian for shit). And we knew this because dog shit in Italy was everywhere, including Ben's shoe.

Dean laughed for the first time in a week. "Good luck with THAT!"

Jake and I were afraid the merda was going hit the fan, so we kind of swayed the group onward to wherever the hell we were going.

§ § § § §

For me, eating in Italy was great. Just about everything I tried was great, except for the fried frogs they tried to get me to eat. Little baby frogs fried whole, eyeballs and all. Their little arms and legs were out-stretched with their eyes looking up at you. The Italians would pick them up and eat them in two bites. These little guys were considered delicacies, but I couldn't eat them. It was one of the only things I wouldn't try.

Dean, on the other hand, was a pizza-only guy. He was safe with a plain pizza, maybe some mushrooms if he was feeling adventurous. This was the usual evening routine, go to the pizzeria for dinner and a few drinks.

Toward the end of our trip, Dean was feeling a little wild. Instead of his usual cheese pizza, he looked over the selection and, feeling a little lucky, he ordered one called *Pizza con l'uovo*. Jake told him he thought it meant artichoke, and that was safe enough for Dean.

The waiter came out with our dinners, including Dean's pizza. He set it on the table like a proud artist displaying his work. He had a huge smile on his face as he set this amazing creation in front of his waiting customer. We all looked at it, and it looked like a plain pizza. Without any warning, and still with the big smile, the waiter reached into his apron pocket, pulled out an egg, and in one graceful motion, he cracks the egg on the side of the table and deposits the raw chicken embryo right smack dab in the middle of this guy's pizza. Like a proud papa, he smiles at Dean and says, "Signore, pizza l'uovo."

Three of us started laughing hysterically, but Dean was furious. The look on his face could have cut through steel. There was his nice, safe pizza now with a slimy, raw egg oozing in the center.

"What the hell is this? I didn't order a goddam egg on my pizza. Get this fuckin' thing out of here."

I thought the waiter was going to cry. We obviously learned another new Italian word, which was *l'uovo*—egg.

Jake calmed him down and we explained to the waiter it wasn't his fault, but bring a plain pizza—quickly.

So much for seeing the world and trying new things.

§ § § § §

Even though we were the visiting team, Jake didn't have too much patience for the home team or their language. One morning, as we were driving into the plant, we hear the definitive sound of a police siren, and the close proximity made it clear they wanted us. Jake pulls over, and even as he's getting out, I told him to be cool.

He gets out and he's standing next to the car as the cops walk over to him. They start talking to him, but he can't understand them and they can't understand him. They were trying to tell him whatever it was he did wrong. I could see his face getting red, and I knew he was about to blow.

He leaned into the car and says, in a loud voice, "These fucking guys can't understand a fuckin' word I'm saying. Can you believe this? What the fuck is this?"

We're in the car trying to shush him, knowing there was probably one word in that sentence they could fully understand. After ten minutes of the three of them yakking back and forth, I handed him the business card of the Italian guy we were actually working with at the plant.

They recognize the company name, and start smiling saying, "Okay, okay. Kanton, okay, *capisce*." They go back to their car, and come back with a nice, neat traffic citation.

They hand it to Jake, and we're in the car telling him to sign it, take it, smile, whatever; let's just do what they say and get out of here.

The one cop looks at his tablet, and reads off of it. "Bus lane. You drive inna bussa lane."

So there it was. He was driving in a bus lane, but who knew? The only sign we knew was One Way Street. It also told us the cops understood Jake and his f-bombs, so it's probably a good thing he observed the cease-fire when he did.

We got out of there, and the folks at the plant took the citation from us and took care of it. But hey, we learned a new road sign.

We continued on with the trip, and it got kind of sticky because the equipment tests ran late so we had to stay a few extra days. We both ran out of currency, but I had an idea that worked out. We were staying in a privately owned hotel, and we had become kind of tight with the general manager, a long haired guy who drank espresso all day and constantly looked like he was wired.

One evening I struck up a conversation with him, and I told him our problem and that I needed cash. I asked him if he could loan me some, and maybe put it on my bill. I was shocked when he said no problem, immediately opened up a cigar box, and handed me twelve hundred Lira—about six hundred bucks. This would hold us over for a few days. I gave myself credit for coming up with that one.

§ § § § §

The trip ended, and we headed for home. Sitting on the airplane, Jake and I realized we never got a chance to shop for our wives. Our problems were solved when the Duty Free cart made its way through the plane. Like good husbands, we found time to shop right there on the aircraft. We joked to ourselves that technically we were still in Italian air space, so we were, in fact, shopping in Italy. We ended up each buying the same thing, a gold and diamond necklace and earrings gift set that actually was pretty nice.

We were pretty proud of ourselves and congratulated each other on a fine act of husbandry. We took our gifts home and each told our wives we bought them something nice in Italy. And technically, that was the god's-honest truth. It would be our secret that we didn't really *shop*.

Fast-forward six months to the Kanton Christmas party. The annual to-do was held at a local hotel, where a good time would be had by all. My wife, Cindy, wearing her fine Italian jewelry, and I walked into the ballroom, and in a few minutes we ran into Jake and his wife, Kristin. We met up with each other, extending the normal greetings to each other.

The girls immediately realized they were wearing the identical gold accessories, and they let us know it in a hurry. I felt the twang of something bad about to happen, and I wasn't wrong.

Kristen smiled at me and asked Cindy, "Did he get you that in Italy?"

"Yeah. You, too, I guess."

"That's what he told me. But I found the receipt, and the bastards bought them on the airplane on the way home. The Duty-Free cart on the airplane. He tried to lie, but I found the receipt in the laundry."

All eyes were now on me, except Jake's, who was staring at the floor, so I did the only manly thing I could think of. "It was Jake's idea. He didn't want to shop while we were there and he had the car keys. I couldn't go by myself. I had to go wherever he went. I didn't know where the hell we were." I whined shamelessly but effectively.

He tried to deny it, and even though it was bullshit, he couldn't. He was toast and his wife let him have it. And I got him. I had extracted my revenge.

Later on, I asked him why Italy was shaped like a boot. We both laughed and knew we were even. It didn't take nearly as long as I thought.

THE EIFFEL TOWER

I had another opportunity to travel to Italy to discuss the equipment in a conference with our Italian comrades. I really had no choice, nor did the engineer from Kanton I had to travel with. The guy's name was Jim, and we left Pittsburgh and went to Milan as instructed.

It was a typical global meeting, with the bullshit dispensed in kilograms instead of pounds. But the Italians knew how to party, and that included the owner, our own li'l Daffy Duck, Mario. Jim and I sat through all the required propaganda, and during one of the evening dinners, Mario had an epiphany.

When he found out we were traveling together and that we had a significant layover in Paris, he told the French sales rep, Philippe, that he would now show the two of us around Paris. Our layover would be changed to a stop-over, which meant another two days away from home. Mario *suggested* that Jim and I stay in Paris for two extra days, and Philippe would be our guide. We had no choice. Philippe had no choice.

As it turned out, Philippe wasn't really a big fan of Americans, and this was pretty obvious once we were away from our Italian leader. His shitty attitude came through loud and clear. We tried to ignore it, and for a while we had some success with that.

But a man can only take so much. We started in the morning, with Frenchie meeting us for breakfast at the hotel. We headed off seeing different sights around the city, starting with the Louvre. Walking through, our host was quick to point out the pieces he liked, and why. He also pointed out a few times that there were no American artists here, and we kind of laughed that one off. Next was a trip around Versailles, and again his oratory included anti-American rhetoric, with things like the gardens were unlike anything America could ever produce.

We, or at least I, was starting to get about sick of this prick's mouth. I hit the wall when he started talking about stopping for lunch, but he said he would not be stopping at McDonald's. "Don't even bother to ask."

I winked at my partner and told him it was game on.

We did indeed stop for lunch, at a typical French café that served typical French food. Our discussion centered on the recent corporate announcement that English was the official company language, and would be required at all international meetings. Philippe was sniveling on and on about this, and how the Americans were surely to blame.

I got fed up with this pretty quickly, and had some advice for my French friend. "Listen, Philippe, if it weren't for the Americans, you'd be speaking German right now, so quit whining."

He just looked at me in silence. Score one for the visiting team.

After lunch, we were driving to the tourist trap Eiffel Tower, and I thought a couple of jokes were in order. "Hey, Phillippe?" I asked.

"Yesz?"

"Do you know how many French soldiers is takes to defend Paris?"

No answer, only a turn of the head and a little French dip of the eyebrows.

"No one knows. It's never been done."

Laughter from the back seat indicated another point for the visitors. Our non-volunteer tour guide was feeling some animosity.

"What's the first weapon given to a new French soldier?" Again no answer, and I even waited for a little while, pausing for effect. "The white surrender flag. Get it? The little white hanky they wave when they surrender." I was waving my hand and my pretend hanky. Another snicker from the backseat.

Frenchie was hot now. He had this little ornery look in his eye that was so cute. I knew I had him on the ropes. I kept quiet though, figuring I'd just let him simmer for a while so he didn't wreck the car.

We get to the Eiffel Tower, and he starts his spiel about what it was, the history, blah, blah, blah.

When he stopped yakking for a minute, I asked a simple question. "What did you say this is called?"

"Zis iz ze Eiffel Tower. Ze Eiffel Tower. Have you heard of it?"

"No, not really. Eif-fel Tower you say?"

He looked at me with little French daggers in his eyes. "Yes. Eiffel Tower," he said as sternly as a Frenchman could.

"Is it new?" I continued my baiting.

"It iz not new. It iz Ze Eiffel Tower! Ze Eiffel Tower, you stupid American."

Okay, now he's into name calling. Jim was poking my ribs, whispering for me to stop. Not a chance.

"The Eiffel Tower, huh? Looks kind of useless. What does it do?"

He started flipping out in his native tongue, waving his little French arms around, until he paused for a second, looked at me, and simply said, "It does nothing."

And with that, he turned and stormed off, stomping his little French feet until he got into his little French car and took off. Drove away as fast he could.

I was laughing as I yelled to him, "Don't drive angry!"

And that was it. He was gone.

"He bagged us! That little prick bagged us!" Jim finally spoke.

"Was it something I said?" I asked.

And as we stood there, stranded, I summed it up. "I've been bagged by better."

We both started laughing pretty hard, because I for one would rather be stranded than led around by that asshole anymore.

We flagged down a cab that took us back to the hotel, and we got the next flight out of Paris. Never heard from Philippe, or anyone else in the French office, for that matter, again.

FIRE IN THE HOLE

Once again I found myself in the great plains of Iowa, with yet another project to install in the refrigerator plant. Actually, Kanton had two going on, with me running one and another guy running another on the other side of the plant. My project was going pretty well, but the other guy's wasn't faring so well.

This thing was months behind schedule with new problems and serious design issues cropping up every day. It had become what we in the technical field refer to as a cluster-fuck. This wasn't one of our core products, meaning it was a system we didn't really do in the US. It had been purchased through another division in England and it was claiming careers left and right. We had an English engineer working there, and he was overwhelmed.

The project I had been working on had finished up and was signed off on, so I headed back to Pittsburgh on a Friday. The week before Easter, actually on Wednesday, I was called into the boss's office and told the project manager for the big blue cluster-fuck had been fired and I would be taking over for him. There was a big, angry meeting scheduled for the next day in Iowa, and I would be attending, with the full management team of Kanton. We would fly into town in the morning and fly back home later that day.

I had sensed this might happen, so it wasn't a big surprise. The big blue beast had claimed another body. Thursday morning came and I was on a plane back to the great Midwest.

The meeting started when we got there, and it was an angry crowd. The English engineer joined us, and the long, long list of issues was reviewed, with a plan to fix them all. I was introduced as the new project manager, and the crew would now work for me.

We went out to the factory and went over the equipment in detail. The machine itself was called a thermo-former, meaning it would, or was supposed to, heat up sheets of heavy plastic and vacuum form them over a mold to make the inside liner of a refrigerator. The customer was limping along with only one older existing machine, and we were basically making scrap all day, every day.

After we met the angry clients, and seeing the job first hand, I knew what needed to happen. I called my boss off to the side and told him I would stay through the holiday weekend and manage the crew that also needed to stay on-site. I didn't have any clothes or supplies, so I would need to buy some essentials to last me thorough the upcoming days. (I do not wash undies in my hotel's bathroom sink.)

He thanked me profusely and told me to buy whatever I needed. He didn't care what I bought, just get this thing working.

With that decided, our management team told them our plan and they left—to be home with their families on Easter. I still had to call home and deliver the bad news that I knew would go over like a lead balloon, but my wife Cindy was used to it by now. The kids would be a little harder to win over, but I didn't really have a choice.

I went to the local Wal-Mart to get a wardrobe and supplies, and I took care of that end of things. I also found a boatload of candy, toys, and presents to pack up and Fed Ex to my family in Pittsburgh. I had a cart full of goodies and presents that I had boxed up and sent home. My Easter was going to suck, but not necessarily for the kids.

Easter morning came, and I had five guys in the plant with me working on rebuilding this English catastrophe. After two days of scouring over it, I could officially say it was a large, blue piece of shit. At one point, I was sitting on an upside down trash can, in the middle of the closed plant, and the English engineer came over and handed me a fag—a hand-rolled cigarette. I lit it up, and as I smoked it with him standing next to me, I started laughing.

When he looked at me, I stopped long enough to hold up my fag and sum things up. "It's Easter Sunday, I'm in a shut-down factory, sitting on an upside down garbage can smoking a hand-rolled cigarette. I MADE THE BIG TIME AT LAST!"

Nobody laughed. The Englishman just nodded in agreement. And the day dragged on.

We had made some improvements over those days so that the machine could supply a limited number of liners for one or two models. Nowhere near the paid-for and promised capacity, but it was an improvement. So I went home the following weekend for a day and a half.

This routine went on for a few more weeks, and it became clear to me and the customer that this thing would never do what it was supposed to, and that it physically couldn't. Too many engineering details to get into, but I knew it wasn't long before me and my engineers were replaced with lawyers. This thing was basically a very, very large boat anchor.

It all came to a head very early one Monday morning. I had gone home for thirty-six hours or so on Friday, so I flew back Sunday night, making it into the plant by seven A.M. As I made my way into the door, I was met by a host of management guys from the plant who were standing there waiting for me. I didn't even have two feet in the door when I was practically grabbed by one ear and dragged into a large conference room and greeted by a host of even more people, most of whom I had never met.

This can't be good, I thought to myself. I could feel the anger in the room.

At that point, the Englishman, my Englishman, walked in. We had a chance to talk quietly for about a minute before this chat got started. He told me our machine had a hydraulic hose burst and blow hot hydraulic oil across the plant aisle and land on the old, working machine and catch it on fire. Now they were completely unable to make product. We had gone from very bad to extremely worse because, not only did our piece of shit machine not work, it also took out the only one that did.

The meeting started, and each one of these strangers took a turn screaming at me. Threats were made, promises of legal action, you name it. I knew I couldn't talk, that I needed to let them vent for a while, and vent they did. They did tell me that the fire started at two

A.M., the alarms went off, the plant was evacuated, and the in-house fire crew was able to control the flames and put them out. Nobody was hurt, and the damage was contained to one area of the old machine.

After an hour of being bitched at, the leader finally asked if I had anything to say for myself. What the hell could I say? I looked around the room, felt the eyeballs drilling me, and said the only thing that came to my mind.

"I think we need to congratulate the plant fire crew for a job well done. That's a hell of an effort."

Looking back, I believe this wasn't what they wanted to hear. A couple of them erupted and stormed out of the room. The guys I usually dealt with were smiling, though, and one of them, my buddy Ben, even winked at me. He knew it wasn't something that I could, or would, accept blame for.

I got up and left the room and went out to the plant to see the charred equipment and our big, blue, boat anchor. I told my guy to get ours in working order and make whatever parts we could. The shit was going to hit the fan, and we needed to be ready. I rounded up all of our guys on-site to start getting reports and tell them not to talk to anyone outside of our company.

This whole thing got extremely ugly, but I didn't wait around to see how it ended. This piece of shit claimed another body, as I quit Kanton a few days later and went to work for a competitor, just like my buddy Jake had done six months earlier.

Chapter 6

GO WITH THE FLOW

Jake actually lured me to my new employer, a competitor of Kanton, also located in Pittsburgh, actually much closer to my home, so my travel to the office was a lot quicker. When I was in town, that is. The airport was still in the same place. We were lucky to have two of the three big guys in our industry located in Pittsburgh.

The big difference now was this company was owned by a large German outfit instead of Italian. This German outfit is actually a pretty large and a hugely popular company, very famous for their pharmaceutical products. Thus the joke was that our group of misfits would cause the headaches and the pharmaceutical guys made huge profits curing them.

Our company was named Kenne Group, or KG for short. We were a part of a division of this large German company and I was hired as a project manager.

One of the funny things that I had to adjust to was working for a major corporation. I was stunned on Day One when my team leader, the boss, told me, "We're not here to make money; our job is to support chemical sales. We've been losing money for twenty years, so don't come in here thinking you'll change things. Just go with the flow."

Well, alrighty, then. I never did get cozy with this unusual business philosophy, but "go with the flow" was something I thought I could handle.

TENNESSEE TAKEOVER

Day Two was spent flying to Knoxville, Tennessee, where I inherited a project from a guy who was moving to another job within the company. This project was a perfect business practice for the KG management: it was losing boatloads of money and a long way from the finish line.

When I arrived, it was three or four weeks late and way, way over budget. The late part is what hurt, since the chemical group was trying to get the urethane business and KG was gumming up the works.

Arriving on site, I met up with the contracted controls engineer, a big, heavy set guy out of Pittsburgh named John James. John wasn't ready for me to change the pace and get his ass moving a little bit faster.

I took him to dinner and explained how we were going to try and finish this fiasco quickly. He accepted it, and we ended up going over the plan and actually just talking in general for a while. It turned out he was a cellist in the junior symphony of something or other. I had never met a cellist, but I could see his passion for his craft.

While we were at dinner, he started talking about the *piece* he was working on. He put his left elbow on the table, and with his clenched fist touching his cheek, he closed his eyes and started playing the arm cello with his right hand. Seeing the arm cello being played much like an air guitar set me off laughing like a madman. I don't know what it was, but seeing a two-hundred and fifty-pound guy playing the arm cello did something to me. Jim was a little befuddled, asking me why I was laughing.

The only honest answer I had was it was my first experience with the arm cello, or any cello for that matter. I finally suppressed my laughter and it was clear that, since I was the only one who got the joke, I was the one who looked like an idiot. Oh, well, certainly not the first time.

§ § § § §

The project we had going was making insoles—a very famous brand of insoles—for putting in your shoes. They had a line that moved little hinged molds around an oval racetrack conveyor, and workers would put little felt-paper sheets on the upper mold halves as they traveled by on the way to get the polyurethane foam injected in the bottom halves.

The day shift had a guy who was hanging the felt sheets with a pretty distinct disadvantage: the poor guy only had one arm. Yes, he was indeed the almost famous "one armed paper hanger." I got to know him over the next couple of days, but never really discussed his situation.

Then one morning I couldn't take it anymore, and I had to be an instigator. I walked over to him and simply said, "Man, you look busy. Busy as a…well, you know."

He looked over at me and said, "Good one, Yankee. I never heard that one before." Then he laughed a little and continued. "Actually, I've heard it before, but no one ever had the balls to say to my face. Congrats, buddy."

So he was okay with it after all and we both had a chuckle.

So far, going with the flow introduced me to my first arm cellist and my first real life one armed paper hanger.

DOG DAYS IN PHILLY

Next up was another clean-up job located outside of Philadelphia, PA. This job had been dragging on for some time, well over a year, and in accordance with the go with the flow and don't make money strategy, this project was well behind schedule and extremely over budget. I was assigned to try to finish the punch list, which is a list of things that the customer claims is not working so they ain't paying. I later learned that the owner of this company had more money than brains, but at this point I was told to make the list go away and try to get our final payment.

I headed off to Philly with my boss, Ed, to meet with the top dog of this little manufacturing company. We arrived as scheduled, meeting the gentleman, named Dick, in the late morning. We started talking about some of the issues, and it turned out I knew his lead engineer from my days working on Long Island. The meeting went back and forth, with Dick getting a little testy once in a while.

No big deal, though; it's certainly not the first time I had to deal with a little prick who was used to treating people like shit. I had thick skin, so it bounced right off me. I made goddam sure I didn't sit in his chair, though, I can tell you that.

My boss, though, wasn't used to being treated so boorishly. In the middle of our meeting, Dick's cell phone rings. He answers it, and quietly says a few words. I hear him say something like, "I'll be right there," or words to that effect. With that, he hangs up the phone and puts it in his pocket. He looks across his desk at us, and as he's getting up, he says, "I have to leave. My dog is sick and he means a hell of a lot more to me than you do." And he walked out of the room.

I looked at Ed, kind of wondering if I actually heard what I thought I heard. We confirmed with each other that he did in fact insult us in the middle of a business meeting.

Of course, we laughed it off like two goofballs. The engineer I knew came in and we talked about fixing things and getting a sign-off. We did fix everything, but the little prick with the sick dog had no intention of paying. Turns out he really wasn't interested in our intentions, but just wanted to try and sue the big German company.

Years later, we ended up in court, and I had the opportunity to tell the jury about his sick dog and his rude comments to us that day. He got so mad he started pounding on the table and yelling at me out loud in open court. Just proved my point a little stronger.

THE PALMETTO STATE

I was traded from the department I worked in to the automotive team, and I was immediately assigned to run one of two projects in South Carolina. This was an odd deal, with me running a job for one manufacturer, and another guy running a similar job one mile away. The customer I was working for actually supplied their parts to the second guy, who used them to make dashboards for a big name Bavarian auto maker. My customers, a Belgian outfit strangely named Selohssa, had opened a new factory in the area and staffed it with young engineers who were all trying to make a name for themselves. The other project was a French company named IAS, also in a new facility, but much more established in the industry. The project I was working on was actually sold in Germany and dropped in our laps here in the US. We were late and over budget before it even started. Still goin' with the flow.

Before I was brought in, a contractor out of the Midwest was hired to install the equipment for us, something we had used before. They sent a crew that included a couple of pipe fitters, a couple of electricians, and one Certified Idiot. The CI was actually a laborer, sent down to do odd jobs for their leader. I wasn't paying directly for the CI, so I was okay with him being there. He was actually a good source of entertainment for us. Working for these young Belgians, we had to put up with a lot of crap, as they were obviously superior to any American. Just ask them, they'll tell you. To this day I don't think they figured out we were screwing with them daily, mostly by sending our CI into their offices to ask for things like a bucket of steam, a left-handed screwdriver, or the occasional k'nuter valve. Looking back, I guess it evened out, since we made each others' lives equally miserable for a few months.

One of the contractors with us was a long-haired biker named Rick. Rick was a good guy to have around, a really hard worker, but he really took a liking to the southern climate. The fact that there was a used Harley store right next to the plant didn't help things much. Rick found a bike that he fell in love with, and since he had a face, he qualified for credit to buy it. So he got himself a gently used Fat Boy. Once he bought the bike, though, it was clear he preferred riding to working.

One morning, he came in way late and his foreman started tearing into him. They argued for a while in the middle of the plant floor, until Rick finally stormed off. The customers witnessed all of this and weren't too happy at all. They weren't so good at the going with the flow thing. And they weren't too happy about this since we were so far behind schedule.

The foreman called the home office for another body, but it would be a few days. This pissed them off even more, but there was more to come. An hour after all this went down, we were standing on the rear loading docks telling the customers how we would recover. In the distance, you could hear the rumble of a Harley coming down the road. As it got closer, I started thinking to myself, *Please, god, no. Not him; not now.*

Prayer unanswered; it was him. Our long-haired friend drove past the plant in high gear with his face pointed straight ahead and his hand held high with the middle finger salute proud and mighty for all to see. We stood there in silence as he drove by.

I looked at the Belgians. "I guess that's a universal language, huh?"

They nodded angrily in confirmation. As we stood there, Rick had turned around to make a second fly-by, with the same morning greeting.

All told, he made four passes before we decided to go inside and finish our conversation. I was losing credibility with these customers, trying hard to maintain that we hired qualified contractors. A total lie, of course.

§ § § § §

Another gem I inherited on this job was a contracted software engineer from the Pittsburgh area named Ralph Richardson. Ralph was a loner, the kind of guy who would pass up a date with a super-model to watch a *Star Wars* rerun on TBS. The Belgians immediately despised him, and I tried to defend him, but he made my life even more miserable. He was a heavy guy, with full facial beard and round, wire-rimmed glasses. He spoke like he was an intellectual, but the words that routinely passed his lips proved he was not. Most of the time, his response to anything urgent or pressing was a very meek, "Oh my."

This was not his biggest downfall, though. That would be his inability to stay awake, no matter that he was set up in the middle of the plant floor, in the middle of the day. We were so far behind sched-ule and the urgency was so thick you could cut it with a knife. I could be knee deep in something, and a Belgian would find me and ask me to come and look at something. We would walk over to the computer area on the plant floor, and there was Ralph, sound asleep. This hap-pened almost daily.

Finally, one afternoon, I had had enough. With Ralph in dreamland, I walked up behind him and slammed the table with a sixteen-ounce hammer. He jumped up and fell to the floor, completely losing it. He even let out a girlish scream that was disturbing in itself.

When he got his shit together, I leaned close to him and quietly but sternly said to him, "Ralph, if you fall asleep in the plant one more time, I'm going to rip off your head and shit down your throat. Do you fucking understand me, Ralph?"

"Oh my."

I couldn't take this guy anymore, either at work or after work. I especially couldn't take eating dinner with him and being forced to listen to his mindless babbling. I had a room on the first floor of the hotel, and I had asked the hotel maintenance guy to take the safety tabs off my window so I could open it. Just wide enough to drag my fat ass out of that son of a bitch. I would use this as my exit route, even parking in the mall parking lot next door to avoid seeing this guy after work, knowing that he would stand in the lobby waiting for me to come out. Imagine seeing a grown man crawling out a hotel win-dow to avoid seeing somebody.

The Germans I worked for had had enough as well, and they actu-ally flew a software guy in from Germany to take over for Ralph. Our US gang looked like even bigger fools, having to be bailed out by the Germans. They actually had this thing about keeping schedules and making a profit, too.

I was able to get the new German engineer a little taste of Ralph, though. We went to dinner to exchange status and general information, and Ralph didn't disappoint me. Although he was full of stupid questions most of the evening, he reached his pinnacle during the main course. He was eating something with sauerkraut, and he actually had the balls to ask our German buddy if they had sauerkraut in Germany. I just wanted to cry, but it sent the other guy over the edge.

"Of course we have sauerkraut in Germany, you stupid fool. Why do the American soldiers call us the 'kraut man' during the war? Are you really this unbelievably stupid?" And he glared at him with daggers shooting out of his German eyes.

"Oh my," was Ralph's wide-eyed response.

Ralph was on a plane the next day.

§ § § § §

I had a technician working for me during the start-up named Tyler. Tyler was a young guy, kind of plain and simple. He was a great worker, and he never complained. We had been on-site for quite a while, and we were now only a week or so before Christmas.

One morning, he came to me with a problem. "Barr, is it okay if I leave for a little while? I have to buy my wife something for Christmas." Apparently he had been married for less than a year and he really needed to take care of things.

"Sure, Tyler. Go do what you have to do. Take your time."

I wasn't going to stand in the way of true love, so off he went. A few hours later, right after lunch, I saw him in the plant and couldn't wait to see what he had bought, so I asked him how he did.

He was quite pleased with himself, and he took me out to the car to show me the "awesome gift" he'd bought for his young bride. We get to the car, he opens the trunk, and pulls out a very large Wal-Mart bag to reveal "the gift," an eighteen-inch Teflon frying pan. He held up this wonderful gift like it was the Hope Diamond.

"What do you think?" he asked me.

He asked, so I told him. "Jesus Christ, Tyler, a frying pan? You got her a frying pan? My god, man, she's going to beat you with that thing."

The proud smile left his face. "Really?"

"Dude, you can't get your lady a freakin' frying pan. C'mon now, wise up. Take this thing back to Wal-Mart, get your ten dollars back and go up the road to the mall. Get her some jewelry. Maybe some earrings or a necklace. Something personal. Take the rest of the day and get your shopping done. I'll see you tomorrow."

And that's what he did. He ended up getting her a necklace or something, but after he left, it hit me that, at age thirty-five, I was now the wise old man dispensing advice to the young buck. And hell's bells, it wasn't even a nice name brand frying pan, but some lame knock-off. I probably saved this dummy's marriage.

§ § § § §

In the eyes of the Belgians, I was to blame for all things bad with the world, at least in their plant. These guys didn't like to hear the word *no*. Or even *maybe,* for that matter. Anyway, toward the end of the start-up, the young guy in charge finally lost it and flipped out on me. He had just had the floors cleaned, painted, painted again, sealed, and waxed. Why he did this in a leased factory building is still a mystery to me. He blew his top one morning when he walked over the shiny new floor in the vending machine area, and spotted a shiny new quarter on the floor. He bent over to pick it up and, much to his chagrin, he discovered he was had. Somebody had super-glued the coin to his landlord's shiny new floor.

Of course, it was my fault, and he came over to me full bore and let me have a bilingual tongue lashing. When he finished, I was able to figure out what he was talking about and went over to the scene of the crime. There was George Washington's mug stuck to his shiny new floor. I immediately started laughing, as did every other American there. Our Belgian buddy got really mad, again mixing his English with some other gargling sound, and stormed away. He stopped for an instant, pointed at me and shouted, "Basically, I hate you!"

This caused more laughter, and off he went to pout, or whatever it is cocky Belgian engineers do when they're embarrassed.

HIT IT WHERE IT LIES

The project manager we had working on the other job a mile away ended up quitting, and I got the pleasure of finishing up that mess. This job, too, was going with the flow, meaning way late and over budget. By now, spring had sprung and we were actually expanding on to the original project. But the customers we worked with at this plant were actually decent American guys, so it was a better place to work. The lead engineer there was named Brett, and he had a good team working for him. Brett and I hit it off, and we were able to get a lot of things accomplished. This included the occasional round of golf. One sunny afternoon, we snuck out to get in a round of afternoon golf. We were knee-deep in a typical round of hacking, but it was better than being in the plant. We weren't the only hackers out there, apparently, because the guys behind us, or beside us, who knows, kept shanking their balls in our fairways.

At one point, I was getting ready to hit, and a ball bounces through the trees and lands about five feet from me. I looked at Brett and he just shrugged his shoulders. I gave him a little "watch this" wave back. I walked over to the stray ball, positioned myself near it, and lay down on my back with the ball right next to my head, with my club dropped off to the side. I played possum for a few minutes until I heard the owner of the Titleist rustling his way out of the trees. I'm laying there with my eyes closed, but I can hear him in the background. I can imagine he's doing the "where the hell is it" scan, when suddenly I hear, "Oh, shit!" followed by the footsteps of him running toward me.

"Oh, no! Buddy, are you okay? Hey, are you okay?"

I can hear Brett in the background, giving the guy an earful about hitting me with his ball.

The other guy gets right next to me, still in a severe panic, thinking he might have killed someone. "Sir, sir, are you okay?" He taps me on the chest.

I'm now to the point where I couldn't keep it going, so I shot up at the guy and yelled at him, "Nice shot, asshole!"

He looked at me like he saw a ghost and just about fainted. Brett and I started laughing, pretty hard. I got up and brushed my pants off and asked him if he was going to play it. He was relieved, and obviously a bit shaken, but he knew he didn't have anything he could say. He apologized a few times, and we asked him to please yell "fore" next time. That's all, just a heads up.

He agreed, but we think he must have given up on that round because we didn't see him or another errant ball that afternoon. Brett thought he probably didn't have a spare pair of underwear with him so he needed to go home.

FLORI-DALE

One of our technicians was a guy who loved the nightlife and loved a good joke, but worked his butt off in the plants. He would zip through things on a start-up, fixing everything he could, as quick as he could. His nickname was Zippo but we also called him by his real name, which was Dale. Dale would go out after work and we might never be sure where he was or when we might see him again. He had a very strict rule when it came to drinking: He would only drink alone or with someone.

One morning, as we were getting into our rental cars and just discussing how none of us had seen him, we heard some rustling in the nearby bushes. We all stopped, turned to look, and what pops out, but our guy Dale, making it back from Tuesday night just in time to go to work on Wednesday morning.

He smiles and says a nonchalant, "What's up guys?" as he walks past us with a little wave. He walks right by us and goes into the hotel like he owned it. We would see him in a little while, no doubt.

We always laughed it off, though, because he always answered the bell when it was time to make these machines work.

One job that he was on with us was in south Florida, at a factory that manufactured boats. He spent the better part of the week telling everybody he had only packed one pair of socks, and he refused to buy a new pair. Or wash the ones he had. He was working hard and sweating his ass off all week, and the socks were obviously paying the price for it.

We finished out the week and made for the airport to head home. As we were passing through security, we see Dale, who was ahead of us, off to the side, getting the "special search" from the security agents. He was sitting in the special search chair and had his shoes off with his stanky feet in the air, as the security agent was on his knees in front of him, checking his shoes and frisking his pant legs. We could see Dale sitting in the chair with his unmistakable, shit-eating grin on his face and his evil snickering. In between the heh heh heh's, he says to the agent, "You're really earning your pay today, aren't you? Heh heh heh heh."

The poor security guy looked like he was going to either puke, quit, or both.

TRICK OR TREAT, MATEY

Another job in South Carolina found me working a long day on Halloween. We had been putting in fourteen-hour days for over a week, so when I left one night very hungry and extremely frustrated, I really wasn't in the mood for any more drama.

It's after eleven o'clock at Taco Bell, and I'm sitting in the drive-through line and finally get my turn. Just before I order, the little voice in the speaker gives me a heads up. "We do not have any beef products, so please order a non-beef item."

I wasn't expecting this, and I admit I did have a chip on my shoulder to start with. Looking at the microphone, and half laughing, I said, "Who's the wizard in charge of ordering meat? How the hell do you run out of meat at a Taco Bell?"

Apparently, the guy on the other end of the microphone was the beef orderer. "Sir, we do not have to explain our business to you. Please place your order."

Oh, okay, an attitude from the little Taco Bell window guy. "Okay, I'll take two beef burritos and a Pepsi."

"Sir, we do not have beef products."

"Are you sure? You sure you just can't find it? Maybe you just misplaced it. How about looking again, Merlin?" I heard a grunt of some sort, followed by dead silence.

All of the sudden, I see a body come from around the corner of the building, coming toward my car at a pretty good pace. It turned out to be the night manager, and he was on a mission. I think he meant to intimidate me, but I guess he forgot it was Halloween. And I guess he forgot he was wearing a pirate costume. Honest to god, a pirate costume from head to toe, including the vest, the knickers, the hat, and even the fake sword at his side.

"Look at you! You're a pirate!" I yelled to him between laughs.

Captain Hook commenced to bitching at me right there in the drive-through line. It's a good thing I was the only one there.

"Sir, we do not have meat, and we do not appreciate your attitude and we do not have to listen to this."

"Oh, you're an angry pirate!" I was laughing my ass off as he continued woofing at me.

He was flapping his arms and bitching about how hard his job was, and how I shouldn't be a smart ass. He stopped blabbering for a second to catch his angry breath, and I was ready.

"Argh, matey...Where's your buccaneers? Argh; there they are, under your buckin' hat!" I even made myself laugh at that one, but he didn't seem to appreciate it.

He was absolutely furious now, an irate pirate, indeed. I was amused at the whole situation, and actually a little bummed that I had no witnesses to this. I mean, here I am at damn near midnight, at a meatless Taco Bell being reamed by a manager in a pirate costume.

This chump was ragging at me like I was the one who forgot to order the meat.

All good things must come to an end, though, and it was pretty obvious I wasn't eating here tonight, so I put the car in gear and started to pull away. I just had to stick my head out the window for one more go at him. "Argh, captain. Methinks I'll go to Long John Silver's for a burrito. Care to join me?" And with that, I honked the horn and drove away, with the angry captain just standing there watching me with his hands on his hips.

I guess there's a first time for everything.

§ § § § §

I had a mechanical contractor working for me, and this one was a local. The project manager they assigned seemed like a nice enough guy, very cooperative but quiet and a little timid. Milt was his name, and one afternoon he showed up in the plant, checking on his crew and the overall progress. I waved to him as he was walking and ducking through the steel structure we erected near the production area. I was in the production manager's office with my buddy, Brett.

The three of us were talking about the job, doing our thing, when Brett quietly says, "Isn't that your guy out there?"

We all looked out the window and there was my guy, Milt, staggering underneath a column support, finally ending up flat on his back with a bloody gash on his forehead. It was time for me to go to my go-to guy.

As I got up, I kind of mumbled something like, "Son of a bitch, not again."

We walked over and there was Milt, with a bleeding lump on his forehead and a dazed look in his eyes. He did have a hardhat on, so he actually thumped his forehead, just below his receding hairline. One of his guys came over, too, and he looked at Milt, and then us, and asked the obvious question. "What happened to him?"

I knew the answer to this one. "The smartest guy here just walked into the building column." I never dreamed I'd be able to use that one again. He was a little shaken but okay, and he put a rag on his wound and went about his business.

As we walked away, Brett asked me what I meant by, "Not again," and I told him how this was my second adventure of a guy knocking himself out on one of my jobs.

I can only assume my man Milt was just going with the flow. At least he didn't start screaming obscenities like the first time I witnessed this.

I guess there's a second time for everything.

THE OHIO CONNECTION

Another job came along in the automotive business, making car seats in the middle of Ohio. Another Japanese-owned company with Japanese management and a local workforce. I would end up spending many months here, since this was a multi-million dollar project with a lot of steel, wires, and pipe to install. We hired the contractor from the Midwest again, less the Harley guy who had disappeared to parts unknown, apparently to never be heard from again, after "finger day" in South Carolina.

We were in full swing, with at least twenty guys working for me. One afternoon, I was checking things out when I walked past a couple of electricians working to run conduit up in the ceiling. One guy was up in a man lift, yelling down measurements to his partner below, who would then cut the pipe to that length.

As I walked by, I heard the upper guy yelling to the lower guy. "Thirty-six and two little black lines."

The lower guy listened and started measuring to make his cut. I walked by, and it took me a second or two to think about what I had just heard. I stopped, and out of nowhere, the contractor's hourly rate sheet suddenly passed through my mind. I was paying over forty bucks an hour for a guy who can't read a tape measure.

This wasn't cool, even by my standards. I know the whole flow thing, but this wasn't happening. I called the foreman over and told him we had a problem and what I thought needed to change. He got really nervous, a little clammy, and walked away. He came back a little while later, and he told me he had called the office and they wanted me to call them. I got to my temporary office and made a call to the company's headquarters.

It turned out the guy in question was actually the owner's nephew, and it was a problem for them to remove him. They had nowhere else to hide him, and they asked me for some help. I couldn't believe this. I usually only catch this crap from my customers, not my contractors. I was willing to play, though, so I made a deal that he could stay on the job, but they had to add a qualified electrician, at no extra charge to me, and junior would do no work, nothing, unless it involved a broom, and absolutely nothing higher than three feet off the ground.

They eagerly agreed. Finally, someone was going to kiss my ass for a change.

§ § § § § §

Part of our equipment package included a few robots that we used to do some of the automation and dispensing for us. With the robots, we purchased the extended installation and start-up services from the specialized technical service group supplied by the robotic company. The company name was RoboMan. The guy they sent was named Harold Bentz, a young, single guy who knew what he was doing, for the most part. He had worked on quite a few of our projects over the years, so we knew each other and worked well together. It cost us a fortune to have him on site, but it really was a specialized piece of equipment. Plus, if you didn't use their guys and you screwed something up, the warranty was shot. So I obviously chose to have him handy.

Near our equipment install area was the smoking area with an old picnic table, and this was a common congregating place both for our guys and some of the plant folks. We were way in the back of the plant, so the main smokers we saw everyday were the four or five women who worked in the testing lab, also in the back. These gals were nice enough, and it made for good conversation once in a while. Since Harold was a smoker, as most of us were, it wasn't unusual to see him over there. We'd even use that table to have our occasional meeting to go over schedules and other things.

Harold had been on the job for a couple weeks, and it seemed like he was getting pretty close to finishing things up. One morning, I was making my walk-through and I didn't see him in the work cell, so I went on a search mission that was unsuccessful. I was starting to get a little pissed, because this wasn't the time for a no-show. I had a deadline to meet and a flow to go with.

An hour or so later, I was over at command central having a smoke when one of the lab girls came over. I told her about my missing Robo-MAN, and she laughed and told me that she was missing a lab-GIRL. Strange coincidence? I think not. The lab girl, whose name was Jenny, told me this wasn't anything new for her partner, if, in fact it was a booty call as she suspected. Problem was, she was very married and had a few kids. We promised we'd let each other know if we heard anything. The day passed and I had no sightings of our Mr. Bentz.

The next morning came and still no Harold. I checked with Jenny and she was still down one lab girl. I had to move on, though, so I called the RoboMan offices and told them I needed a new guy sent out because I was one RoboMan shy of a load.

Of course, they didn't have anyone sitting around waiting for me to call, so I'd have to wait until they found someone. This went over like a Get Well card in a funeral home, but my complaints fell on deaf ears. I made my way over to the smokers' post, where the plant crew was taking their break. This is where I found out what happened to my overpriced technician.

Apparently, his time spent at this old wooden table had sparked a love connection between him and the lab girl. They ended up hooking up in his hotel room, which was in one of the two hotels in this little spot on the map. Husband of Lab Girl noticed his wife wasn't home with the kids, and he went looking for her. I guess her track record wasn't the cleanest of slates, so HOLG went right to the Comfort Inn, where he spotted her car in the parking lot. The RoboMAN, meanwhile, drove a pimped up old black Dodge Charger, with big fat tires, a big white stripe down each side, and Michigan plates. A moving billboard, basically. HOLG had waited for his bride to emerge from the den of iniquity, and when she did, all hell broke loose. Seems RoboMAN was with her, and HOLG went ballistic, forcing Robo-MAN into his chariot and fleeing at a high rate of speed. He hadn't been seen or heard from since.

Sounds like a Charlie Daniels' song, but they told the story in a matter-of-fact tone that implied this wasn't unusual. Pretty amazing turn of events, but I was royally screwed here. I tried calling the RoboMan offices again, saying they really needed to get me another tech, but I didn't tell them what I knew about our young Harold or the fact that I didn't think he'd be returning to Ohio anytime soon.

Why does everything have to happen to me?

All was not lost. My boy Harold called me later in the afternoon, apologizing for not being at work and thanking me for not ratting him out. I could have lectured him, but when it came to his well-being, I mostly didn't care. I just wanted him to finish his job and go home, so I could hopefully do the same.

I made the suggestion that he return to Ohio with another car, stay at the other hotel, and maybe trying to use a different name. He did return to the plant the next day, taking me up on the different car advice, but I'm not sure about the other stuff. Still didn't care, I was just glad he got his ass back to work. I made him promise to keep his junk in his pants until he finished his job. He agreed and got back to business. From then on, he looked over his shoulder a lot, I can tell you that.

Lab girl's story had a different ending. Not sure of the details, but she didn't come back to work for a week or so. The Japanese weren't as forgiving as I was, since they didn't like the whole no call/no show thing. She got demoted to some pee-on job pushing a broom.

Rumor had it those two answered a few rogue booty calls over the weeks to come, but he came to work for me and I still mostly didn't care. It made for some great conversation at smokers' central, though.

§ § § § §

We weren't the only ones who had equipment in this factory. One of our competitors had an old system running on the other side of the plant. I watched it operate, and it seemed like it was a lot of work to keep running, and according to the plant manager, it was a money pit, as well. I never really paid attention to that area anyway. Until…

One evening, I was at one of the local pubs, all by myself, having a few drinks in the company of no one. This particular night was spent at an out of the way tavern in town. I wasn't there long before I decided to call it a night, so I left the pub and went to the parking lot and got in my car. I had put the key in the ignition when the back door opened, scaring the shit out of me, and in plopped a drunken, middle-aged woman.

Before I could say anything, she started ragging on me at full bore. "You son of a bitch! I know who you are! You walk around the plant all high and mighty while we kill ourselves trying to do our jobs and your machine doesn't run for shit! You fucking General guys are killing us. That piece of shit machine sucks and you walk around like you're the king of the plant!"

Now she was in full sob, with boogers and snot working their way out of their respective crevices. And the tears. Oh, my god, the tears. She was pissed. Problem was, she was pissed at the wrong guy. General was the name of the company that supplied the other equipment. I let her catch her breath before I tried to reason with her. I tried to figure out a place to start, but it was abundantly clear I was in a battle of wits with an unarmed opponent.

"I don't work for General. I work for Kenne, babe. I understand your anger and frustration. Funny way of making a point, though."

She looked at me with a quizzical look. The Coors Light quizzical look, to be specific. She murmured, "Huh?"

"Yeah, hon. I don't even work for General. How much have you had to drink tonight? You should be more careful about whose fuckin' car you jump into. What's your name?"

"Carol," was her answer, followed with some beer tears and sniffles.

"Well, Carol, I'm not sure what to say now. Why don't you go back inside and have a few more cocktails, because obviously you need more alcohol."

"Okay," she mumbled. "I'm sorry. I thought you were someone else."

"Get out, Carol."

As she was getting out, I gave her a last bit of advice. "Stay away from the peach schnapps—it's only forty proof!"

She staggered away, apparently taking my advice.

I told this story the next day to the gals at the plant, and they laughed hysterically. It turns out I wasn't the first one who got her wrath in a drunken rage. Her alcohol-induced theatrics were well documented all over this little town, and she was kind of like the town she-drunk, in the mold of Otis on the *Andy Griffith Show.*

It was unanimously agreed amongst the locals, though, that I was the first to have her jump in the back seat of a car and start a one-sided argument. I accepted this honor, as I would be a part of local folklore for years to come.

I made it a point to find her the next day, and I have to admit, as ass-faced as she was the night before, she looked a lot better than she should have. She didn't even recognize me, though, which I guess was a blessing. I headed back to my side of the plant, trying not to look all high and mighty.

§ § § § §

Being part of a large corporation, with its endless supply of rules and regulations, was a huge culture shock for me. Some of these guys were here ten or twenty years, and going with the flow was all they knew. All the diversity training and safety training had brainwashed them into corporate robots that did the corporate thing to the extreme. What this all meant was they could avoid hard work by waving the "safety first" flag and not have any fear of dealing with repercussions.

I got schooled on this one afternoon in the plant, and I mean big-time schooling. During our start-up, the technicians had been slowly doing their thing when we discovered a small leak in one of the chemical lines. The chemicals in question were not really harmful, but in large quantities you might feel some trouble breathing. Some people might get sensitized to them over time and with repeated exposure to this stuff, called TDI.

It was nothing new; a small amount of material had leaked onto the floor. It might have been a cupful at most. Again, in a chemical processing line, this was normal. Typically, you'd clean it up with a little rag, tighten the leak, and move on. Not our boys. We had been in the middle of the start-up, in our roped off equipment area, but the rest of the plant was business as usual. There were people doing their jobs all around our little oasis, and even a few people working with our guys to help out.

I hadn't noticed my two tech service reps had disappeared when they spotted the little puddle on the floor. Twenty minutes later, they come walking out of the locker areas and calmly walked toward the scene of the crime. Remember, we're talking about a cup of brown liquid on a two-hundred thousand square foot concrete floor. My guys calmly walked through the plant and finally arrived at the little puddle, ready for action.

There was one small problem, though. Correct that. It was actually a very large problem. You see, they were each wearing complete protective gear, covered from head to toe in a bright white Tyvex suits, facial masks with breathing filters, gloves, and shoe covers. I'm all for safety, but this almost made me cry.

I started telling myself, "No, no, no, no," and started walking, and then running toward them to try and stop them as soon as I saw them.

I failed. They got to the spill, knelt down on all fours, and started wiping the little spot with some paper towels. This wasn't really a problem except for the fact they were working not more than five feet from a group of plant workers who were wearing shorts and T-shirts!

It took only a few seconds to sink in, but one by one, the plant people finally realized they were looking at supposedly trained professionals in full body protective suits. When it dawned on them they were working as usual next to our Three Mile Island clean-up crew, they freaked out. I mean they really freaked out. One guy ran over to the spill alarm, pulled the lever, and ran like hell out the back door. He was immediately followed by two hundred of his closest co-workers.

These folks didn't need a big excuse to get out of work at any time, and we just gave them one on a silver platter. My two safety-conscious-corporate-do-gooders had managed to shut down an entire plant.

As I watched the workforce flee from the building, I became nauseous and immediately began searching through my mental files for excuses, to try and determine the best response to the high level ass-chewing I would surely be receiving in both Japanese and English. It was a sickening silence that came over the plant as my two white-suited colleagues wiped up the spill. They were already gone when the plant spill team showed up, as they do whenever the spill alarm was set off, a requirement of the plant owners.

Fortunately, I knew these guys, too, so when they came over and I pointed to the little spot on the concrete floor where the spill used to be, they laughed it off. The plant manager, though, did not laugh it off. Not at all. Nor did his Japanese management, who called me into a room and let me have it. (I did have the sense NOT to sit in the chair furthest from the door, learning my lesson on Long Island.)

I had a great relationship with the Japanese, and I think this saved me from getting too much of a reaming. The sweat beads started flowing because the factory only made what they needed to ship, maybe keeping one day's worth of inventory. Every hour's production was already planned for shipment to the main assembly plant. No car seats, and the assembly plant shuts down. This causes a lot of puckered sphincters across three states.

When I found my guys, all clean and safe, I thanked them for their riot-causing overreaction, and they basically told me it was our company's written procedure that they had to follow. I didn't think it was in there that they cause a plant shutdown, but I wasn't in the mood to argue. We made a pact that the next time they saw a puddle, they would call me and I'd have it taken care of. Since it meant they most likely wouldn't have to do anything, they agreed. Another problem solved.

§ § § § §

I took the Japanese VP, whose name is something-something Oshimura, but "Call me Oshi," and a plant engineer to dinner one evening at one of the two restaurants in town. It was a steak place called The Barn. The Barn was literally a reconstructed barn that had the whole country décor going on. Country style round tables with country style wooden chairs, with country dressed waitresses, and decorations and memorabilia hanging throughout the place from way back in time. During our dinner, we were having a nice conversation when my eyes wandered a bit. As Oshi was quietly talking, I looked over his head at the wall directly behind him. I gazed half-heartedly at an old newspaper hanging behind him. It took a few minutes to sink in, but when it did, I almost started choking. It was a front page reprint of the local newspaper from August 14, 1945.

JAPS SURRENDER!
NIPS ACCEPT DEFEAT

I could feel myself starting to sweat like a whore in church wondering how I could keep these two guys from looking at the wall. As we talked, the newspaper seemed to get bigger and bigger. It got to the point I could only see the word *Nips*. During dinner, I made sure I mentioned to them a couple of times that I wasn't from that town.

We finished our dinner, and when we got up, I purposely pointed to something behind me, showing them some stupid lantern hanging from the wall. This forced them to walk forward, away from the Nips-paper.

They looked at the lantern for a second, and then Oshi says, "Barry-san, look here." And he walked over to the newspaper and pointed right at it. I pretended to read it for the first time, making an "I can't believe it" look. They smiled at me a little and I kind of shrugged my shoulders.

"What are you gonna do?" I asked them. Fortunately, they just smiled shrugged it off.

Oshi said he still liked to eat there, and usually did once a week or so.

§ § § § §

Another embarrassing Japanese insult moment was a few weeks later, when one of our older technicians was on-site working for us. He was a nice guy, named Rege, but he was a little short on tact. He liked to claim he was an American Indian, but he looked more Polish to the rest of us.

Anyway, I walked over to Rege and one of the Japanese engineers talking one day near the command post in the plant. I got there to hear Rege asking the guy something about life in Japan, and he told him things about where he lived, his house, the usual. Then he asked Rege if he'd ever been to Japan.

Rege gave the only answer he knew. "No. I've never been there, but my grandfather flew over it in forty-five." He then made the whistling sound of a bomb dropping while his hand made the unmistakable bomb-dropping motion.

Our Japanese friend looked kind of squeamish; his eyes got big and round and he quickly scurried away.

The real me was laughing my ass off on the inside, but project manager me had to speak up. "Rege, why did you say that? Jesus

Christ, you can't insult the clients like that. He's gonna make our lives miserable, or he'll tell the chemical guys we insulted him and they'll make our lives miserable."

"Well, he asked me so I told him."

"Couldn't you have just said no?"

I normally would have been on damage control, but I let this one go, hoping the customer would, too. I never heard from him, so he either let it go or was too frightened to talk to us anymore.

§ § § § §

I checked into the hotel one Sunday night, as I usually did whenever I'd go home for a weekend. I liked to be back first thing on Monday, so Sunday became a travel day. I arrived around ten at night, and at the front desk was the usual Sunday night staff, an older lady named Irene. Irene and I were well acquainted with each other, seeing as I had showed up there for so many months.

This time, though, while I checked in and made my usual small talk, Irene seemed to have a little extra jump in her step. She proceeded to tell me that this was her last night at work, as she was retiring to spend more time with her grandkids. I was happy for her, and we talked for a while as she got me checked in. She was so excited talking about her retirement I thought she was going to burst. To see this kindly old woman so happy to be done working was refreshing.

I signed in, took the key for room 225 and off I went, after a little hug from Irene. The old gal was floating.

I get up to 225 and put the key in the slot, the latch unlocks, and I push open the door and take a step inside. I noticed the screaming first. Very angry screaming, at that.

Son of a bitch, I did it again. Walked in on a pair of local fornicators. Just as I did last time, I gave the ol' "deer in the headlights" look and hoped they weren't armed. There was a small lamp on in the room that shed a little beam of light on the young couple who were apparently just getting ready to snuggle. This one was a lot better looking than Alice the Goon in West Virginia so many years ago.

She tried to pull the covers over herself as she let out a barrage of obscenities at me that would make a sailor blush. She was m-f'n me up and down, peppering it with about six other obscene man-words while she kept thrusting her right arm at me. I remember hearing *asshole* a lot. She stopped screaming at me long enough to figure out that hotel maids tuck in the sheets so tight it takes two arms and a leg to pull them out. She worked at this while yelling at her man to find out "what the fuck" I was doing.

I started apologizing, of course, and fortunately, I still had the little key-card holder in my hand that said Room 225 written right on it. I was trying to show her and tell her it wasn't my fault, but I could tell she didn't want to hear it, being naked and all. By now I had already seen all the way to Beaver County, so I back-stepped out of the room and he came out with me.

I showed him my key card, and he kind of laughed. "That old lady fucked up, dude," were his only words for me. He opened the door to go back in and I could hear his lady on the phone.

She was spewing obscenities worse than before, and as I walked away, it hit me. *Irene! Holy shit, poor Irene. Her last night and she's getting laid into by the angry guest in 225.*

I headed back down to the front desk, with my heart wrenching for ol' Irene. She was so excited about her last night on the job she double dipped on the room assignment.

I walked up to her ready to apologize like it was my fault. When I got there, she was still on the phone getting hers. Finally she put the phone down, with a very distraught look on her face.

She told me she was so sorry. That couple had just checked in right before me and that's why she had that number in her head. At first I thought she was going to cry, but I told her not to worry about it, and I even thanked her for letting me get a little unexpected peep show on a slow Sunday night. I then proceeded to tell her about my previous walk-in on a love struck couple, which she couldn't believe had now happened to me twice.

She laughed so hard, it was hard to believe she was ready to cry ten seconds ago. We yukked it up for a while, until she calmly reached down and pulled out a bottle of bourbon. Ah, yes, of course…nothin' says, "It's my last day," like Wild Turkey. Apparently Irene had been drinking for a quite a while, being her last night and all. Judging by the level in the bottle, it may have had something to do with her assigning the same room to a couple different guests, not to mention the emotional light switch she was turning on and off while we were talking.

I had a belt or two with her, and again, I hugged her before heading off, trying a new room. This one was empty, thank god. Now that I knew Irene was down there with her Wild Turkey, I got in and closed and locked the door behind me. The chances of someone trying to get into my room were pretty good. Fastening the little chain across the entrance, I thought to myself, *I have to stop doing this shit.*

Chapter 7

LET'S MAKE A DEAL

The corporate machine put the brakes on the whole go with the flow thing, and they put a general manager in place who was told to start making money or start making empty offices. Dan Foller was his name, and he ended up getting things turned around. It took him a while to convince the career flow goers, but eventually most of them got the hint.

Shortly after he took charge, I was put on the sales staff when he needed a replacement for the automotive market. This meant I would be traveling for a change, but I was already used to it. It meant a new travel routine, and a new style of overtime. The OT Blues that was required with the sales job was an upper class sort of partying. Golf courses, nice restaurants, and the occasional foreign country. Every now and again, though, I was reminded of my roots and the fact that I still had some dues to pay.

AIRPORT ETIQUETTE

I was taking a trip to see a customer in the Nashville, Tennessee, area, and for good measure I took one of our project managers. The conventional wisdom was that by taking a rep from engineering, I could give the appearance of a unified team. Plus, the guy with me, Frank Stolman, had worked with this customer before, and it would help to break the ice. He had been a long time flow goer, but was a real good guy. Frank was really personable, but kind of slow-witted, at least when it came to budgets, schedules, and other pertinent ditties that his job threw at him. But he was a great people person, and this helped him fly under the radar for a couple of decades.

Frank and I met at the Pittsburgh airport, and together we headed to the tram that takes you to the gates. Off the tram, we make our way across the center terminal area, like the rest of the afternoon lemmings, with me walking a couple of steps in front of him, just kind of talking about nothing in particular. As we were walking toward our concourse, I see a drop-dead gorgeous blond walking right at us. She was obviously a US Air stewardess, and she was absolutely stunning. Every man in the terminal was turning his head to look at her and even a few women were, too. She slowly got closer to us, and as she passed me to the left, she looked even more stunning than before. What a smile.

She got a step or two past me when I heard a deep thud, a grunt, and another thud. I heard people gasping and a couple of "oh my's!" Then a few people were running toward me from the front and sides, but they passed me up and went behind me. I turned around to look and, in a flash, I realized Frank wasn't with me. Another split second and I see him. My "Ace in the Hole" is lying flat on his back with both hands holding his head.

A quick glance at the three-foot diameter concrete column in front of him and the daffy look on his face told the whole story. He had walked into the column when the blond walked by. I didn't even have to ask. Here's what I instantly surmised: He turned his head to stare at her and he brained himself when he thumped the column in full stride. This would've been the first thud that I heard. The counterforce of this momentum snapped his head back, but drove his chest into the column, resulting in the loud grunt. And since my high school physics teacher taught me that every action has an opposite and equal reaction, it's safe to say that Frank ended up flat on his back after his melon hit the column, knocking him to his ass, and causing the third thud that I heard. This all ran through my head in about a second, maybe two, tops.

As the crowd gathered around him, I couldn't help but notice the beautiful blond was the first one there. She knelt down and was asking him the usual questions one asks a grown man when he walks into a cement column. He looked a little groggy, but really no worse for the wear. He sat up, with the help of Blondie, and the crowd gave a weak round of applause. I stood there half embarrassed and half pissed off. I looked at him with the look of "what the fuck did you just do?"

He got up on his feet and he started laughing, pointing at the blond and half-heartedly shouting at her, "You almost killed me! What were doing, smiling at me like that?"

She gave him a little apologetic (sympathetic?) smile and went on her way. We stood there for a minute, as the crowd dispersed and we went to our gate. I didn't say a word until we got there, finally asking if he was okay.

"That was embarrassing," was his only answer.

"You think?"

Travel Tips in Detroit

I traveled to the Detroit area with another salesman for a joint sales meeting. We were flying back to Pittsburgh with a couple of hours to kill, when Todd, the guy I was with, decided he wanted to stop at his old stomping grounds, a strip bar called the Air Strip. He told me he used to stop by this place quite a bit when he was a rep for the chemical group.

So, what the hell; we went in. We were sitting by ourselves in nice comfy chairs away from the stage when a young girl started dancing on the little table between us. The music was playing, and she was doing her thing, as Todd gave her the approving smile of the northern land shark. The gal did her thing, and she knew she had a fish on. When the music stopped, she stepped down off the table and sat down next to Todd and said a shy little hello.

He smiled at her, said hello back, then asked her a simple question. "Do you take tips?"

I damn near died. *Do you take tips? Did this horse's ass just ask a stripper if she took tips?*

She looked at him and tried to be as restrained as possible.

Not me. I spoke up loud and clear. "No, Todd. She doesn't take tips. She does this for fun. Jesus Christ, what the hell kind of question is that?"

The girl looked relieved that I said something. Todd started mumbling and fumbling for a bill, but I kept going. "No, mister, I shake my bare ass for fun! I stopped eating years ago. I just needed somewhere to spend my afternoons, so I thought, 'Why not dance naked?' Who the hell needs money? Not my landlord!"

Todd turned beet red, and he should have, and the dancer got a few bucks and walked away, laughing her bare ass off.

I gave him some more shit over this monumental brain fart, and he tried to defend himself with some inane babbling. But the damage was done, more than he knew. You can't un-ring a bell, as they say. I tried to let it pass, but the whole trip had been just like that golden moment, and I had to vent.

At no time in my life had ever wished so hard that I had a rolled-up newspaper in my hand.

SOUTH CAROLINA'S GULF STREAM

I was trying to sell a job to my old friends in South Carolina, and my man Brett was the program manager working me over on pricing. That was always a part of it, but the good thing was, since we had a good relationship, we were able to really define the scope of the whole project. The dollar value ended up being in the eight hundred thousand dollar range, but after three or four trips down south, I thought we were pretty close.

Brett and I went to dinner one evening with one of his guys, Steve, and together they planned on beating me down some more in price. During dinner, that's what happened as we talked back and forth and eventually agreed on a general price.

I thought it was a done deal, but Brett threw in one more caveat. "Dude, I think we're pretty close here but the only way were signing this contract is on the back of a fishing boat out in the gulf stream."

Ah ha. The deal-breaker. I smiled at this, and I knew he meant it. We had talked about it before, always threatening to go fishing, and now it was time to shit or get off the pot. I looked at him and Steve, and as I raised my glass of wine, I smiled and said, "Can do."

I flew home the next day and met with Dan, our GM. I told him we had a great meeting, agreed on a design and all the technical issues, and we even got pretty damn close on the price. I then told him about the non-written stipulation of the need to catch tuna in the Atlantic Ocean. Dan didn't flinch, and was actually all over this. He immediately said he'd get it set up, and we would go the following weekend off the coast of Charleston. He told me to find a big-ass condo to rent, and we would get a couple other customers and the sales manager to join us. The company had no problem doing business on the open water.

We ended up in a high rent condo with five bedrooms and all the luxuries you can think of. We flew down and met the guys there, as well as a couple of other clients.

Saturday morning we got up early and headed down to the docks, where we all boarded the boat for our guided fishing adventure. We got out to our spot, and when the captain anchored the vessel, telling us to get ready to fish, I stopped my guys from fishing and the three of us huddled together at the back of the boat. "No deal, no fish," I told them.

As Dan and the others chatted with the crew on the front of the boat, I continued my negotiation. "Okay, guys, we're on the back of a boat in the gulf stream. I believe we were at eight hundred and sixty grand. Do we have a deal?"

They both smirked and chuckled a little bit, and then Brett speaks up. "We'll accept that price if you extend the warranty period."

"Done."

"Done it is."

And with that, he stuck out his hand and we shook in agreement. Steve and I then shook hands, and we kind of congratulated each other. I could see Dan out of the corner of my eye, checking us out. That was that, and now it was time to fish.

I went to the galley of the boat to grab three beers out of the cooler and Dan came over to me. "Did I just see happen what I think just happened?"

With three cold beers in my arms, I quietly filled him in. "It's a done deal. We agreed on eight sixty. I have the contract back at the condo and he'll sign it when we get back."

Dan smiled big and wide and pumped his fist. He gave a thumbs-up to our sales manager and all the boys were smiling. "This is why we do these things, Barr. Nice work."

We dropped about five grand on the weekend of fun, but we got the order. We had a great day on the water, and Dan even talked about going to Alaska some day to do some serious fishing.

The boys raised their drinks in agreement. "Alaska's cool; we're in."

DEUTSCHLAND

I had to go to Germany with my non-tipping colleague Todd, to the home office near Cologne. We met a couple other guys from our office there, to join in a company sales meeting. I was paired with

Todd, and he was hell-bent on shopping for certain items to maintain his lifestyle.

These certain items included German coffee, German chocolate, and Mephisto shoes. Now I believe you can buy these shoes anywhere, but Todd needed to get these shoes in Germany in the worst way. And the worst way it was. We had meetings all day, and afterwards we would head back to our hotels. But since I was paired with Todd, I had the pleasure of shadowing him as he shopped around Cologne. I'm not much into shopping as it is, but to shadow a guy around and watch him nitpick merchants who can't understand him was like a sentence in hell. After three or four days, I was beside myself watching this grown man shop like a teenage girl. Hours spent picking and choosing something that had to be just right, then putting it back when he saw the price tag. The hunt for Mephistos sent me over the edge. We were in the shopping district, and I had tagged along for yet another hellish trip. At one point, Todd was in a shoe store looking for the perfect Mephisto, and I decided to wait outside.

I was leaning against the wall, watching the Germans walk by. Feeling totally hopeless, I started asking the passersby to shoot me. I stood there, alone, and just started asking people, "Excuse me, can you shoot me?" No answer.

"Gotta gun? Can you shoot me?" Not even a look. They keep walking by.

"I need to be shot, can ya help me? Anyone. Any one at all?" Nothing.

I continued to babble. "Ladies and gentlemen, we have an American who needs to be shot right away. Any takers?" They just walk past me like they don't understand. Not even a maybe.

This wasn't working either. No, that would be too easy. I look up to the heavens and put my arms out and give a loud, "Why me, lord?"

At that point I get a tap on the shoulder, and it's a little old German man. "Excuse me, son. I speak a little English and I hear you ask for shooting. Why you ask for to be shot? Is everything okay?"

I started laughing a little and he smiled at me. I certainly didn't have enough common words to tell him about Todd and the whole week-long shoe search, but I told him as best as I could how I went from shop to shop while my friend looks for shoes. "Mephistos," I told him, pointing at the shoe store.

"Ah, Mephistos," he replied. He smiled and touched his temple, then said, "Come with me."

He took me two doors down to a little beer garden where we sat down and he ordered us a couple beers. We made good conversation, albeit a bit slow, but I was surprised that this guy had no problem taking an unknown American into a local pub for a drink. I tried to further explain the whole Mephisto situation, and I think he got it. We had been drinking for an hour or so, and we didn't know, or even ask, each other's name.

My new friend would occasionally talk with the locals, in their native tongue, and I'm sure he explained how he found me and how I was asking to be shot. I heard him say "Mephistos" a couple of times and he was even making the hand motion with his fingers to show a gun, and all the guys laughed. It was strange, but they all seemed to know exactly what I was going through. I was one of the guys, and this was the way to shop.

A little while later, a frantic-looking Todd came in, with his shopping bags in hand, and found me and my new German buddy sitting at the bar.

As he stood there looking at me like an angry wife, my new pal pointed to Todd's bags, held up his beer and yelled, "Mephistos!"

Everyone else in the bar did and said the same thing. "Mephistos!" And the whole place erupted in a loud chorus of cheers. Todd stood there looking stupid, not knowing what the hell was going on.

STILL IN OHIO

Our Japanese customers in Ohio were planning on building a new factory in the southern US, closer to their customer. We were trying to get the equipment business for the new facility, and I spent a few months working with them on specifications and of course, pricing. After months of haggling back and forth, it came time to get serious in negotiations. I was invited to meet with the Japanese division VP, my old friend Oshi, in his Ohio office. So I went to his office for a four o'clock meeting. Oshi was living in this small Ohio town, as were quite a few Japanese guys. It was typical for the Japanese to be assigned to work in the US for a five-year stint, and this was the case with Oshi and just about every other Japanese engineer I knew there. I had known him for a few years, so we were comfortable with each other and knew each other well. I knew that being invited for a four o'clock meeting was a ploy to get me off my game, but that was amateur hour. I would sit in the lobby for an hour or so, not meeting with Oshi until at least five. This didn't bother me, because I also knew every single person in the office, if not the plant. People would see me in the lobby and sit and talk forever. Finally, though, Oshi stepped out and invited me into his office. I had a proposal for him that was about forty pages long, covering well over seven digits in total price. I knew it would be a long night, but since we already had millions of dollars in equipment already installed in this plant, I figured I would have to give in a little, but I was expecting to walk away with the order.

I quickly found out Oshi came to play as well. He was tough on me, and I tried the old "bend but don't break" approach, but we slowly padded along. We were in his office for quite a while, and before we knew it, it was nine o'clock. We were still negotiating, back and forth, pissing each other off then calming back down. Finally, at a little after ten, we had reached an agreement. We agreed on a price, delivery, warranty, everything. We were both so freaking relieved that we both slumped back and our chairs and smiled at each other.

Then the unthinkable happened. Oshi got up, walked over to his little cabinet and pulled out a bottle of Johnnie Walker Green Label. I looked at him and said, "Yeah, baby!"

At first I didn't realize that I said that out loud, but he smiled at me and said, "Yeah...baby," and we both laughed.

So we drank scotch out of Styrofoam cups in his office until one-thirty in the morning, when we finally called it an night.

When we left the plant, my new drinking buddy hugged me in the parking lot and I had the pleasure of calling my boss in the morning and telling him that I actually got a hug from a Japanese VP.

ALASKAN REWARDS

The much-talked about fishing trip to Alaska became a reality. Our GM, Dan, and the sales manager put it together, and another salesman and I took some clients to an isolated lodge in Alaska to do a little salmon fishing. I took Brett and Steve from South Carolina, and we added a few other big spenders to the list. We flew to Seattle, where we all met up, and then took a flight to Ketchikan, Alaska. Once there, we were picked up by a private float plant to take us to the remote lodge that was only accessible by a plane that can land on water. How cool is that?

We arrived at the lodge, and the staff met us at the docks and took our luggage. We took in the sights for a few minutes when someone asked if we were interested in knowing where the bar was. You never saw a dozen overweight white guys run so fast.

The lodge had it worked out so that each pair of guests was fishing with a guide. We all headed out our first morning, with my buddy Brett and me paired up with an older gentleman who would be our guide for the week.

He told us his name was Slice, and when we eventually asked how he got the name, he held up his hand to show that there was any empty space where is pinky finger used to be. "I'm not allowed to clean fish anymore."

He put us onto the salmon and halibut, and we were reeling them in left and right. One of the conversations we had while we were in our little john-boat in the bay, an extension of the Pacific Ocean, was kind of funny. We were talking about the mountains, the climate, the eagles in the trees, when Brett came up with the question of the day. "Hey, Slice, how far above sea level are we?"

Slice looked at me, and then he sheepishly looked at Brett. He was embarrassed to have to actually speak the answer, but I gave him a wink and a supportive nod, and so he told him. "Well, Brett, we're at sea level."

I looked at Brett and started laughing. "You asshole! We're in a freakin' boat in the Pacific Ocean and you ask how far above sea level we are? That's like asking a stripper if she takes tips!" I was the only guy in our group who got that one, but I laughed out loud anyway.

Brett was truly embarrassed by this obvious brain fart, and it showed. He muttered a few choice words at me and we continued fishing.

When we got to the dock, we stepped up and out of the boat and Slice called out to Brett. "Hey Brett, now you're about a foot above sea level."

"Thanks, Slice. Now I have two asshole fishing buddies."

HAVE A CIGAR

Good or bad, I took many trips to Germany, as did a lot of the guys in sales and management. One of the things I learned from working for Dan was the art of enjoying a fine cigar every now and again. Whenever I was in Germany, I made it a point to get some Cuban cigars, since they were kind of cheap and easy to find. Of course, it was always a fifty-fifty chance they would get confiscated by the customs agents.

Usually I'd only get a half dozen or so, but one particular time we were planning a golf outing for our better customers, and I was bringing a whole box of Monte Cristos in for the event. It was more than a few hundred bucks I had invested in these stogies, so I was a tad puckered going through customs in Pittsburgh.

I played it cool and made my way through customs, declaring about ten bucks worth of chocolate. The agent started looking me over. "What were you doing in Germany?" he asked.

"My company had a global sales meeting," was my calm, cool answer.

"Who do you work for?"

I pointed to my luggage tag that showed the company name. Since it's a real popular name in Pittsburgh, the agent recognized it and seemed to lighten up. "You don't have a bunch of cigars in there, do you?" he joked to me.

My heart started racing and my mind wasn't far behind. I honestly didn't know what to do next. *Holy shit I'm busted! How does he know? Oh my god, what do I say? What do I say? Think! Think. Say SOMETHING!* "Yeah, I wish. I get candy for the kids but I never get anything for myself." I thought this was a pretty smooth answer.

And so did Mr. Customs Man, 'cause he smiled in agreement and told me to go on and have a nice day. That was a little too close for comfort. It didn't stop me from doing it again, but it was close.

GERMAN ADVENTURES

Our Japanese friends were once again in the market for a new production line. I was working this one pretty hard, with the help of my German colleague and good friend, Dieter. Dieter and I were leading the charge from our respective locations, and my Japanese contact, Oshi, was the lead from Ohio and Japan. They wanted to meet in our Cologne offices, see our facility, and run some kind of machine test. After this, they wanted to see some of our equipment in production at some European factories.

Dieter arranged all of this, covering two weeks of travel that would take us from northern Germany to Bavaria, into Austria, and finally back to Cologne. It was a long two weeks at that, and there were a total of three of them, two Japanese guys and one American guy. Oshi brought one of his young Japanese engineers, as well as the head American engineer. Dieter and I made for a group of five, pretty large when traveling through Europe.

After our meetings in Cologne ended, we got on the high speed train to Munich. The five of us all settled into the first class section and off we went.

During this trip, though, I was knee deep in a separate contract negotiation with a company located in Kentucky. Making things a little crazier was that the headquarters of this company were in Spain, and that's where the purchasing manager was who was trying to lowball me. I had Dieter's cell phone, and the Spaniard and I were discussing the machine pricing and usual details. So here I am, on a high-speed train in Germany, with a German guy's cell phone dickering over a half-million dollar contract with a guy in Spain for a plant in Kentucky. As an added twist, I had two Japanese and one American customer sitting behind me in different stages of snoozing/head bobbing.

There are a couple of problems inherent with cell phones on a high-speed train. Number one, the train is barreling through the countryside at approximately a hundred and fifty miles an hour and the noise is kind of intrusive. Number two, there are a lot of tunnels on this journey. Every time we got into a heated point of discussion, we'd blow through a tunnel and I'd lose the guy, so he would have to call me back. I made my way to the club car so I could talk louder without my customers hearing me negotiate with another customer on their time.

After the fourth or fifth time we got cut off, Spain guy called me back, a little irked. "Meester Metzler, are you in Germany or Africa? Why do you keep cutting off?"

I didn't know whether to laugh or cry. Dieter did, though, and he was laughing at me pretty good. I explained to Spain guy that I was on the train heading south at a pretty good speed, and the tunnels were everywhere. Fortunately, he seemed to understand and we made it a point to have another try at three P.M. the next day on the same phone. I promised him I would be primed and ready.

The next day came along, and we were in southern Germany, or rather Bavaria, as they prefer, and we visited a couple of factories to show our guests the equipment. With my eye on the clock, we were heading from a plant in the Austrian region to our hotel. It was two forty-five. I mentioned to Dieter, quietly, that I had another phone meeting with Spain guy, on his phone. We weren't on a train today, but rather in a Euro version of a minivan. Dieter was riding roughshod over these country roads like he was on a freakin' horse, with our customers in the back bouncing around like sacks of potatoes.

At three o'clock sharp, his phone rang. Spain guy was ready to go again, so we picked up where we left off. We were going through the pricing, going back and forth with our offers and counter offers. I could feel the van bouncing around as I held a hand over one ear and the phone to the other. This went on for a few minutes, with numbers being yelled out back and forth. We got to a point where it seemed like we were close on a price, and that's when I realized the van was stopped next to a massive hayfield, and as I looked out my window, I saw my two Japanese guys and the taller American guy standing in the middle of the field. Just standing there, doing nothing, like they were waiting for a bus. I started to panic, thinking they were sick or something. I looked over at Dieter, and with Spain guy still talking to me, I asked him what was going on.

"They told me to pull over so you could have some privacy," he whispered to me. I was relieved and flattered. I actually wanted this to happen but didn't have the balls to ask.

I continued with Spain guy, and we reached an agreement and made a deal. He would fax a purchase order to my office in Pittsburgh.

When I hung up, I looked over at Dieter. "Holy shit, I did it. Thanks for the phone."

"That was one of the craziest things I've seen. Have you ever done anything like this to get an order before?"

"Not really, no. Not like this. Just on the back of a boat so far."

It was then I remembered the guys standing in the middle of the field. "Look! They're still out there." And there they were, two little Japanese guys and a tall American guy standing in a grassy German field, doing nothing.

We both laughed pretty hard, partly at the sight of these guys standing in a hayfield and partly because we had totally forgot about them.

I called them back over to the van, and as Oshi got in, he asked, "Barry-san, did you get the order? That seemed like tough negotiation."

I told them I got it, and they all cheered for me and rubbed my shoulders. Dieter laughed and started the van up and off we went to our hotel to celebrate.

§ § § § §

One of the stops we had to make was to take our customers to a plant in Bavaria that they were actually in a partnership with. The corporate leaders in Japan wanted our guys to stop and meet the people in this plant since they had signed some sort of limited partnership to produce parts for each other. "No problem," we told them. "We'll take you there."

So that's what we did. Dieter drove to the factory, and since he spoke the language, he got out and went to the security office with Oshi. They had a discussion with somebody in charge, and they walked back over to us, as we all got out of the van. We were going to make a plan to come back and pick them up.

When they came back over, Dieter announced there was a small problem. He spoke to directly to Tom, the American guy with them. "Tom, we have bad news. You are not permitted to go inside. Only the Japanese." Oshi nodded in agreement.

Tom looked at him the same way we all were, kind of like a "You gotta be shittin' me" look. Oshi apologized to Tom, but we told him it was okay, that we would find something to do and be back in two hours.

The three of us went to a café and got a coffee to kill time, but Dieter and I made sure we did a respectable job of busting this guy's balls. Talk about blatant discrimination.

Tom wasn't too happy, and he kept asking us why he couldn't go in the plant. After listening to him woe for an hour, I finally tried to cheer him up.

"Listen Tom, who knows why? I'm still trying to figure out why kamikaze pilots wore crash helmets."

He laughed and decided to relax and forget about it.

As we sat and had our coffee, Dieter asked me again if I ever experienced anything like this before.

"Nope." I told him. "Another first."

§ § § § § §

After ten days with our guests, it was time to part ways. We were to drop them off at the Munich offices of one of our competitors, who were also going to try and get this same order we were working on. This was another first, dropping off a melting pot of customer heritage at a Bavarian factory. But, what the hell, we did as we were asked.

We went, again, to a security office, where Dieter and Oshi got out and did the talking with someone who must have been waiting for them. We said our goodbyes, shook hands, and off they went. The two of us then went back to the train station for another train ride north. As we drove away, I asked Dieter if everything was okay with our guys going to the competitors.

He laughed a little, and with a snicker, he told me he took advantage of the language barrier. "Yesterday, when I spoke to the guy, I told them we would be there precisely at eight-thirty in the morning." It was now almost noon. "He was a little upset to be waiting so long. But I told him we had no choice because the Japanese were suffering from a virus and were very ill and throwing up and shitting a lot."

I started laughing. "Why the hell did you tell him that?"

"Because now he will only talk to them for an hour at the most, instead of the four or five like he planned, and return them to their hotel so they can sleep."

That was genius and it was all arranged in German so they had no idea what he told them.

"Congratulations, my friend," I told him. "Another first."

We made it back to the Cologne area, where I would spend the weekend. I was invited to visit with Dieter and his family for the weekend, as I have a few times in the past. They picked me up at the hotel and off we went. I went with them on Saturday to the Rheine River area, where there were parks and a nice river walk.

We were on the river walk, enjoying the morning air when I spotted something that I hadn't seen in Germany but sorely missed from back home. A coffee stand. The Germans make great coffee, but you just never see it "to go." I saw the little stand and immediately got a jump in my step and waltzed over to get a "roadie."

Standing next to the little shack was something you see a lot of in Cologne, and that is a beggar. It was pretty common to see guys in raggy clothes with cups in their hands looking for spare change. I was pretty excited to get a coffee, so when I did get it I was feeling pretty darn good about myself and life in general. I paid for the coffee and was given a couple of Euro coins back in change, so I stepped over to the beggar, and in one smooth motion, I plopped my change in his cup and gave him a little wink as I turned and walked back toward my companions.

As I walked away, though, I could hear the guy saying something to me, in a kind of loud voice. *I just gave the bum some coin and he's giving me attitude? What, it wasn't enough?*

When I joined my hosts back on the trail, Dieter looked at me and said tersely, "Come; let's go."

As we walked, I could still here the guy barking at me in German. "What's his problem?" I asked Dieter.

"He's not a beggar and you've just ruined his coffee."

*You gotta be shittin' me...*I felt bad about it, so I wanted to make it right. "Oh shit! I should buy him a coffee."

"No, no. Keep walking. He's very angry right now and I don't think a new coffee will help. He is quite insulted that you thought he was a beggar."

So we picked up our pace a little, and headed along the river pathway.

"Another first for me; how about you?" I asked my buddy.

He laughed, as did his wife, Edith. "Oh, yes; absolutely another first. You know, you should consider writing a book someday."

WHAT HAPPENS IN VEGAS...

Part of our job was the annual conference and convention that was held at various locations in the US. As a sales engineer, we would be asked to present papers or give informational speeches at these soirees.

One of my favorite places to attend these things was, for the obvious reasons, Las Vegas. We would get a good turnout and you could talk to and see a lot of industry people under one roof, but best of all, you could get lost really easy. Disappear like Houdini, then show up and make like you've been in the hall all day.

One particular Vegas show, I was asked to present a paper on one of the new technologies we were pushing. It was really a glorified sales presentation, but what the hell, we would get our name in the program. The conference itself was held in the Paris hotel, but I was staying next door at Bally's, basically because everyone else wasn't. I was scheduled to give my paper around two in the afternoon, so I hung out alone for a while to practice it and basically make sure I memorized it well enough not to embarrass myself or my family name.

An hour or so before my time, I was in the lobby area, leaning against the wall in a quiet, out of the way place near the box office windows, which were closed at the time. I noticed as I was standing there that there was a little sign placed on the floor that announced the Bobby Vinton show that evening was canceled. Short and sweet. Show Canceled was all it said.

I'm standing there, in a black suit and tie with a pretty plastic name badge on my lapel, reading and re-reading my speech. Just then, two older ladies come over toward me, and they look at the sign with obvious disappointment showing all over their little old faces.

"Excuse me, sir," one of them said. "Why is Bobby's show canceled?" They were both looking at me with puppy dog eyes and broken hearts.

I figured out that my suit and name tag made me look kind of official, especially to two old ladies from Paducah.

"It's sad, ladies. Very sad," I said to them, with a very serious look. I then made the international sign for *drank too much* by holding up my cupped hand to my mouth and tilting it back and forth.

Their eyes popped open, their mouths dropped, and they gasped in unison. "No! Oh, my god, no." They were devastated.

I made the *it's a shame* look with my eyes and gently shook my head. "It's heartbreaking, I know, ladies, but he just can't go on stage tonight. You can get your refund here later today."

They stood in silence, and just looked at each other. They quietly thanked me, then turned and walked away, arm in arm, dejected and confused by this sudden turn of events.

I just looked around, wondering why in the hell I just did that.

TIME TO GO

After all the time I spent at KG, I could sense that the tide was changing and that the papa company wasn't looking to keep this division around much longer. Out of the clear blue, I got a call one weekend at home, from an old buddy named Bob Renton. Bob and I had worked together at Kanton, and in fact, he was actually hired years ago by my buddy, Jake, who had left a few years earlier. Bob called me to offer me a job for yet another competitor, located out of state. I could work from home and be a sales manager. The best kind of sales manager, though; no employees or anyone to really manage except myself.

I thought about it for four or five seconds and jumped on it. I would miss working for Dan and a few others, especially Dieter, but I went in on Monday and resigned. It's all a continuous cycle. Actually, guys in our industry are like Christmas fruitcakes. There's not really a whole lot of them around; it's just that they get passed around so much it looks like there's a bunch of them.

Chapter 8

Reading departure signs in some big airport
Reminds me of the places I've been
Visions of good times that brought so much pleasure
Makes me want to go back again
If it suddenly ended tomorrow
I could somehow adjust to the fall
Good times and riches and son of a bitches
I've seen more than I can recall

—Jimmy Buffett, Changes in Latitude, 1977

EVERYTHING AIR

As a long-time traveler, I've had my share of incidents in airports, airplanes, airport ticket counters, airport bars, and even with airport security. I've met my share of airline employees, and I can tell you that for every one that will be nice and help you, you'll find ten that will screw you over in a New York minute just because they can. But I'm not bitter; I've learned it's usually not personal. Usually.

To the ordinary public, air travel seems like a fun and glamorous pastime. My various colleagues and I can tell you that that's a crock of shit, especially since 9/11.

I honestly think that if the Wright brothers would have had any inkling of what's going on today, especially in places like Newark, Chicago, or London, they would have ripped up their aircraft blueprints on the spot and burned the little paper shniblets until there was nothing left but ashes.

§ § § § §

The early days had me traveling weekly or bi-weekly to the little town outside of Peoria, Illinois. It became second nature to go to the airport on Monday morning, and get a flight to Peoria with an open return.

One trip had me on a mid-morning flight that wasn't the typical traveler's first choice for the ride over to the great Midwest. Today, I was the only passenger on the plane, which was a little puddle jumper that had about ten seats on it. I could only surmise there were a lot of people who needed a ride back on this aircraft; otherwise, this flight would have been cancelled like a used postage stamp. As it was, I got on with the pilot and co-pilot and they asked me if I wanted to sit in the front row and put a headset on. This was pretty sweet, so I was all over it.

We take off, and I'm amazed just listening to the chatter back and forth as we get airborne for our flight to Peoria. When we get to the descent, the tower starts telling them the numbers to go left or right, up or down; the usual, I guess. All was going well, and we were coming into the runway. All of a sudden, these alarms started going off, little sirens and some computer voice that kept repeating, "Alert! Wind shear! Alert! Wind shear!" I about shit my pants right there in 1A.

The pilots didn't seem too concerned, but in a split second the nose of the plane shot straight up to almost ninety degrees in what had become my first aborted landing. I could hear the voices saying, "Abort landing, US (and some flight number)." At this point, I made the decision to let them worry about the plane and I'd worry about keeping my shorts clean.

We went straight up, made a sweeping right turn and came right back in for the landing. I still had the headset on and the voices never got excited or raised, which probably was a big factor in helping me with my personal challenge on that aircraft. We circled around and they brought it in for a textbook landing.

When we stopped, the co-pilot took the headset from me. "You weren't supposed to hear that."

The look on my face was probably what made them laugh so hard. I'm glad they enjoyed it, though. I was puckered for a week.

§ § § § §

I was making my way back to the job site in Illinois on another typical Monday morning journey, just like I had done for three or four months before this. This time I stayed with the big planes, which was a good thing, but I had to fly through Chicago, which was a bad thing. I got there easily enough, and it was what we would classify as a great flight. A good flight is one where the plane lands and you can walk away from it. A great flight is good flight, but they can use the plane again. So, it was a great flight.

I was going through O'Hare Airport, one of the busiest in the world, just walking down the concourse like the other losers when I heard something strange over the public address system. I stopped to listen a little closer.

"MISTER BARRY METZLER—PLEASE PICK UP A RED COURTESY PHONE FOR A MESSAGE.—PAGING MISTER BARRY METZLER—PLEASE PICK UP A RED COURTESY PHONE FOR A MESSAGE."

I couldn't believe it at first. Was that me? I stood there and heard it again. *I think that was my name.* But who would be paging me at O'Hare Airport? I moved over to listen again, and there it was. It WAS me and I was being paged at O'Hare! Me! I'm SOMEBODY! Hear that? That's me, baby! I felt like Steve Martin in *The Jerk* when he saw his name in the phone book for the first time. I'm SOME-BODY!

Okay, I thought, *now that I've established that I am, in fact, some-body, who the hell would be paging me in Chicago? Only one way to find out.*

I walked proudly, like a paged man should, over to a red courtesy phone for my message. I did a little head turn to make sure people saw me at the red phone.

I swear I could hear the whispering behind my back. "Oh, look, that guy must be the one who got paged. He must be one important son of a bitch. Lucky bastard."

I picked it up, told the lady my name, and she told me to hold on for a call. *Ha! It was a full blown call, not just some message! That's right...a live call, baby.*

I heard a click and said hello.

"Hey, fella, what are you doing in Chicago?" It was my boss, Phil.

"I'm going to Galesburg like I always do. I mean the plane tickets were delivered to my house on Friday, so I figured I'm still needed on the job, right?"

"Yeah, well, listen, guy. They have a big mechanical issue and the software guys don't need to be there for a week or so. Come on back home and come into the office."

So there it was. The boss had tickets sent to my house, like we always did, so I went to the airport like usual. But now I had to get a return trip to Pittsburgh so I could go to work.

I found the next flight to Pittsburgh and went toward the gate. When I went back to the ticket counter I tried to tell the girl that I was the one just paged. Me. Red courtesy phone. I was the one.

She seemed like she mostly didn't care, though. She gave me my boarding pass and I went home to go to work.

My fifteen minutes came and went, just like that.

§ § § § §

I was in the little airport of South Bend, Indiana, one winter's day, waiting in line to get my boarding pass for the trip home. I was just kind of just standing there, waiting, when the guy in front of me stepped up to the counter and I took notice of him for the first time. He was short, skinny little guy, with a bald head sporting a little ring of hair around the sides from ear to ear. When I coyly inched forward to listen, I heard his nasal whine and the accompanying lisp. This guy sounded exactly like Mr. Peabody from the *Mr. Peabody and Sherman* cartoon. He was holding a cage that was occupied by his little mutt, about the size of a large rat. He was attempting to raise hell about something, but he was failing miserably.

The problem, I quickly learned, was his dog was chucked in the cargo hatch, and apparently our Mr. Peabody was assured it was a heated compartment. Judging from the looks of the dog, the heater wasn't working on that flight.

The little guy was furious and doing his best to let the counter guy have it. "I wath told my dog would be put in a heated compartment. Look at him. He'th frothzen! Hith water bowl ith frothzen tholid!"

And it was at that. The little dog was shivering in his cage, with ice crystals hanging from his stringy fur.

Peabody kept at it. "Look at my dog. He'th thtill thivering!" Holding the cage up high, he tried to show the man behind the counter that his sad little mutt was shivering.

I couldn't see his face, but the business end looked frozen to me. The counter guy still wasn't fazed, and in reality I guess there wasn't much he could do about it now except let the guy vent for a while, so that's basically what he did. He looked concerned and listened.

Mr. Peabody wasn't done. He stopped to catch his breath, and that's when he again held up the cage but now he turned it so the dog's ass was facing the guy at the ticket counter and his little ugly mug was facing me. The poor little dog looked at me, shivering, with this sad, hopeless look. I think he was ashamed of his owner and the fuss he was raising, but his day was about to get worse. Way worse.

Holding the cage up high and now backwards, he yelled some more at the counter guy. "Look at hith testhicles! They're frothzen! Hith testhicles are frozen!"

Mr. Peabody held them up in front of god and everybody. "Look at them!"

And I shit you not, the dogs balls were crusted in ice.

This was about all the guy behind the ticket counter could take, though, because when Peabody held up the cage and put the little dog's crystal balls on display for all to see, he busted out laughing, hard. I mean really, really, hard. He was obviously holding it in for as long as he could. With the little dog looking at me so pathetically and then hearing the counter guy losing it, well, it set me off, too, and I started laughing hysterically.

Mr. Peabody turned and gave me a Mr. Peabody glare, but I couldn't stop laughing, and I honestly felt bad for the little bastard. I mean the dog, of course. That poor thing had absolutely nothing going for him that day, and I swear he knew what was happening.

Mr. Peabody demanded to see a manager, and the counter guy disappeared behind the wall to get his shit together and find a manager. By the grace of god, I was helped by another agent, and with tears in my eyes, I walked away, with Peabody trying to get satisfaction from the supervisor, but I'm not sure what they could have done for the dog and his testicular problem.

§ § § § §

I had a connection in Chicago, and as usual, I was delayed. Just to keep things in perspective, if you're delayed more than four hours, the term is *stranded*. Less than four hours is *delayed*. This particular morning, I was delayed, but I could see stranded from here. After getting my share of lies from the airline, it was obvious I had some time on my hands, so I decided to kill it the best way an Irishman could, and that is to go get a Bloody Mary. It was noon somewhere, so off to the bar I went. I sat down and ordered my cocktail, hoping to mind my own business.

As I sat there, I was watching a group of drinkers who were watching TV and really getting into the *Price is Right*. Bob Barker was doing his thing and these guys and gals were yelling out prices, "higher" or "lower'" and anything else that helped them help the contestants. These folks were really getting into it, and I got drawn in. A guy sitting near me looked over and said something like, "That's a hell of a bid." I nodded in agreement.

A few minutes later, he said something else to me, and for some reason, I decided to fuck with him and his friends. "This is a cool show, man; what's it called?" I asked.

"Dude, this is the *Price is Right.* You don't know the *Price is Right?*" He was amazed.

"No, man. I've never seen this show. Is it new?" I could play dumb as well as anyone.

"Dude, this show has been on forever. That's Bob fuckin' Barker!" He then turned to his friends and told them all how this guy next to him had never seen the *Price is Right.* They couldn't believe it.

"You've never seen the *Price is Right?* Have you been in a coma for the last twenty years?"

"I travel a lot and don't see much TV," was my lame excuse. The bartender kind of winked at me, probably because we were the only sober guys there.

They all gathered around me, pointing at the TV and telling me what was happening and why. It was comical to hear someone half lit up describe why the little Swiss mountain man was angling up an incline when the contestant missed a price. Bob and his babes provided some serious entertainment, and as it turned out, I didn't have to buy a single drink after that. My new friends took good care of me. The Price *Was* Right.

§ § § § §

A cold blustery morning had me on a flight to Indianapolis, which I was doing on a semi-routine basis. It was usually a nice, easy flight, though, so it wasn't that bad. I was sitting in my aisle seat, waiting for the boarding to complete, when a middle aged woman stopped right in front of me and started waving her ticket at me. "You're in my seat. I have 9E; look," and she waved her ticket in my face some more. "You're going to have to move," she not so pleasantly advised me, with a shitty little scowl.

"Ma'am, I'm in 9D. You have the middle seat. But I'll be glad to get up for you."

She didn't want to hear this at all. She looked at her ticket, looked at the little sign above the seats, and let out an angry sigh. No apology, no "excuse me," nothing. She sat down and complained about having to sit in the middle, like it was shame to her family.

The doors closed, and as we're sitting there, she taps me on the arm and I look over at her. "There's ice on the wings."

"Excuse me?"

"There's ice on the wings. Look."

So I looked out the window and, sure enough, there was some ice and snow on the wings. In the dead of winter, no less. Go figure.

So I gave her my best frightened look and said quietly, "Oh, my god...No! It can't be. We better tell the captain." And I started moving around in my seat like I was trying to find someone up or down the aisle. I was bobbing back and forth, just saying, "No...No...Oh no. We can't take off. Ice...Oh no. Where the hell's the captain?"

When she witnessed me going from quietly reading the paper to freaking out, she almost fainted. She was worried and afraid, losing her righteousness, and was now brought down to earth.

The plane pulled out of the gate, and I gave her a little look. "Say a prayer," was all I said, and I closed my eyes.

She started trying to get a stewardess to tell the captain about the ice issue. When one of them walked down the aisle, she screamed at her. "Miss! Tell the pilot there's ice on the wing!"

Everyone around us heard her and looked at her like the lady in the *Airplane* movie—the one where everybody stood in line to smack her.

The stewardess looked at her and smiled. "Ma'am, it's winter. Of course there's ice. We'll go to the de-icing station before we take off."

"Oh," was all she said.

I'm sure she felt plenty stupid now, but I kept my eyes closed, figuring we were even.

§ § § § §

My buddy Mick and I were into the Lemon Drops for a while, but we really took a liking to them at thirty thousand feet. The Lemon Drop, of course, is a fruity slug of vodka that, when properly assembled and consumed, tastes like the little lemon candy that everybody loves. The proper way to do these is to get a shot of vodka, a lemon slice, and some sugar.

Me and Mick were off to a job in Dallas, and we had our usual seat assignments in the front of the plane. The first class cabin was about half full, with about six of us, all told. After we took off, the stewardess came around and asked if we wanted something to drink. We ordered the Lemon Drops as usual, but we had to explain to the young lady what we needed to make the Lemon Drop. She brought out a little tray with all the ingredients, and we got busy. A couple of guys behind us saw what we were doing, and asked us about these Lemon Drops. We enlightened them, and now we had two more Lemon Drop customers.

We got more set-ups, and the four of us did a toast and the shots. The other folks in the cabin saw the four of us doing shots and having fun, and they wanted in. A little hand wave and the stewardess brought out six set-ups for Lemon Drops, with a few beers. Now she too was curious as to this Lemon Drop thing, so she disappeared into the galley and came out with more vodka, lemon slices, and sugar.

Enough for seven, as a matter of fact. Mick had convinced the stewardess she should try one. So she scooted into the seat next to him, and then we six passengers and one employee did a toast and a shot. This happened a couple more times, and before we knew it, we had a party going on.

There were chips, pretzels, snacks, and drinks all over the cabin, and the stewardess assigned to serve us was now one of us. Mick was hitting on her like he was in a bar, and she was loving it. She must have had four of these Lemon Drops, and she was showing it. Her giggling and laughing were pretty obvious, but since her colleagues were back in the coach cabin actually working, she didn't seem to care.

The rest of us were having a good time, and eventually we ran out of vodka in first class. This is where our girl made her mistake. We convinced her to go back to coach to get some more vodka, and when she did, she was clanging down the aisle with a pretty obvious bounce.

She came back in a few minutes, but she had company in the form of her partner, or boss, an older woman who wasn't too happy with her behavior.

Mick looked at her and declared, "Uh oh, it's Officer Buzzkill."

She did bring some vodkas, though, but we had to sit through a stern lecture on, "This is not a bar, it's an airplane," before we were allowed to have another round.

Yeah, yeah, wish I had a nickel for every time we heard that.

Those were the days.

§ § § § §

Flint, Michigan, is one of those places where nobody *wants* to go; you *have* to go. Well, I *had* to be there on a Monday morning, so I had to fly out of Pittsburgh on a Sunday night. I left a pretty happening picnic with my family to catch a flight at ten P.M. This flight wasn't anything glamorous, and US Air agreed by assigning a dumpy little aircraft, a turbo-prop puddle jumper with the wings on top of the cabin and propellers on each side. Cramped seating was a given, just to make things a little more uncomfortable.

As I sat in the back of the plane, I watched as two five-hundred-pound women boarded the plane and started lumbering, sideways, down the narrow aisle. They ended up sitting in the row directly in front of me. This really didn't bother me, and I actually felt bad as they tried to squeeze their sizable backyards into the little seats. It was a full flight, so spreading out was out of the question.

All was quiet until the flight attendant made an announcement over the loudspeakers. "Ladies and gentlemen, we'll be pushing off shortly but we need to remove some fuel from the aircraft so we can meet the weight requirement for take off."

You could hear the gasps throughout the cabin.

Remove fuel? Are you nuts?

She got back on the microphone to try to explain that we needed to remove weight from the plane, when I quietly started waving my hand in the air. I'm in the last row, so only she can see me. As she started talking again, I caught her attention by waving my hand some more, and then I started pointing at the half a ton of dead weight in front of me. We made eye contact and I made the "Are you kidding me?" expression.

It was obvious what the message was, and she got it. Right in the middle of her announcement, she cracked up and started laughing so hard she had to stop talking and turn away from the cabin. She ducked into the little galley in the front of the plane, and I could still see her laughing. Everybody in the plane was watching her, too, wondering why she lost it trying to explain why we had to get rid of fuel to safely take off. What could possibly be funny about that?

She finally composed herself and got back on the mike, not looking at me in any way, shape, or form. But, in the end, this is an airline, so common sense never had a chance. The fuel was out, the heifers in, and we took off an hour late.

§ § § § § §

TWA was my ride of choice for the weekly and bi-weekly flights to and from a job in Iowa. The typical go-home routine was Friday morning out of Cedar Rapids to St. Louis, then St. Louis to Pittsburgh. Making this trip was usually a quick and painless way home, even if it was for only thirty-six or forty-eight hours or so. It was usually an uneventful great flight. Usually.

This warm, sunny Friday started out like any other, and I made it to St. Louis a little after noon, as usual. I was at the gate for the second leg, waiting to board, and it looked like any other Friday afternoon flight. They opened the doors and I made my way to my seat, which was an aisle seat in the first row in first class, good ol' 1D. Our aircraft of choice today was the MD 80, which was basically a DC 9 that was stretched out a little longer. It probably held one hundred and thirty or so passengers, and it looked to be a little more than half full today. When they closed the doors to push back from the gate, I was alone in my row, so I was able to spread out and relax.

The plane took off, and it took about sixty seconds for me to realize that something wasn't right. The plane was bouncing and shaking, with the wings dipping from side to side. I had made this trip often enough in the last few months to know what to expect. This wasn't it. I could see the flight attendants and I could see that they knew something wasn't right. I looked out the window to see the Mississippi River below, and it was close.

Normally on this flight, when we crossed the river, we were at a pretty good altitude and I could maybe see boats in the water, but not the guys fishing in the boats. Looking down today, I could see the boats, the fishermen and what they had for lunch. I've never been this low as we crossed the mighty Mississippi. We kept bouncing and shaking, dipping and swaying as we made it across the water into Illinois. At this point, the pilot opened the cockpit door and whispered something to one of the stewardesses in the jump seats. She then unbuckled her safety belt and headed down the aisle to the rear of the plane. I wasn't missing this, so I scooted over to the next seat to see what the hell she was up to. She got to the very back of the plane, and started feeling the rear service door with flat hands, just like the fireman taught us in grade school.

The pilot was turned around and looking straight back at her, just like I was, when she turned her head back toward the front. Across the entire length of the plane I could see her mouth these words to the pilot: "IT'S HOT. IT'S HOT." He then signaled her back to the front, and he whispered to her again before closing the door.

In another few seconds, the captain made an announcement that we were having a mechanical issue with the aircraft, and we would be returning to Lambert Field for landing and that we should all remain seated with our seat belts securely fastened.

No problem there, chief. I slid back to my window seat and buckled in. As we made the shaking turn, it almost looked like we weren't high enough to land. The plane was still bouncing like crazy, with the dips and sways scaring the shit out of us. Not a word was spoken, and I'm not even sure if the people in coach realized what was really going on here. I'm not an aircraft engineer, but I knew our plane was apparently on fire.

As we made it toward the airport, I could see, at least on one side, that all activity at the airport below was stopped, with the runways cleared and fire trucks rushing around the tarmacs. We crossed the Mississippi, again, even lower than before, and I thought for sure we were going to be toast. I looked over at the flight attendant and she gave me little wink but I could see that she and her partner were holding hands.

We were getting closer to the runway, and the plane was climbing and dropping, like we were trying to maintain a land-able altitude. The shaking and erratic bouncing never stopped, and the sound of the engines going from really high to really low added to the drama. We got near the runways and we seemed to stop dipping long enough for the pilot to slam the plane onto terra firma and we rumbled down the runway to a quick and dead stop. I could see the emergency vehicles rushing toward us when the captain made the calm, cool, announcement I've only heard once in my life. "EVACUATE THE AIRCRAFT IMMEDIATELY."

The flight attendants sprung up from their seats, and the one closest to me told me, "Get that hatch open."

So I grabbed the emergency door, pulled the red handle and opened it up, just like the little card instructed. I chucked it out onto the runway, and a giant yellow chute appeared out of nowhere and unraveled to the ground, creating the big slide that was now our exit plan. There was a young lady behind me with a little girl about two years old or so. Before I headed down the slide, I told her to slide the baby to me before she jumped. So I slid to the bottom, stood up, and faced the door above me. She then slid her baby down the slide and I caught her, stepping back away from the slide. The lady landed, crying like crazy, and grabbed her kid from me. People started coming fast and furious down the slide, and within a minute, there were busses for us to get on.

We could see the firemen on the backs of their trucks and high up in their booms, wearing the shiny silver suits spraying the back of the plane with foam. When our bus filled up, it took off and calmly drove us back to the terminal, where we got off and were escorted back into the gate area. After a few minutes, our Pittsburgh-bound group was re-assembled at the gate and waiting for some information. Out in the distance we could see our wounded duck sitting there, with the ass end covered in white foam. Eventually, they towed it away, out of sight and out of mind. It was really a sight to see, with a lot of people sitting and crying. Praying was a pretty popular pastime, too.

A gate agent finally came out to try to calm some nerves, explaining that the auxiliary engine located on the back of the plane at the base of the tail fin, the one that provides power for the cabin lighting and controls, had "malfunctioned."

You say "malfunctioned," I say "caught on fire and almost killed us all."

We were then told that they were trying to find another plane to fly us to Pittsburgh, and they mentioned the obligatory one hour, which I knew was a lie. It's Friday afternoon in St. Louis; where in the hell were they going to find a spare airplane just sitting around?

I knew we'd have some time to kill, so I figured I'd spend it with my old friend, Mary. Bloody Mary, that is. A few of the other passengers had the same idea, and we ended up at the bar laughing about our brush with death.

It was in the bar that I realized this had been only a good flight. My first non-great flight! And, actually, it was on the fence as a good flight, because we didn't completely walk away; we jumped out of a chute and were bussed away. We took a vote at the bar, however, and good flight won in a landslide.

After a little while, I went back to the gate, where there were about a dozen people left. I can only guess that the majority of the passengers headed to the Greyhound Bus station, because there weren't a lot of us left. I looked around, trying to find the mother and daughter I had helped a little earlier. She never said a word to me, not on the ground or on the bus. Now she was gone. Oh well.

I did see the pilot and co-pilot leaning against the wall, so I wandered over to chat. "Hey, guys, nice job."

I got a nod and a "thanks" from the pilot. I did have a couple questions for these guys, so I thought now was as good a time as any to get them out there. "I have a couple of questions…" I started.

"Okay, shoot," the pilot offered.

"First off, we took off and landed, so, technically, that constitutes a flight. Will we get our frequent flyer miles for that near-death experience?"

They were both a little shocked to hear that question, but they started laughing at the thought of it and said they would indeed make sure we all got our miles for that *thing*.

"Second, assuming we do get another bus to fly us home, can we agree that the drink cart should be complimentary to those of us who remained loyal to air travel?"

This one hit home. The captain, to his credit, started laughing and said he thought it was a good idea, but he'd think about it. The co-pilot just looked at me kind of funny.

A couple of hours passed and they announced they had a plane for us and we'd be boarding shortly. By now, the majority of people who had boarded the flight that morning were gone and we were now down to about a dozen of us. Though smaller in number, we were all friends now, and we were all hoping my talk with the big guys would do some good on this flight. I still had a first class ticket, so I knew my drinks were free, either way. I was standing up for the little guys, but I'd bag them in a flash if I had to.

We got on the plane and it was a weird atmosphere. Everyone was in a goofy mood, even the flight crew. A lot of joking around by everybody. I took a seat in coach to hang out with my new friends. They closed the doors and the pilot welcomed as back on board, congratulating us on earning double miles today.

We got airborne, and at the ten thousand feet, the pilot got back on the speakers. "Well, folks, we're climbing to our cruising altitude and everything looks good for our trip into Pittsburgh. Upon request, we have decided to open up the drink cart today and make all cocktails complimentary for you loyal passengers who've stayed with us. Please enjoy with our compliments."

And with that, we erupted in cheers, and the stewardesses made record time getting that thing out. They didn't even bother to put it away, which was another first. It was like a real party, and we were having a ball.

At one point, one of the stewardesses got on the speakers system and announced for everybody to assume the crash position. And we all did. We all lunged and sprawled across our seats like we were in a plane crash. The *true* crash position. Everybody laughed and it was basically like that for the entire two-hour flight. We landed safely, and when we got off the plane, the stewardesses hugged each of us, and the captain and co-captain shook hands with everyone. This was a great flight.

§ § § § § §

We have a saying in my family; it's kind of a simple one with a simple meaning. "Time on the bench," is it, and it means that something you've done will get you time on the bench. As in, when you die and get to the Pearly Gates, St. Peter will look at his list and say, "Oh oh, remember this? You can't come in right now. Go over and sit on that bench for a while and we'll let you know when you can enter." That's what we referred to as "time on the bench."

Whether I liked it or not, the St. Louis airport was a regular Friday afternoon hangout for me. This Friday was no different, except I had one small problem with my connection. I didn't have a seat on the next flight, and I was stand-by for the next few after this one as well. It was really starting to look like I wasn't going to get home this day. I was a little upset over this, seeing as how I made this flight about every Friday for how many months and now I can't get a seat?

They did tell me I was "right on the top" of the stand-by list, which was the usual bullshit story they fed everybody. I decided I'd wait this one out in the bar until it was time to board the next flight and see if I was going to get lucky.

I ordered a beer and sat at the corner of the bar by myself, looking at the TV and biding my time. To my right were three annoying guys yukking it up and having a great time. They were drinking their beers and telling stories of how their wives wouldn't believe they were drinking in a bar on a Friday afternoon, how great this bar was, and what a good deal it was to "get a shot for a dollar more."

It was painfully obvious that they were rookies, and this was their first business trip. "I can't believe we're drinking beer on a Friday afternoon! This is great!" one of them must have said that four or five times.

"My wife would blow a gasket if she knew what I was doing right now," another one would chime in.

They were getting louder and more obnoxious by the minute. Even the bartender was sick of them, but they did have cash, so he tolerated them. Here I am pretty much stranded, after yet another brutal road trip, and these Bozos are having the time of their lives. For some reason, it really was pissing me off.

It gets worse. As I sat in silence, stewing over my predicament, I heard something from these clowns to piss me off even more. These morons had seats on the flight I couldn't get on. I overheard one of them asking the other what time their flight arrived in Pittsburgh.

What? You're going to Pittsburgh? You're on that flight?

The guy then took his ticket out and looked at it, gave him the time, and put it back in his shirt pocket. As I watched this, I started to boil, but then it hit me: all three of these rookie yahoos had their tickets sticking out of their shirt pockets with their names typed on the ticket jackets. I set down my beer, focused my eyes and did some inconspicuous studying of their shirt pockets. They were laughing and joking it up as I was memorizing the names on their tickets. Typed nice and neat, just like their moms did to their underwear at Boy Scout camp, and sticking out there for anyone to read. Big-time rookie mistake.

I motioned to the bartender that I would be right back, and he gave me the okay nod. I left the bar and walked about ten feet over to the bank of pay phones that lined the wall. I called the 1–800 number of the airline, and when I got the operator, I told her I needed to cancel my flight.

"Yes, ma'am, I need to cancel my flight, and my two colleagues,' as well. It's flight 356 from St. Louis to Pittsburgh, today. Yes, my name is Morton. Robert Morton. Yes, that's me. Okay, the first one is Richards, Mark. And the last one is Cooper, Chad. Yes, we're going to have to re-schedule, but I'm not sure what time just yet. We haven't finished our meetings today. Hopefully soon, though."

She was very nice about it and was very appreciative for me calling. Some people just don't show up and don't even bother calling. She would gladly cancel for all three of us, and she again thanked me for having the courtesy to call.

I hung up and casually walked back over to the bar, slugged down my beer, and threw a few bucks on the bar. I turned to leave and the Three Amigos were still having their little party.

Have fun, boys. You like drinking in this bar so much? Well, today's your lucky day!

I walked down to the gate, and kind of stood there, just lurking, if you will. About five minutes passed, and the agent made an announcement. "Pittsburgh passenger Metzler—please come to the podium. Barry Metzler, please come to the podium."

Hey, that's me!

I went over to the little counter and she had a boarding pass for me. I was all smiles, and she was, too.

"It's your lucky day. We just had a couple of seats open up, so you're on the plane. Have a nice flight."

*Huh! Luck, my ass..."*All right, thanks." I took my ticket and sat down while she called a couple of other people who just got lucky, too.

We boarded the plane, and as they were finishing the boarding process, we could hear some kind of commotion at the end of the jetway. Three guys were just discovering what it meant to be screwed at the airport.

They closed the doors and off we went. I gazed out the window with a little shit-eating grin on my face, and a realistic thought crossed my mind. *I'm definitely doing time on the bench for this one.*

§ § § § § §

Returning from an overseas flight, I was making my way through JFK airport in New York. It was only a two-day trip, so I had only one bag, one of those garment bags that you put the clothes in on hangers and then fold it over to be a carry-on. A popular piece of luggage in the nineties.

This quick trip didn't require a lot of clothes, so I had bottles of wine shoved in there where the clothes would have been if I had them. My Italian buddies made sure I took home the good stuff, usually Borolo. After lugging this thing around the world and through the airport, coupled with the fact that I hadn't gotten much sleep over the past few days, I was in a kind of a pissy mood.

So when I got to the customs agent, with my bag clinking and clanging, and slicing into my shoulder, I wasn't really in the mood to talk. He went through all my documents painfully slowly, looking at me and passport, at my bag, at me again, at my passport, at my shoes, then my passport again until he finally graced me with a spoken work, in the form of a question.

"Do you have anything to declare?"

"The Mets suck."

Not a good idea to say this to a Mets fan with a badge, and now a bit of an attitude. I got pulled into the special room, where I got the special search. They jawed at me for a little while, took three bottles of my Borolo, and set me free. The lighter bag actually helped me out as I now had to haul ass to my connection to Pittsburgh.

Lesson learned, I guess.

§ § § § § §

In the mid-nineties, a flight departing from Milan had me crammed in the coach cabin with a full load of international losers. At least I had a nice aisle seat, so I thought I'd be able to snooze for at least a little bit of the ten-hour flight. Sitting next to me was an older gentleman, and another, younger guy next to him who was probably in his fifties. They didn't speak English, so I assumed they were Italian. There were two guys sitting behind them that they must have been traveling with, because they would occasionally speak to each other, albeit quick and short.

The flight attendants came around with the meals, and as usual it was pasta or chicken. I took the chicken, but when she asked my seat mates the pasta or chicken question, they looked at her and kind of spoke to each other in their native tongue. Being the world traveler that I am, I leaned over to provide my best translation services. I looked at my guys next to me and said "Pasta o pollo?" which meant, of course, "pasta or chicken?"

They looked at me with the same look they gave her. I pointed to my chicken and said "Pollo...pollo." They were just looking at me not knowing what the hell to do.

She stopped me and said, "They're not Italian, they're Bosnian. They're refugees trying to get to the States."

This was one the most heartbreaking moments I ever had traveling. These poor guys had fled their homeland with basically nothing, and they looked lost and frightened. It was up to me to make it better, I thought.

I held up my chicken and nodded and smiled at them. "Okay?"

They smiled and nodded. I did this for the guys behind us, too.

"Bring them all chicken," I told the stewardess. "And get the drink cart here as fast as you can, okay?"

She knew exactly where I was going with this. "You got it," she said in agreement.

So we're all sitting there eating our chicken, and these guys are tearing it up. It looked like they hadn't eaten a real meal in days. Halfway through, the drink cart showed up and I ordered a beer. The girl gave me one, on the house, since this was an international flight.

I held up the beer to show my new friends and give them a look like "You want one?" The older guy next to me smiled, shook his head, and then made the hands-to-pocket motion that he didn't have any money.

"No problem," I told them. "No problem." I looked over at the stewardess, and we were on the same page. "Give these guys a beer, please," I said to her as I motioned to the guys next to me and behind us.

She was more than happy to start dishing out the beers, and these guys were in heaven. They were letting out the ahs and the ohs, and gladly accepting the free drinks.

The stewardess looked at me and actually thanked me for taking care of these guys.

"No problem at all," I said. "Make sure you keep these beers coming to us, okay?"

"Absolutely," she replied. "If you need one and I'm not around, ring the attendant bell for me."

And that's what we did. I was determined to let these guys relax for a while and have a few drinks. After all the shit they've gone through, with a war-torn country and fleeing to safety, they deserved a little fun. We partied for three or four hours, with the drinks flowing and the peanuts and chips even making a huge hit with them. They were singing songs, trying to get me to learn the words, and I was doing the same with English. It was actually a lot of fun, and some of the other passengers chimed in. We all sang different songs in different languages at the same time, but the alcohol made things sound a lot more harmonious.

After we socialized for a while, it was now time to take a nap and that's what they all did. They slept like rocks, each and every one of them. While they were sleeping, the stewardess came by and we had a little talk. She told me there were refuges on most of the flights out of Italy, and most of the people were going to St. Louis.

I did have one simple question, though. "Who's paying for their trips? I know my ticket was almost a thousand bucks."

She told me the airline donated the flights, and some religious charity was taking care of them once they landed.

When my new buddies woke up, I turned them on to sandwiches and coffee, which was also another free treat they thoroughly enjoyed. We arrived in New York, and when we got off the plane, I walked them through customs until we had to split up, since I was a US citizen.

We shook hands, and the old guy who sat next to me actually hugged me and wept. He said something in his language, and then, "New York, USA," with the smile of a little kid.

I meant to tell them not to talk shit about the Mets to the customs agent, but I forgot.

§ § § § §

I had a flight to Nashville, and I was going to check in with a couple of bags at the ticket counter. I strolled on up to the counter where there stood a dedicated US Air employee, a middle-aged lady, with cats-eye glasses and a genuine bouffant hairdo. I said a little hello and put my ticket on the counter right in front of her. "I'm going to Nashville, but I'd like to send this bag to Boston," I said. I then set down my other bag and said, "And I'd like this bag to go to Atlanta."

She gave the Mother Superior airline-employee look, complete with the wrinkled nose. "Sir, we can't possibly do that."

I leaned forward toward her. "Oh, yeah? You didn't seem to have a problem doing it last week."

I guess I was still a little bitter from the last trip and was having trouble letting go.

§ § § § § §

Delta had a direct flight from Atlanta to Pittsburgh, and on this fine day I was on it. I'm sitting in my aisle seat in the second row, just minding my own business and looking at the newspaper. I notice that boarding has come to a dead stop, and I look up to see a woman in her sixties standing in front of me with a very distressed look on her face. I silently watch as she painfully looks at her ticket, then up to the left, then back at her ticket, and up to right. I just watch as she does this over and over, with the grumbling behind her getting a little more irritated and louder with each passing second. Finally, I make eye contact with her and ask the obvious question. "Ma'am, are you looking for something?"

Completely befuddled, she squeaked out an answer. "Yes. Where is row twenty-six?" I gave her a solemn look and said to her, "Well, ma'am, this is row two. My guess is twenty-six is back a little further. Go down the aisle and when you get to twenty-four or twenty-five, start looking really hard."

She thanked me and off she went.

§ § § § § §

Another flight, another aisle seat in the second row, and another idiot. Same thing as before; I'm sitting there minding my own business when the boarding line came to a dead stop. I casually look up, and there's a forty-something women standing there eye-balling her ticket, then up to the row number, back down at her ticket and, well, you get the picture. I look up at her, knowing what the deal is before I even ask. "Do you need some help?"

"I'm looking for row nineteen," she answered.

"Oh, boy, good luck! These rows are all numbered randomly so it could be anywhere. I got lucky and found mine pretty quick, but keep looking. It's gotta be somewhere!"

It goes to show you that they don't teach common sense.

§ § § § §

I was on a cross-country flight, nestled comfortably in first class with my usual aisle seat. The guy next to me in the window seat made a chaotic entrance to the plane, followed by more chaos as he positioned himself in his seat. I could tell by the way he dressed and acted that he was above the rest of us commoners, and he obviously thought very highly of himself. He unpacked his reading materials, snacks, and other things into the seat pocket in front of him, moving my newspaper without a saying word. Getting settled, he pulled out his earplugs, his eye mask, and of course, a little neck pillow. He actually pulled all of this equipment from a single little case he produced from his monogrammed bag. Serious flier, this guy.

As we took off and got into the flight, he positioned all his gear in the appropriate body area and started his power nap. A few minutes later, the stewardess comes by with the meals. She comes to my row and asks me if I wanted the chicken or pasta, and I told her I'd try the chicken. She started to ask Mr. Important next to me, but he obviously couldn't hear her.

After a couple of failed attempts, I offered up my assistance. So I leaned over a little bit and tapped the guy on his arm. He rustles a little, rolls toward me and takes off his mask and earplugs and gives me *the look.*

"What?" he snarls at me.

I point toward the stewardess and ask him, "Do you want the meal?"

He leans real close to me and asks, "What are my choices?"

He thinks I'm his servant, I guess. So I look at him for a minute and give him a stern answer of my own. "Yes or no." I just keep looking at him with a completely straight face.

At that point, the stewardess starts laughing right there in the aisle as she watched the little situation play out.

She finally stepped in and gave the guy his dinner, and to this day I still don't think he got the joke.

§ § § § §

A security line head scratcher came up when I was in Cincinnati headed east for the twenty minute or so flight. I made it to the security line with my little carry-on, and the little old lady TSA agent pulled me and my bag aside after it went through the X-ray machine. She dug into my bag and pulled out my Speed Stick deodorant, which was all by its lonesome self in a Zip-Loc baggie, just like President Bush had ordered.

She looked at me and shook her head. "Is this yours?" She held up my Speed Stick for all the world to see.

"Yes, it is. I admit it. It's my Speed Stick."

"You can't do this. This bag is illegal. It's too big. The bag is too big."

I looked at her in stone cold silence as the obvious retorts hung in the air like gigantic beach balls. I just stood there looking at her as she held up the bag with my Speed Stick. I knew if I tried to fight this nonsense, I was in trouble. That's exactly what she wanted, for me to get shitty and fight back.

I recalled my breathe deep therapy and immediately put it into action. "What do you mean the bag is too big, ma'am?" I asked her nice and calm.

"The law says you have to use a one quart bag. This is two quarts."

"Who knew? Besides, that's the only item in it, so we're even," I said to her as I pointed to my contraband.

"Doesn't matter. The bag's too big and I have to confiscate this."

I looked at her and garnered a little smile. "Well then, ma'am, if you taking my Speed Stick makes this world a safer place, then who am I to argue?" I winked at her, hoping common sense would rear its much-needed head, but I got no response.

She didn't see the humor or irony as she scowled and silently walked away with my deodorant.

§ § § § §

Small town airports are always unpredictable, because they have these security agents who want to be like the big city agents, and they sometimes feel that if they don't find any weapons or even an over-sized Zip-Loc bag, they would try to create enough inconvenience that any potential terrorist would get so fed up and pissed off that they would scrap their plans and pursue other career opportunities.

Greenville-Spartanburg Airport was one of them. They'll make you go through rows and rows of turns and twists, even if you're the only one there. No shortcuts. All nice folks, though, but they bring rural mentality to the big-time security scene.

I had taken a trip to see my friend Brett in South Carolina. During the trip, he and his wife had invited me to dinner at their house, and I always accepted as I always enjoyed their conversation and visiting with their little girls.

Our dinner was fresh salmon, and Brett had a freezer full from a trip to Alaska he had just taken with his dad. This was really great fish, so when he asked me if I wanted some to take home, I jumped all over it. It was all frozen, so when I got back to my hotel I was able to put it in the little freezer I had in the room. Morning came and I was packing for my flight home, which meant finding a creative way to pack my frozen fish. I think I had about seven or eight pounds of it, all told. I had some newspapers lying around, so I wrapped the fish in a plastic bag, and then a layer of newspaper, then another layer of plastic, and so on. I also borrowed a towel or two from the hotel to add to the wrapper. I was hell-bent on making sure my frozen fish was just that when I got home.

I get to the airport, walk through the maze at security, and get ready to throw my bag onto the belt for the trip through the X-ray machine. There are two elderly TSA agents on duty, one he-agent and one she-agent. She's at the screen; he's at the end of the conveyor. I put my shoes on it, my computer, and finally my carry-on bag.

I get through okay, and go to the end to wait for my stuff. My shoes get through, so I grab them and put them on. My computer and bag make it to me, so I grab them. The roller bag starts coming through and the belt stops. Officer Granny reverses the belt to get another look at the X-ray screen. She sends it through again, and, again reverses and studies the screen. I know what she's looking at, and I'm wondering how it's all going to play out.

She looks long and hard at the screen, then asks for help. "Mel, you want to come over here, please? There's something fishy here."

I swear to god that's what she said. "There's something fishy here."

Officer Mel walks over and they both study the monitor. They send it forward and backward to try to get a better look at this thing. Mel finally agrees. "You're right, Dottie. Let's see what this fishy thing is."

I'm looking around, really glad I'm the only one here right now. I wished Brett was here to witness this, though.

So Mel takes my bag and very politely asks me to join him over at the search table. He takes my bag and opens the zipper to pull open the flap.

I had the fish in the middle of the packed clothes, for the obvious insulation value. Mel puts on his rubber glove and goes in. He digs around a little and pulls out his hand, holding my tightly wrapped block of newspaper-covered frozen fish.

He takes it out and starts unwrapping it, layer by layer, until he finally gets to the frozen salmon fillets, and he holds it up for me and Dottie, who's just joined us, to see. They both looked at me, so I gave the obvious response.

"AH-HA! You got me. I'm smuggling frozen fish. I'm busted, I admit it. Great work, everybody."

Now they could have been really shitty about this or they could have taken it like it was meant to be. Thank god, they chose the latter. Mel and Dottie both started laughing.

"Oh, my good lord, it IS fish," Dottie mused.

"I'll be damned," was Mel's input. And they both laughed a little more. I explained what it was and why it was in my suitcase, and they agreed it wasn't illegal and let me wrap it back up and head to my gate. Mel took a specially keen interest in my improvised version of an insulated wrapper, and he looked it over and even made note of the borrowed towels. He predicted it would still be a frozen hunk when I got to Pittsburgh. Hearing that from Mel certainly boosted my confidence. They ended up being pretty cool about it and told me to "have a nice day and enjoy the fish," as I left the security area.

§ § § § §

In the late summer of 2006, I was in Cedar Rapids on a sales call, traveling with a European colleague. Having wrapped up our business, we had planned to go our separate ways, as I was flying out of Cedar while he wanted to drive to Chicago and spend a couple of days there before heading across the Atlantic.

I woke up early, in no big hurry because I had a late morning flight to Chicago, with a follow-up connection to Pittsburgh. I turned on the TV to get my daily dose of current events, when we all heard about the breaking news that British security agents had discovered a security threat that involved liquids on airplanes. The TSA had just raised the threat level from orange to red.

Seeing this chaos on the tube immediately raised my own mood level from relaxed to puckered. I knew I needed to get the hell out of here and get to a major airport if I had even a snowball's chance in hell of getting home. I rushed out of the hotel and to the airport, where I was told of the "no carry-on" rule, so I checked my bag to

Pittsburgh. I was able to get an earlier flight to Chicago, and that made me feel a little better.

I arrived in Chicago, and start looking for flights to Pittsburgh on the monitors. As expected, all I see are the words CANCELLED or DELAYED next to the majority of flights in and out of O'Hare that day, including mine. This was quickly turning into a nightmare. The overall mood in the airport was as tense as I had ever seen. Passengers, employees, security, you name it. And those wearing turbans were getting openly abused everywhere. I saw a guy in the men's room who was taking a leak and just started screaming at some Muslim guy who was trying to do the same. Very intense.

The truly ironic situation, though, was happening just outside security. I was on the safe side of security, but as I walked around the concourse, you could clearly see what was going on. There was a complete ban on liquids, so people had to throw them away or consume them before entering security. Now just think about that. How many tourists, domestic and foreign, do you think pass through this fine city on any given day? And how many of these visitors are stocking up on American liquor?

I stood there and watched as groups of travelers were gathered around in circles, laughing it up and drinking as much booze as they could in the shortest time possible. The brown bags were being passed around by literally hundreds of travelers, all of whom would be soon trying to get on these cancelled or delayed flights. When these folks get done drinking, they're going to be so pissed off and liquored-up, who knows what could happen.

I'm not sure this is what they meant by banning liquids, but it was the start of an extremely long and ugly travel day. I couldn't get on a flight for the life of me. Mine was cancelled, and all the others were already over-sold. I spent the night in Chi-Town, getting a $400 hotel room, and the hotel staff actually convinced me I was lucky to have it. I might have been lucky to have that room, but that's all I had. My bag was somewhere between Cedar Rapids and Pittsburgh. I ended up getting home the next day, without luggage, but in one piece.

I heard there were numerous arrests at the O'Hare airport for some reason, though. Wonder what could have caused that?

§ § § § §

My youngest daughter, Shannon, and I were watching the news one evening, when the anchorman reported, "The Transportation

Security Administration had just raised the threat level from yellow to orange, effective immediately."

She was like, ten, and didn't understand this. "Dad, what does that mean, the threat level is raised to orange?"

I struggled for the right words for a second, and then gave her the straight poop. "Well, honey, it means I have to take my shoes off when I go to the airport now."

"Oh. Okay."

PHILADELPHIA INTERNATIONAL AIRPORT

February, 2008

It's a bitterly cold February morning, and when I heard the alarm go off at three-thirty A.M. I knew this day was going to suck. I leave the house and walk in the snow out to my car, where I do my scraping and chipping so I can get the door open. Shoes are wet, socks are wet, fingers are frozen. It's not even five yet, and I'm heading to the airport to catch a five-thirty flight to Philly and, hopefully, get to Dallas. If all goes right, I'll be having lunch in Texas with my customer. If all goes well, that is.

Something always goes wrong, in some way, shape, or form. The Philly flight takes off on time, so that's half the battle. As usual, we land at the very last gate in B concourse and I need to get to the very last gate in the D concourse. With my wet feet and wrinkled suit, I start the trek across the terminals. When I make the turnout of B concourse, I feel the uncomfortable rumble in my lower abdomen that's trying to tell me something. No sense fighting it, because I know, *it's time.* It must be noon somewhere.

Anyway, I'm going to excuse myself at this point and go into this smelly men's room. Hopefully I can get through this without any incident and continue with my trip. I'm really not in the mood for any situations just yet.

It's just too early and I've been doing this way too long.

Breinigsville, PA USA
18 January 2011
253473BV00002BA/5/P